Academic Tribes and Territories

SECOND EDITION

SRHE and Open University Press Imprint
General Editor: Heather Eggins

Current titles include:

Catherine Bargh *et al.*: *University Leadership*
Ronald Barnett: *The Idea of Higher Education*
Ronald Barnett: *The Limits of Competence*
Ronald Barnett: *Higher Education*
Ronald Barnett: *Realizing the University in an age of supercomplexity*
Tony Becher and Paul R. Trowler: *Academic Tribes and Territories (second edition)*
Neville Bennett *et al.*: *Skills Development in Higher Education and Employment*
John Biggs: *Teaching for Quality Learning at University*
David Boud *et al.* (eds): *Using Experience for Learning*
David Boud and Nicky Solomon (eds): *Work-based Learning*
Etienne Bourgeois *et al.*: *The Adult University*
Tom Bourner *et al.* (eds): *New Directions in Professional Higher Education*
John Brennan *et al.* (eds): *What Kind of University?*
Anne Brockbank and Ian McGill: *Facilitating Reflective Learning in Higher Education*
Stephen Brookfield and Stephen Preskill: *Discussion as a Way of Teaching*
Ann Brooks and Alison Mackinnon (eds): *Gender and the Restructured University*
Sally Brown and Angela Glasner (eds): *Assessment Matters in Higher Education*
John Cowan: *On Becoming an Innovative University Teacher*
Gerard Delanty: *Challenging Knowledge*
Chris Duke: *Managing the Learning University*
Andrew Hannan and Harold Silver: *Innovating in Higher Education*
Norman Jackson and Helen Lund (eds): *Benchmarking for Higher Education*
Merle Jacob and Tomas Hellström (eds): *The Future of Knowledge Production in the Academy*
Peter Knight and Paul Trowler: *Departmental Leadership in Higher Education*
Mary Lea and Barry Stierer (eds): *Student Writing in Higher Education*
Ian McNay (ed.): *Higher Education and its Communities*
Elaine Martin: *Changing Academic Work*
Moira Peelo and Terry Wareham (eds): *Failing Students in Higher Education*
Craig Prichard: *Making Managers in Universities and Colleges*
Michael Prosser and Keith Trigwell: *Understanding Learning and Teaching*
John Richardson: *Researching Student Learning*
Stephen Rowland: *The Enquiring University Teacher*
Maggi Savin-Baden: *Problem-based Learning in Higher Education*
Peter Scott (ed.): *The Globalization of Higher Education*
Peter Scott: *The Meanings of Mass Higher Education*
Anthony Smith and Frank Webster (eds): *The Postmodern University?*
Colin Symes and John McIntyre (eds): *Working Knowledge*
Peter G. Taylor: *Making Sense of Academic Life*
Susan Toohey: *Designing Courses for Higher Education*
Paul R. Trowler: *Academics Responding to Change*
Melanie Walker (ed.): *Reconstructing Professionalism in University Teaching*
David Warner and David Palfreyman (eds): *The State of UK Higher Education*
Diana Woodward and Karen Ross: *Managing Equal Opportunities in Higher Education*

Academic Tribes and Territories

Intellectual enquiry and the
culture of disciplines

SECOND EDITION

Tony Becher and
Paul R. Trowler

The Society for Research into Higher Education
& Open University Press

Published by SRHE and
Open University Press
Celtic Court
22 Ballmoor
Buckingham
MK18 1XW

email: enquiries@openup.co.uk
world wide web: www.openup.co.uk

and
325 Chestnut Street
Philadelphia, PA 19106, USA

First Published 1989
Reprinted 1993, 1996

First Published in this edition 2001

A catalogue record of this book is available from the British Library

ISBN   0 335 20627 1 (pb)   0 335 20628 X (hb)

Library of Congress Cataloging-in-Publication Data
Becher, Tony
    Academic tribes and territories : intellectual enquiry and the culture of
    disciplines / Tony Becher and Paul R. Trowler.–2nd ed.
        p. cm.
    Includes bibliographical references and index.
    ISBN 0-335-20628-X – ISBN 0-335-20627-1 (pb)
    1. Universities and colleges–Great Britain–Faculty. 2. Universities and
    colleges–United States–Faculty. 3. Universities and colleges–Great Britain–
    Curricula. 4. Universities and colleges–United States–Curricula. I. Trowler,
    Paul. II. Title.

    LB2331.74.G7 B43 2001
    378.1′2′0941–dc21   00-068750

Typeset by Graphicraft Limited, Hong Kong

Printed and bound in Great Britain by
Marston Lindsay Ross International Ltd,
Oxfordshire

Contents

Preface to the First Edition

This book began with a mild obsession. In 1959, I read – and, in common with a number of others, was profoundly irritated by – C.P. Snow's *The Two Cultures and the Scientific Revolution* (1959). Having myself been trained in philosophy, I took the view then, as I do now, that it offered a superficial and conceptually flawed polarization between the worlds of the sciences and the humanities. That experience triggered off a concern to establish that there are many more numerous and more subtle boundaries than Snow's polemic allowed within the world of scholarly enquiry, and many bridges across what he chose to depict as a grand canyon of the intellect.

It was not, however, until a further 20 years had passed that I found a way to develop more actively my interest in mapping the variegated territory of academic knowledge and in exploring the diverse characteristics of those who inhabit and cultivate it. If I owe the physicist who wrote *The Two Cultures* the debt of making me think about the question, I owe the anthropologist Clifford Geertz, more than anyone else, the inspiration of how to get to grips with it. It was his unpublished paper, 'Towards an ethnography of the disciplines' (Geertz 1976, partly reproduced in Geertz 1983), that set me off on the investigation on which the present study is based.

Having once identified the means, the opportunity followed closely. I am beholden to the University of Sussex, where I was by then teaching, for giving me 9 months' study leave in 1980, and to the University of California for awarding me a Visiting Fellowship to the Center for Studies in Higher Education at its Berkeley campus for 3 of those months. I was able during that period to undertake a substantial part of the fieldwork for my investigation. I was not, however, in a position to follow it up more than sporadically for the subsequent 6 years, until another period of study leave and another Visiting Fellowship to Berkeley allowed me to complete my data collection and to do a great deal of relevant background reading. The wide range of sources listed in my bibliography is a tribute to the excellence of the University of California's multi-campus library system. During both periods of active research, I was also indebted to the Nuffield Foundation for awards under its Social Sciences Small Grants Scheme which contributed towards the costs of travel, typing and other research expenses. In the intervening years, two colleagues in particular – Burton R. Clark of the University of California at Los Angeles and Eskil Björklund of the Swedish National Board of Universities and Colleges – encouraged me to develop my emergent ideas and sponsored me to write about them. Their support helped significantly to sustain my commitment to the enterprise.

I have always found dialogue a more congenial mode than soliloquy of generating and shaping ideas, so I am in the habit of asking the more indulgent and long-suffering of my friends to comment on the drafts of most of what I write. On this occasion, no less than 10 of them were prevailed upon to read critically through the whole of the book in draft: Michael Black, Roger Blin-Stoyle, Barry Cooper, Mary Henkel, Eric Hewton, Dorothy Jerrome, Robert Murray, Trevor Pateman, Sheldon Rothblatt and Martin Trow. Their comments, individually and collectively, led not only to numerous improvements in style and clarity but also to my recognition that a sizeable part of the original text needed to be jettisoned and another substantial element restructured. I am deeply grateful to them for the trouble they took and the help they gave me – and so ought any reader to be, for a much improved exposition.

The plan of the book, as it now exists, differs significantly from the one I had in mind when I first embarked on my systematic study of the cultures of academic disciplines. At the time, I saw myself as putting together a series of perhaps six to a dozen different ethnographic accounts, each attempting to portray those who worked in a particular field and the particular field they worked in. But as the enquiry proceeded and the piles of data accumulated, it became clear that some of the most interesting features of the investigation lay in the comparisons and contrasts between different groups, and that the process of marking these demanded an analytic approach, as against successive portrayal.

The decision to focus on recurrent and apparently significant themes across disciplines brought a major change in its wake. When the key issues began to emerge and to become more clearly identifiable, it was obvious that my data were not sufficiently exhaustive to allow me to pronounce on every theme with equal conviction or with comparably persuasive supporting evidence. This was especially the case when I came to consider in detail those aspects relating to the nature of knowledge, as against those concerned with the workings of the academic community. To do the argument proper justice, it was clear that I could not rely on my own field material alone, but would have to draw extensively on the research findings of others.

In consequence, my exposition now rests on a combination of two main categories of testimony: that drawn from my first-hand enquiries into different disciplines, and that which derives at second hand from a diversity of written sources. I hope I have made the distinctions between them evident enough in the process of quoting them: but the reader will soon be as aware as I am that the balance between the two shifts quite markedly from place to place in the text. The interview material comes most strongly into its own in Chapters 4, 5, 6 and 8; Chapters 1, 2, 3 and 7 call more extensively on the relevant research literature. The majority of previous enquiry has focused on the natural sciences (on my rough estimate, science-related investigations outnumber by about two to one those in the humanities, social sciences and applied fields taken together). A subsidiary consequence is that they also seem at times to dominate my account. I have tried as far as I can to offset this bias, but the material available has not always allowed me to do so.

For those with a taste for methodological issues, the way in which I collected my field data and the longer-term research implications of the study are reviewed in the Appendix. Here it is only necessary to mention that I built up my understanding of the different subjects in my chosen sample by asking practitioners in each of the relevant fields to share with me their own ideas, perceptions and experiences. Altogether, I interviewed just over 220 academics, spanning 12 disciplines and 18 institutions in two countries (Britain and the USA). I owe my largest debt of all to those colleagues, for so willingly giving their time and so generously contributing their thoughts to my enquiry.

Tony Becher

Preface to the Second Edition

The invitation to prepare a second edition of what is now a well-established text provided an opportunity to reflect on over a decade of profound changes in higher education across the world and to consider their implications for the academic tribes and their disciplinary territories. As we comment in Chapter 1, during the late 1980s and 1990s there were major geomorphic shifts in the landscape on which those territories lie. One of the tasks we set ourselves in preparing this new edition was to take into account the adaptations of the academic tribes to these environmental changes: adaptations made sometimes reluctantly, occasionally enthusiastically and often unconsciously. Another was to integrate some of the latest research on the academic professions into the account, while a third was to interrogate some of the assumptions underpinning the original research with a view to assessing their robustness in this changing environment.

Clark overstates the thesis of the first edition of this book when he characterizes it as arguing that bodies of knowledge 'determine the behavior of individuals and departments' (Clark 1997: 24). Such determinism is certainly very far from our current position. The changes in the HE system worldwide have meant a growth in the strength and number of forces acting on academic cultures, enhancing the externalist rather than internalist character of the influences on them. The activities of the evaluative state, the slide to performativity and the need to 'chase the dollar' are just three examples of factors that have meant important changes in academic practices and attitudes worldwide. The decline in donnish dominion (Halsey 1992) has meant a parallel decline in the significance of disciplinary knowledge as a force.

Meanwhile changes to the higher education system, the internal character of universities and to the very meaning of higher education have resulted in a highly differentiated, more permeable, system in which close engagement with the disciplinary knowledge core through research is only one academic activity among very many. For a good proportion of academics it is not a significant aspect of their work at all. The idea of the ivory tower, still current in popular discourse, will today elicit a wry smile from almost every faculty member everywhere.

As if to reinforce this change of emphasis, theorizing about the ways in which recurrent practices, values and attitudes are shaped and articulated has shifted focus, partly under the influence of broader intellectual trends. The post-structuralist spotlight on the significance on agency and discourse in social construction has shone more brightly over the past two decades, including – though less frequently than elsewhere – into HE institutions as research sites (Trowler 1998a; Prichard 1999). The way we conceptualize knowledge or, better, knowledgeability, is itself touched by this way of seeing: epistemological forms are themselves subject to social interpretation and construction and so the complexity and mutuality of causality becomes apparent.

This shift has been augmented by the new attention paid to micro-social processes in developing quite localized meaning systems and practices (Gherardi 2000). Viewed from this perspective it becomes quite perilous to make generalizing statements about practices among academics in particular specialisms.

The emphasis on the epistemological in social construction has thus been squeezed from two directions: by real-world changes and by theoretical shifts. Like academics themselves, whose claims to exceptionalism no longer find a sympathetic audience in the contemporary context of postmodern delegitimation, the 'special' signficiance of disciplinary knowledge has been diminished. It has not disappeared though; it remains a signficant factor to be taken into account in attempting to understand the academic profession, albeit one which needs to be understood in a slightly different way than was once the case.

The book remains an enquiry into the nature of the linkages between academic cultures (the 'tribes') and disciplinary knowledge (their 'territories') and so excludes detailed discussion of other influential factors in conditioning faculty cultures in higher education. However, we wanted to consider how far the relative importance of epistemological factors affecting cultures had changed over time. Given that there has been considerable diversification of higher education since the mid-1980s we also wanted to introduce more material from lower status institutions and disciplines than was present in the first edition, no longer relying so heavily on the transferability of conclusions derived from the study of an elite group.

In all of this, however, we had no intention of writing a completely new book, and hence of losing the insights and the use of data that had made the first edition so successful. While Paul Trowler took most of the responsibility for preparing the new material, he was conscious of the strengths in the original work and the quality of the prose in which it was presented. Revisions have been careful, therefore, and apart from a completely new first chapter are largely confined within the original structure of the book. Where appropriate, we have included many new references to the research literature after 1989, and deleted some of those that stretched back for more than a generation: however, we have retained most of the original citations on the grounds that they provided an important part of the database for the original text. We hope that, far from fundamentally changing – or worse, damaging – the original, we have retained its qualities while updating and adding something new to it, which readers will find valuable.

There are some new names to add to those to whom we owe a debt. They include John Skelton at Open University Press for his continuing enthusiasm and support for our work, and to Emma Sangster at the SRHE whose careful and thorough preparation of the statistics on staff and students in the UK was invaluable in updating the book. Finally there is the debt to our families, who by now are only too well aware of the consequences of engagement in this sort of project.

Paul Trowler and Tony Becher

Abbreviations

AAUP   American Association of University Professors
AUPSW   Association of University Professors of Social Work
CVCP   The Committee of Vice Chancellors and Principals (UK)
DES   Department for Education and Science (UK) (later reorganized into the DfEE, see below)
DfE   Department for Education (UK) (later reorganized into the DfEE, see below)
DfEE   Department for Education and Employment (UK)
ESRC   Economic and Social Research Council
FRS   Fellow(s) of Royal Society
HEFCE   Higher Education Funding Council for England
HERI   Higher Education Research Institute (USA)
HESA   Higher Education Statistics Agency (UK)
ICT   information and communication technology
LSI   learning styles inventory
NAA   new academic appointees
NCES   National Center for Education Statistics (USA)
NCIHE   National Committee of Enquiry into Higher Education (the Dearing Committee and Report, 1997) (UK)
ORU   organizational research unit
QAA   Quality Assurance Agency (UK)
RAE   Research Assessment Exercise (UK)
SPRES   State Postsecondary Review Entities (USA)

1

Landscapes, Tribal Territories and Academic Cultures

HE in the post-industrial environment

The first edition of this book, published over a decade ago, mapped the territory of academic knowledge at the time and traced the links between the academic disciplines into which that knowledge had coalesced and the cultures of the academics engaged in them. Since then there have been major shifts in the topography of academic knowledge and more significantly, in the very landscape in which it lies: not only in higher education (HE) institutions and systems at the national and international level but also in the socio-economic contexts within which they operate. We can describe these shifts as structural in the sense that, as they occur, there are changes in long-standing sets of practices in different locales among the academic tribes which are the concern of this book. Structures have the characteristics of both rules and resources (Giddens 1984) and, as we shall see below, there have been important developments in various aspects of both in recent years.

This chapter begins by tracing the nature of the fundamental, geomorphic, changes in HE, and goes on to provide an initial overview of the implications for the academic tribes and their territories, setting the scene for our closer re-mapping of academic knowledge and cultures in later chapters. As in the first edition, the main focus is on HE in the UK and USA, though we argue (with Neave and van Vught 1991; Dill and Sporn 1995; Slaughter and Leslie 1997 and others) that it is possible to discern international convergence in many of the trends we identify in this chapter, at least in the developed world.

Cameron and Tschirhart (1992) have described the new HE system as operating in a post-industrial environment characterized by turbulent change, information overload, competitiveness, uncertainty and, sometimes, organizational decline. For HE institutions this has meant high levels of competition, scarce resources and new associated costs, as well as unpredictable fluctuations in enrolments and revenues. For academics it has sometimes meant the need to search for new, positive identities and new roles in which to find refuge from the storm of change (Henkel 2000: 136). The term 'post-industrial' also points to broader socio-economic changes, which have important impacts on HE: the shift of economic character in the developed world that will see, for example, a loss of 10–15 million manufacturing jobs in the USA in the first decade of the twenty-first century, with predictable social consequences (Tierney 1999: 6). Below we draw on a range of literature to explore the following set of interrelated changes in the characteristics of HE associated with post-industrialism: globalization; 'massification'; altered HE-state-industry relations; marketized relationships; managerialism within universities; and, finally, substantive disciplinary growth.

The globalized landscape

Globalization is a term with contested meanings (Cole 1998; Urry 1998: 5). Here we understand it to refer to the development of global flows of information and resources along networks transcending nation-states' influence and disturbing nationally-organized systems and practices. Such networks intimately connect the local and the global and may have any combination of physical, social and economic characteristics. International transport systems exemplify the first of these, while the internet and SuperJanet, its academic sub-network, as well as the increasingly global invisible colleges (Crane 1972) of academics exemplify the second, social globalization. The fact that a scientific discovery in a university in one country will be exploited to make a technical advance by a company based in another and put into production in yet another country, chosen for its low labour costs and offered for sale by that company's subsidiaries throughout the world illustrates economic globalization. The term is also used to refer to 'virtual' globalization: that sense of the global which comes to inform personal identities, perspectives and everyday practices (Baudrillard 1985; Kumar 1997).

The globalized landscape has fundamental consequences for HE. It is creating new patterns of incentives and disincentives, new opportunities and dangers, new structures and constraints. Slaughter and Leslie argue that 'the changes taking place currently are as great as the changes in academic labor which occurred during the last quarter of the nineteenth century' (1997: 1) and this is probably not an exaggeration. They identify four consequences of globalization for universities:

1. financial constraint by the state on discretionary activities such as HE, necessitated by fierce international competition
2. the growing centrality to HE of technoscience associated with international markets
3. tightening relationships between governments and multinationals related to product development and innovation

4. increased focus on global intellectual property strategies within multinationals and established industrial countries, representing a new environment for university research

(Slaughter and Leslie 1997: 36–7)

The globalization of HE has seen growing convergence between the UK and USA as well as among other countries in the areas of science and technology policy, access, finance and university autonomy. In each country there is more rapid technology transfer, increased movement of products and processes from the university to the market, a blurring of the boundaries between public and private sectors of HE and a greater emphasis on applied science in universities. In each country the HE curriculum is becoming more vocationally-oriented while at the same time an expanded HE system means more opportunities for access for lower status groups.

Meanwhile HE is acquiring a 'borderless' (CVCP/HEFCE 2000) character in other senses: ones related to the 'market' for students. Traditional universities seem likely to be threatened by global 'mega-universities', such as the University of Phoenix (USA) and the Open University (UK). Eleven such institutions accounted for nearly 3 million students in the mid-1990s (Daniel 1996: 10). They are characterized by their capacity to deliver distance teaching at degree level to large numbers of students. Increasingly they employ new 'knowledge media' (Eisenstadt and Vincent 1999), which allow the dynamic creation, accessing and sharing of knowledge on a global scale. The ability to offer the whole curriculum through these new technologies, rather than simply small chunks of it, is more cost effective both for institutions and for students, giving the mega-universities a strong global market position. In the longer term the influence of knowledge media may be even more radical: 'Some claim . . . that the knowledge media created by the convergence of computing, telecommunications and the cognitive sciences change fundamentally the relationship between people and knowledge' (Daniel 1996: 17).

For some authors the internationalization of their provision will be crucial for universities to retain their competitive position in the future (Lee 1999).[1] Brian Fender, chief executive of HEFCE, noted that 'We are all aware of the development in the US and elsewhere of major virtual and corporate universities' (Goddard 2000: 6). Others, however, remain more sanguine about the threat posed by global 'e-universities' (Thompson 2000). Certainly it seems unlikely that the more extreme visions of globalized HE will be realized: the national rather than global nature of legal systems, professional accreditation in health care and other areas and the localized nature and appeal of some knowledge forms will ensure that this is the case. Reports of the imminent demise of physical universities are likewise premature (at the very least). Though Levine worries about the death of HE as we know it, asking 'if we can do all of these things electronically, why does higher education any longer need the physical plant called a campus?' (Levine 1997: 16), other authors present good reasons why the future will not be so different from the past. Brown and Duguid for example note that 'obituaries are now regularly written not just for tools, but for well-established practices, organizations, and institutions [including universities], not all of which seem to be fading away' (Brown and Duguid 2000: 3). For these authors, specialists in the social dimension of new technologies, the obituary writers are too concerned about information and overlook the social context which helps people understand what that information means and why it matters:

> envisioned change will not happen or will not be fruitful until people look beyond the simplicities of information and individuals to the complexities of learning, knowledge, judgement, communities, organizations and institutions. That way, it seems more likely that change will reorganize the higher education system, rather than simply disorganizing it.
>
> (Brown and Duguid 2000: 213)

The phenomenon of massification

Despite its flaws, Martin Trow's (1970) classic formulation of HE systems as having an elite, mass or universal character is much cited in HE research. According to this categorization the British HE system became a 'mass' one in 1988 when its age participation index surpassed 15 per cent, while the American system passed the 40 per cent barrier to become a 'universal' system in the mid-1960s (Trow 1972). The UK system, in the late 1990s, was stable in the lower 30 per cent area, its move towards 'universality' having been at least temporarily halted.

Qualitatively and quantitatively, however, both systems have been transformed during the past decade. There were 1.8 million HE students in the UK in 1998 (HESA 1999) and 14.3 million in 1997 in the USA (NCES 1999). There has been an increase in enrolments of around 13 per cent per decade in the USA for the past 20 years and a much bigger jump in the UK: a 91 per cent increase in the number of first-year enrolments between 1982 and 1992 for example (DfE 1994), though that rate of growth subsequently slowed. This has meant an increase, though not proportional, in the number of academic staff in the system: a total of 128 000 in the UK in 1997/8 (HESA 1999) and 1 150 000 in the USA in 1995 (NCES 1999), as against around 100 000 in the UK and 800 000 in the USA in 1976.

Meanwhile the composition of both students and staff has changed. In the late 1990s compared with a decade earlier HE students in both countries are more likely to: be female (53 per cent in 1998 in the UK and 56 per cent in the USA in 1997); come from minority ethnic groups (10 per cent classified as black or Asian in the UK and 27 per cent in the USA in 1997/8); and be older (59 per cent over 21 in the UK and 58 per cent in the USA in 1998).

As a result of changing demographic characteristics students are likely to be less well prepared for HE than was the case, and this has meant adaptation of the curriculum and the provision of more and better support services for them. Meanwhile academic staff are more likely to have come from professions outside academia and more likely to be involved in vocational subjects and new disciplines and domains of knowledge, partly because of the disciplinary dignification and programme affiliation that accompanies massification (see below and Chapter 7).

Looking at the two countries' systems as a whole, it is clear that while externally subject to globalization they have become internally increasingly diversified and diffused (Teichler 1988; Clark 1995). The American system has always been more diversified than its UK counterpart, with a large number of institutions having overlapping functions but distinctive missions and different academic standards. That system includes the highly prestigious 'Ivy League' private universities as well as less prestigious public universities and two-year colleges, each with its own cultural configurations and associated sets of rewards and frustrations for academic staff (Clark 1987b). The de-regulatory HE policies of UK governments in the late 1980s and early 1990s have had the effect of making the UK system more like a 'frog pond' of competing institutions rather than the 'separate campuses of the University of the United Kingdom', as Trow puts it (1987). Diffusion in HE encompasses the blurring of boundaries between HE and other education sectors, between HE knowledge and demotic knowledge and the intellectually 'downward' trajectory of teaching and learning in some parts of the system: 'dumbing down' as it is popularly known. Such characteristics are typical of post-industrialism more generally: the shifting boundaries and relativization of knowledge-claims, social status and different areas of social life (Bloland 1995).

Finally a shift in the perceived purposes of HE has accompanied its massification. In both the USA and UK there has been an increasing emphasis in government policy and rhetoric on the vocational functions of HE, in terms both of its role in supplying qualified students for the professions, industry and commerce and in terms of its research function. This has meant the de-emphasizing of its other roles, those concerned with the general development of individuals' minds and capabilities, contributing culturally to the community and enhancing knowledge and understanding for their own sakes rather than for utilitarian ends. In the UK this priority is as clear in the Labour government White Papers such as *Learning to Succeed* (DfEE 1999) as it was in the Conservative White Papers of the 1980s, for example *Higher Education: Meeting the Challenge* (DES 1987). The attack on academic staff control of the 'products' and processes of HE, 'producer capture' so-called, and the instrumentalist view of HE as the servant of business remain at the forefront of policy developments. For Ron Barnett (1997, 2000) this 'slide to performativity' clearly represents not just a shift in the HE curriculum towards operational competence as opposed to academic competence but a fundamental shift in power relations in terms of who defines what counts as useful knowledge and whose discourses achieve dominance.

The regulatory state

The expansion of HE towards a mass system and beyond has demanded a steadily growing proportion of public expenditure. According to Dearing (1997) there was a 45 per cent increase in expenditure on HE in the UK in the 20 years to 1996. With that has come increasing state concern with 'quality' and a consequent intervention in the affairs of universities. As the British Quality Assurance Agency puts it:

> When the HE system was small and largely uniform, and made a relatively small claim on public funds, reliance upon implicit, shared assumptions and informal networks and procedures [for quality assurance] may have been possible, and sufficient. But with the rapid expansion of numbers of students and institutions, the associated broadening of the purposes of HE, and the considerable increase in the amount of public money required, more methodical approaches have had to be employed.
>
> (QAA 1998: 6–7)

As a result there has been an increase in accountability and an emphasis on efficiency and economy with, at the same time, a loss of the exceptional status and individual autonomy of HE. The Research Transparency Exercise in the UK entails a further extension of surveillance and accountability, requiring universities to quantify the amount of time their staff spend on different types of activity. Small wonder, then, that HE researchers have begun to refer to the 'evaluative' or 'supervisory' state (Neave 1997; Sporn 1999). This change is compounded by a drastic cut in funding for students: Dearing's (1997) estimated 45 per cent increase in total expenditure incorporated a 40 per cent reduction in expenditure per student over the 20-year period 1976–1996, a figure with which other analysts broadly agree (Brookman 1992; Watson 1996; Williams 1996). Meanwhile staff salaries have seen a relative decline and academic posts have been less likely to be securely provided on a long-term basis: Halsey (1992) notes a reduction in those academics with salaries wholly protected by university finance from 84 per cent in 1970 to 77 per cent in 1980. In the UK the 1988 Education Reform Act breached academic tenure and 1992 saw an end to the self-regulation of universities. Popularly interpreted as a 'promotion' for the polytechnics, the abolition of the binary divide in 1992 was a way of levelling down rather than of raising the playing field (Trow 1992: 214; Slaughter and Leslie 1997: 43). As state funds have begun to dry up, universities have had to search elsewhere for income, so that between 1980 and 1991 in the UK the percentage of university funding from private sources increased from 10 per cent to 20 per cent in 1991 (Williams 1995: 181). Increasingly too there has been an emphasis on a 'bid and deliver' system of public funding in the UK, which has seen financial allocations tied to tightly specified performance (Martin and Irvine 1992), this being one aspect of the application of new managerialism in HE (Deem 1998).

Meanwhile in the USA much the same picture obtains, with governmental intervention increasing and per capita funding declining. At the State level there has been increasing intervention, with numerous states implementing policies designed to regulate academic quality. In Federal government there have been debates leading to the creation of State Postsecondary Review Entities (SPRES), characterized as inaugurating a new era of governmental control (Dill and Sporn 1995: 6). McGuinness (1995) has shown how the fiscal crisis which began in the USA in 1990 set the scene for the decade. Demand began seriously to outstrip resources, the state withdrawal from providing the major part of HE funding accelerated, and a variety of constraints began to affect universities. However the situation is not entirely new. According to the RAND Corporation the United States has been underfunding HE since the mid-1970s (1997: 10). Between 1987 and 1992 state appropriations per full-time student fell by 13 per cent (Quinn 1993: 51). Within a generation there will be a USA funding shortfall of US$38 billion – almost a quarter of what it will then need (RAND 1997: 14).

The triple helix

In parallel with the state-HE developments there have been important changes involving the incursion of industry into state-university relations. The work of Michael Gibbons *et al.* (1994; 1997) is significant in depicting the dynamics of this change, though he uses sweeping strokes and a broad brush. Gibbons and his collaborators argue that private industry has been gaining the advantage over universities in technological development and exploitation, not only because of its ability to invest but because it is not restrained by now-outmoded disciplinary structures which make up 'mode 1' knowledge. Increasingly science involves 'mode 2', transdisciplinary, problem-oriented knowledge, the characteristics of which are that:

- knowledge is produced in the context of application
- transdisciplinarity is the norm
- heterogeneity and organizational diversity are common
- there is enhanced social accountability
- there is a more broadly based system of quality control

This second knowledge mode is considered extremely important for institutional communities of academics.

Mode 2 does more than assemble a diverse range of specialists to work in teams on problems in a complex applications-oriented environment. To qualify as a specific form of knowledge production, it is essential that enquiry be guided by specifiable consensus as to appropriate cognitive and social practice. In Mode 2, the consensus is conditioned by the context of application and evolves with it. The determinants of a potential solution involve the integration of different skills in a framework of action, but the consensual form it takes may be only temporary, depending on how well it conforms to the requirements set by the specific context of application (Gibbons 1997: 94).

Although the 'natural' home of mode 2 knowledge appears to lie outside the university, Etzkowitz and Leydesdorff (1997) offer hope to academics. They refer to the 'triple helix' of academia–industry–government relations, which they see as a key component of any national or multinational innovation strategy in the late twentieth and early twenty-first centuries. In the contemporary context innovations are increasingly likely to develop holistically rather than in a linear fashion, to involve this triple helix, to be transnational and interdisciplinary. There is co-evolution of technologies and organizations. As a result the system as a whole is developing and university research is evolving in ways that will incorporate it as part of the technoscience knowledge-production loop. Turpin and Garrett-Jones (1997) show that universities are tending to develop formal commercial arms which are increasingly likely to evolve into loosely knit organizational networks, largely unbound from their university and industrial antecedents. Clark's study of five entrepreneurial universities (1998) identifies the types of organizational change he believes necessary to adapt to this new environment. His five pathways of transformation involve (1) strengthening steering from the university's core; (2) expanding the developmental periphery; (3) diversifying the funding base; (4) stimulating the academic heartland; and (5) developing an integrated entrepreneurial culture.

Marketizing knowledge

The marketized HE system is characterized by:

- deregulation of the system, reduction in the monopolistic position of universities and a threat of new rivals, including private industry and information technology on a global scale
- increased power of 'customers': students, employers and the government acting as a core buyer
- increased rivalry among competitors

(Dill and Sporn 1995)

In 1983 Burton Clark helpfully portrayed the main sources of control in HE in the USA, Europe and the UK as occupying different positions (see Figure 1.1). As noted above there has been a move in recent years in both the UK and the USA towards the market, or more accurately 'quasi-market' (Woods *et al.* 1996) point of this triangle:

Figure 1.1   Clark's continua of influence over higher education

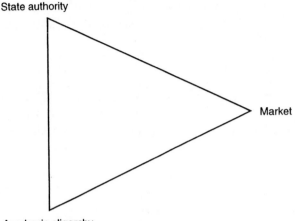

State authority

Market

Academic oligarchy

Source: Clark 1983: 143

> Policies and statutes [in the USA] moved from an ideology that de-
> fined the public interest as best served by shielding public entities from
> involvement in the market, to one that saw the public interest as best
> served by public organizations' involvement in commercial activities.
> (Slaughter and Rhoades 1993: 287)

The UK universities have travelled a much longer distance than their US
counterparts from an 'academic oligarchy' or 'collegial' character (Dill 1992;
Eustace 1994; Dearlove 1999) towards a marketized system yet with considerable accompanying state intervention. British students have moved from
being 'consumers in waiting' to fully-fledged consumers since the introduction of student fees in 1998. Their location within the 'largest single market
in the world' (Sporn 1999), the European Union, means that students can
move freely across a European HE network. There has been a discernible
movement towards 'academic capitalism' (Slaughter and Leslie 1997) in
which market-like behaviours become common at both the institutional
and the academic staff level. Some, but by no means all, universities are
becoming more entrepreneurial and less and less reliant on state grants.
'Chasing the dollar' (or the Euro) has become an increasingly important
part of the academic's role in such institutions, at least in some disciplinary
contexts and at some professional levels.

   In the face of these pressures universities are required to 'develop more
creative, adaptable, and efficient means of organizing academic work' (Dill
and Sporn 1995: 16). Examples include the push to establish more sophisticated and well-managed organizations for the procurement, support and
administration of contract research, reflecting the need to generate mode 2
rather than mode 1 knowledge in the attempt to stay competitive. There is

also growing pressure for better quality teaching and support services relevant to students. Universities are likely too to become wary about protecting their intellectual property, though Dill and Sporn argue that they will not close up entirely: the ideal of knowledge production for the public good is still extant in large parts of the system.

Meanwhile there is evidence that marketized relationships have led to the commodification of knowledge: its treatment, discursively at least, as a 'thing' capable of being bought and delivered in module-sized chunks, with learning outcomes being the unit of currency (Trowler 1998a, 1999). In such a context academic staff may be viewed as exchangeable deliverers of learning outcomes rather than as subject specialists with unique contributions to make. From a managerialist point of view such a trend can be seen to have very attractive characteristics.

Economy, efficiency and effectiveness

Managerialism involves a framework of values and beliefs about social arrangements and the distribution and ordering of resources. It provides a guide and justification for managers' and leaders' behaviour (Hartley 1983: 26–7) – behaviour that is oriented to efficiency, economy and market responsiveness and which calls for the direction of employee activities towards these ends by managers. Some of the key tenets of managerialism relevant to the current discussion include the following:

- there is a strong orientation towards the customer and the 'market', at least in the language used by managers
- there is an emphasis on the power of the top management team to bring about corporate change and its legitimate right to change cultures as well as structures and processes
- the management of change is seen primarily as a top-down activity, though 'neo-managerialism' involves steering at a distance through devolution of responsibility within strict parameters, careful monitoring of staff and cost centre outcomes and control through fostering internal competition
- in education, a conceptualization of knowledge and learning is adopted which is atomistic, mechanistic and explicit.

There are a number of variants of managerialism, including neo-Taylorism; the public service orientation; the public management approach; cultural approaches; competency approaches; 'new public management'; and 'new managerialism' (Pollitt 1993; Ball 1997). Each of these may be articulated in a 'hard' or 'soft' form (Trow 1994). The sources of managerialism are multiple too, with mixed origins in New Right ideology, management theory and elsewhere (Pollitt 1993; Fairley and Patterson 1995). Braun (1999) notes that two different managerialist models have been emerging across the countries studied in his research with colleagues: the client/market model and the efficiency model. The latter is predominant in Germany, France, Italy and Switzerland while the former is more evident in the US, England and the Netherlands (Braun 1999: 248).

According to many writers on the English and North American systems there has been a move to what Hoggett calls post-bureaucratic control (Hoggett 1991: 244), a form of 'new public management'. Within university institutions this has meant the development of corporate strategies, strong central management teams, a proliferation of cross-institutional support units concerned with quality assurance, teaching and learning, staff development and so on. The result has been to shift the focus away from the academic department in terms of initiatives and to impose a greater scrutiny of the department's documents, practices and policies from the centre, including the appointment of committees to monitor departmental research activities and strategies (Patrick and Stanley 1996). Increasingly departments and academics are expected to meet corporately determined standards. This has important impacts on the distribution of power in universities: 'A senior administrator spoke of central audit giving him the authority to "open the black box" of academic decision making and to see to it that academics could justify the procedures (or lack of them) that they had' (Henkel 1997: 140).

However, this is moderated by an awareness of the need to balance academic strengths in departments against centralism: to avoid killing the goose that lays the golden eggs. Henkel found that, in the six UK universities her team studied (four chartered, two unchartered), all showed significant movement towards acting as a corporate enterprise in the context of a largely state-regulated market. This involved a – not-necessarily conscious – mix of bureaucratic and post-bureaucratic modes of management (Henkel 1997: 136). What such a change implies in practice is a form of 'centralized decentralization' (Hoggett 1991; Henkel 1997) in which there is a considerable degree of autonomy at the periphery, nonetheless within centrally-defined parameters designed to ensure careful 'steering at a distance' (Kickert 1991). This is achieved through objective-setting, the use of performance indicators, bid-and-deliver contracts and the monitoring of outcomes. Post-bureaucratic managerialism, then, is distinguished by its 'tight-loose' character (Ramsden 1998a), a pattern found not only within universities but also at the system level, hence Neave's (1997) comments about the 'offloading state'.

In the USA too, Rhoades (1997) shows how management prerogatives have grown and academic power has declined in US universities, though as he suggests (1997: 4): 'Many, if not most, faculty are unaware of the scope and significance of the restructuring that is going on in higher education . . . Many faculty still believe they are independent professionals. At least they act as such.'

For Rhoades, academics are not proletarianized: however they are nonetheless increasingly 'managed' professionals. Rightly, in our view, both he and Slaughter and Leslie (1997) portray this situation not as static nor as part of an inevitable trend but as an ongoing negotiation of professional autonomy and managerial discretion. Professions are dynamically constructed (and deconstructed) in this way rather than having or lacking objective characteristics that bestow 'professionalism' on them, as early theory on the professions claimed. There is constant struggle over academics' terms of employment, so academic capitalism needs to be conceptualized as processual rather than static in nature:

> knowledge, theory, expertise and altruism are not enough; organizational, political, and economic skills are equally, if not more, important . . . [It is necessary to focus on] active agency, particularly at their [professionals'] intervention in the political economy, to gain a greater degree of control over their work lives and income streams, through, for example, state licensure laws.

> (Slaughter and Leslie 1997: 140)

The overall balance of operational discretion, though, has been consistently tipped towards managers in the USA in recent years, much as it has in the UK. Halsey (1992) writes about the 'humbling' of the academic profession and Ramsden talks about a 'shift from academics as professionals to academics as proletarians' (Ramsden 1998b: 351). Trowler (1998a) found important changes in the labour process of academics occurring at NewU (the acronym given to the post-1992 English university which was the locus of Trowler's ethnographic study). These included work intensification, degradation of working conditions, bureaucratization and power shifts towards managers and administrators. Slaughter and Leslie agree (1997: 40): 'Overall, the system lost autonomy because of major changes in governance structures, and professors lost many of their prerogatives with regard to control over their work.'

The situation appears to have been exacerbated in recent years by the managerialist applications of information technology. Rhoades (1997) finds more evidence for academic deskilling than for enskilling as a result of the application of ICT, with faculty being professionally marginalized in crucial decisions about whether, and how, to introduce and use educational technology. There is generally no contractual provision for such decisions and managers have been able to exploit this void so as to increase their span of control:

> Instructional technologies are more than just new methods of delivering instruction. They are means by which managers can bypass full-time faculty's influence and claims on the curriculum . . . Managers are creating a curricular realm over which they have more discretion and control.

> (Rhoades 1997: 265)

In another sense too IT applications are important in the academic world. Roderick Floud (1999) predicts that by 2002 the technology of surveillance will be so developed that it will be possible to quantify the cost of producing a graduate in different universities and even in different university departments. Publishing such information and making decisions on the basis of it will have crucial political and policy implications as well as generating unintended consequences in terms of institutional and individual behaviour in HE.

Managerialism's three key aims are economy, efficiency and effectiveness, defined in particularly loaded ways. The pursuit of these has had a substantial, often painful, impact on academic communities. Far more than previously, academics are likely to find themselves 'overextended, underfocused, overstressed, underfunded' in the words of one North American university principal (Vest 1995, quoted in Clark 1998: 146). Academics are expected to work longer, on a greater variety of tasks with fewer resources. There has, in short, been an intensification and degradation of academic work. Rhoades reports that between 1987 and 1992 contact hours increased in every category of institution except liberal arts colleges (Rhoades 1997: 267). This trend over the 1990s is confirmed in data collected for the Faculty Surveys conducted by the Higher Education Research Institute at UCLA 1998–9 (Higher Education Research Institute 1991; Sax *et al.* 1999). McInnis (1996, 2000), reporting Australian data, notes that academics are nowadays working 2–3 hours longer per week on average than they did 15–20 years ago, and the longer hours are accounted for by non-core activities. These often involve searching for financial resources no longer provided by the state but achieved instead through consultancies, teaching on fee-paying summer schools, engaging in marketing activities and so on. Indeed, the search for resources is one of the most important contributing factors to their work intensification (McInnis 1996; Slaughter and Leslie 1997). McInnis's 1999 Australian survey data (McInnis 2000) showed that the percentage of academics satisfied with their job dropped from 67 per cent to 51 per cent between 1993 and 1999; those who felt stressed increased from 52 per cent to 56 per cent; 69 per cent said that academic support for students (largely related to the increased and changing student intake) was the main source of increased work hours with 55 per cent claiming a substantial increase in their working hours in that 5-year period. Though McInnis notes that the decline in academic work conditions, levels of satisfaction and career outlooks has been dramatic by any measure, he is at pains to counter the simplistic view that academics are all in the same boat. Diversity is a key characteristic of these changes. In the USA the situation also seems quite complex, with increasing levels of stress among academics mainly related to domestic and health issues (possibly a function of an aging faculty) with, at the same time, heightened levels of satisfaction with the overall 'climate' for faculty in higher education (Sax *et al.* 1999).

To generalize, deprofessionalization of academic life is clearly occurring, while traditional ideas about the special status and knowledge claims of academics have rapidly become outdated. Kerr (1989) is almost certainly right to point a cautionary finger at the experience of school teachers and the school system in both the USA and the UK. In the classroom, teachers

have experienced deskilling through the process of separating the conceptualization from the execution of lessons, increasing bureaucratization and
managerialism, central control of the curriculum and extensive audit and
control of their work. Meanwhile the use of league tables of pupil achievement and of financial efficiency, together with a whole range of other
statistics, has had innumerable unintended consequences, many of them
deleterious but most of them quite predictable. Callahan's (1962) historical
account of the 'cult of efficiency' in the early years of this century in the
USA would provide informative reading for many of today's HE policy
makers and those HE managers impelled by managerialist ideology.

Patterns of growth and fragmentation

For Burton Clark (1996b) the growth in knowledge and the consequent
explosive growth in disciplines and their fragmentation into sub-disciplines
is probably the most important, but often-overlooked, change affecting HE
in recent years, adding to its complexity and proving more powerful in its
effects even than the system's 'massification' and marketization. Disciplinary growth can be measured by the number and types of departments in
universities, the change and increase in types of HE courses, the proliferation of disciplinary associations, the explosion in the number of journals
and articles published and the multiplication of recognized research topics
and research clusters. A five-country study of graduate education and academic research (Clark 1993) found that the number and variety of disciplines, specialties, and inter- or multi-disciplinary subjects is on the increase
everywhere, while the 1992 *Encyclopedia of Higher Education* (Clark and Neave
1992) reported a vast expansion in overall academic output (a point also
discussed in Chapter 5). There are now over 1000 maths journals covering
62 major topic areas with 4500 subtopics. More academic works of history
were published between 1960 and 1980 than in all previous time. Similarly
in chemistry more articles were published in two years in the mid-1990s
than in all the years prior to 1900. Overall there appears to be a growth in
output of around 4–8 per cent annually in most branches of science.

A number of related processes are at work here, as Metzger (1987) shows
(see also Chapter 7). Subject parturition means that new fields develop from
older ones and gradually gain independence. These may develop from one
discipline or a number. Examples of the latter would include many of the
areas of study that developed in the 1970s and 1980s such as women's studies,
race and ethnic studies, education studies, development studies and, more
recently, Deaf studies. Such fields gradually develop distinctive methodological approaches, conceptual and theoretical frameworks and their own
sets of internal schisms.

Subject dispersion also occurs, so that disciplinary areas grow, or are
'grown', to cover more ground. Meanwhile programme affiliation (the integration into university education of subjects such as law) and subject

dignification (increase of status and therefore acceptability within the academy) together mean that the notion of what is a 'suitable' subject for HE widens and new types of academic department and degree courses are created.

As well as growth there is also decline. Physics and chemistry in their pure forms have found it difficult to recruit students in recent years, partly as a result of changes to school syllabuses and weaknesses in the school system (Clark 1997; Henkel 2000). The response to such pressures in many universities has been the development of new domain-based degrees such as environmental sciences and sports sciences, which require less specialist knowledge and have greater market attraction.

Knowledge organization and expansion can operate in its 'well-muscled' organizational form independently of, and sometimes counter to, trends in the student market, managerialist imperatives, government policy and other structures. The resulting changes are largely internal to universities and can be very powerful. They comprise: 'a line of influence that has its own determinants and wide-ranging effects that shape higher education institutions from bottom to top' (Clark 1996b: 418).

For universities in straitened times disciplinary growth simultaneously offers the prospect of greater market attractiveness, promotion up the university status ladder and, more negatively, escalating costs and re-shaped internal patterns of power, influence and resource allocation.

As Clark (1993) contends there is structural differentiation and a closely related elaboration of academic professionalism within which academics 'specialize their interests and commitments in a widening array of subjects and institutions' (p. 266). He argues that the driving force behind this is the academics themselves who, in pursuing scholarship, differentiate organizational networks as well as ideas and literatures. Such a position could, however, be said to ignore the larger forces shaping academic institutions and academic life: those associated with post-industrialism and postmodernity which lie outside academics' immediate control as well as other 'externalist' forces discussed in this chapter. Clark's approach too, though helpful, is at a high level of analysis and so misses some of the detail of disciplinary differences in relation to the power of academics to mould the shape and content of their disciplines. The study of politics offers an example: 'Because political science is so deeply imbricated with political practice, its history as an organized body of social knowledge has been tied more than any other social science to situational conditions' (Katznelson 1997: 319).

Changing landscapes, shifting territories

These shifts in the landscape of HE have significant implications for academics, their various tribes and disciplinary territories. We will now delineate in general terms the most clearly apparent trends within academic life and work.

The impact of the geomorphic and territorial changes on academic staff has been substantial. However, the relationship between the identifiable shifts in the landscape on the one hand and academic cultures, work conditions and disciplinary communities on the other is dynamic, complex and far from tightly-coupled. The landscape metaphor turns out to be a particularly appropriate one: land exists without an observer, but landscape does not: the 'scape' is the projection of human consciousness, the way the land is perceived and responded to (Bowe *et al.* 1994). In the interaction of social structure and human agency lie the roots of the unpredictability of social life. It is important, then, to remember the role of agency in change: the important role of the reception, interpretation and implementation of new policies and responses to changing environments by academic staff themselves.

For some analysts (Henkel 1997; Trow 1989), in the face of the fundamental change in the transition from elite to mass HE and the simultaneous reshaping of state-public services, academics in general, and those in the UK in particular, are struggling to hold on to values and practices from the past. These include elite, or 'pre-modern' values and 'modes of specialisation, divisions of labour and institutional governance that stem from the dominance of the discipline in concepts of academic identity and professionalism' (Henkel 1997: 142). However responses to change are not usually so monochromatic. We can expect to see a variety of reactions from different groups of staff, and even from the same individuals and groups at different times. These will include not only negativity and resistance, or a burying of the academic head in the sand in the hope that things will change for the better, but the enthusiastic adoption of change in some cases and the strategic undermining and reworking of it in others.

For some the consequences of the above changes include deprofessionalization and loss of the bonds that once tied the academic 'community': a slippery term, as Hillery (1955) and Kogan (2000) demonstrate. Clark (1987a) sees differentiation and fragmentation as the third phase of an intellectual movement in American HE. In the first phase academics were hired hands. Around the 1870s a semi-integrated professionalism began to take root, located in the establishment of universities rather than colleges. Since 1945 there has been a greatly differentiated profession reflected in the night-and-day contrast between the research universities and community colleges. The same can be seen in the move from full-time to part-time work with part-time 'gypsy scholars' piecing together an academic livelihood. This has been accompanied by a shift from scholarship to teaching, where discipline matters much less and the job role becomes increasingly similar to that of secondary school teachers. There are large resulting differences in workload and orientation, while at the same time existing controls are 'thrown out of whack': 'If knowledge is power, then new knowledge is new power, expanded knowledge is expanded power, and fragmented knowledge is fragmented power' (Clark 1987a: 273). However according to Clark there are 'interlocking cultural communities' – a collective comprehensiveness that is integrative despite the forces for specialization. The analytical handle here is the idea of integration through overlap (see also Chapter 4). Others agree that despite disciplinary fragmentation there are still unifying factors, sustained by intellectual exchange, which help to ensure that the centre of the academic community still holds (Kogan 2000).

It is clear that, taking a system-wide perspective, recent years have seen a diversification of the academic profession into even smaller and more different worlds than was previously the case: post-Fordist patterns of employment have led to fewer permanent jobs and greater diversity at the periphery (Henkel 1997; Rhoades 1997). Clark remarks on the elaboration of academic professionalism in the context of structural differentiation (Clark 1993), among whose consequences one can identify an increased rigidification of the division of labour, more varied conditions of employment, greater differentiation in staff contracts and roles and more tightly defined areas of responsibility. Academics are increasingly stratified, with more internal hierarchies and divisions stimulated by the need for managerial flexibility (though there are important shades and subtleties to all this).

These divisions are not just the short-term consequences of policies such as the UK Research Assessment Exercise: they are symptoms of more fundamental forces, including the fragmentation of research arising from both the greater emphasis on teaching needs in mass HE systems and the political imperatives of economy and efficiency (Clark 1991). The resulting pattern of change is an important issue for the central theme of this book. The rapidly changing disciplinary fundament, explored briefly above, has had dramatic effects on many of the longer-established as well as the newly-developed academic tribes in recent years.

For McInnis (1996), greater role specialization is an important means of mitigating the effects of work intensification and diversification. But it is also clear that from an individual's perspective there has been an extension, intensification and fragmentation of the job role, even for core academic tasks such as course design and delivery. The demands on permanent full-time academic staff have multiplied:

> Academics find they must, for example, not only generate new courses; they must cost them, determine and stimulate markets for them, evolve new ways of delivering them and ensure they can stand up to hard external scrutiny. The stress on old assumptions about the nature and organisation of work are becoming more difficult to resist across the world.
>
> (Henkel 1997: 139)

The impact of these extra tasks and the additional time they involve varies with the individual's academic rank (Slaughter and Leslie 1997) and the type of parent institution (Clark 1987a). For most academics, however, the cognitive consequence is far greater than it appears when measured simply in terms of the number of hours worked. As we saw above, surveys of academics in numerous countries suggest that they experience considerable psychological pressure in their attempts to do more with less. Only 9 years after the publication of his book, Boyer's four scholarships of integration, discovery, application and teaching (Boyer 1990: 17–25) need to be supplemented by the 'scholarships' of leadership, management, administration and entrepreneurialism, which now form an inescapable part of the modern academic's agenda.

Maps of academic tribes and territories need to take this diversity into account and to incorporate the increasingly important category of part-time staff into the analysis. This is a group often excluded from accounts of faculty worlds, as they were by Bown and Schuster (1986) for example. Rhoades argues that part-time faculty have been sidelined in the literature and marginalized by full-time faculty in the contest over professional status: stereotypically they 'simply deliver instruction' (Rhoades 1997: 263). Their teaching is discredited in a number of ways (by omission, by not being acknowledged as professional experience, by not counting for salary/seniority calculations, etc). But in reality far from being a minor and marginal part of the system they are becoming central to its operation. In the UK in 1997–8, 14 per cent of academic staff were part-time (HESA 1999); the average figure for the USA in 1992 was already 27 per cent (Haas 1996: 344), though this has risen to as much as 50 per cent in public 2-year colleges (NCES 1999). As well as diversification in the terms of employment, there is greater diversity in the composition of academic staff. While Finkelstein *et al.* note that in the USA this diversity includes 'race/ethnicity [and] nativity' (1998: 17) this is less true in the UK (see Chapter 7).

We have already noted the diminished span of control that academics have over their work and environment (Halsey 1992; McInnnis 1996, Rhoades 1997). Associated with this are the greater levels of surveillance and control of their work and their much greater accountability for what they do. They have autonomy still, its limits are ever more clearly defined and policed by the centre: both the centre of the institution and the political centre and agencies associated with it. There are other pressures on the academic community, too, related to the concern about intellectual property. The collegium has come under pressure as knowledge capital has increasingly been patented and protected by Industry Liaison Officers, acting as the guardians of university interests (Webster and Packer 1997), rather than as a freely available contribution to the public good.

However, the outlook is not wholly pessimistic when seen from the perspective of the academic tribes. While much of the writing in the field has addressed their diminishing span of influence and power as well as their declining status and rewards, it remains possible that the increasingly global character of knowledge media and the newly-acquired skills of universities in exploiting them will serve to strengthen the academic world and increase its span of influence. Nor should the pressures of massification and creeping managerialism be interpreted purely negatively. As Winter notes (1995: 130), new situations can present real opportunities to shed oppressive practices as well as to realize new possibilities. 'Contradictions not only generate "problems" ... they also generate spaces within which power can be contested and reforms can be won': a point encapsulated in the Chinese symbol for 'crisis', which incorporates the signs for both threat and opportunity (Daniel 1996).

In the area of curriculum and teaching and learning, while subject review by the QAA in the UK has brought increased surveillance and accountability, with corresponding intensification of academics' work, it has also had some positive effects, generating a collective conception of educational quality and better awareness of the importance to students of a coherent experience (Henkel 1997). Arguably it has also brought an increased sense of community in adversity: a sort of Dunkirk spirit among academics (Kogan, 2000). Mechanisms of audit and control have provided further benefits in terms of equal opportunities for academic staff. Gender regimes in universities have traditionally been profoundly unwelcoming to women and had allowed the unacknowledged exploitation of their work. Greater scrutiny and transparency through audit and assessment exercises have made this harder to bring about (Davies and Holloway 1995). Likewise the changing curricular structures, which have led to shifting borders and border territories in HE, have sometimes yielded positive outcomes for women and other previously marginalized or exploited groups (Deem 1996). If, as Henkel (2000: 180) argues, those who became academics in the 1980s and 1990s were effectively joining a different profession from those who joined in the 1960s and 1970s, it was not only or altogether a diminished one.

Levels of analysis

To see how these diverse aspects of cultural change relate to the rest of the book, it may be useful to conclude by giving some attention to the notion of levels of analysis in academic concerns. Becher and Kogan (1992) argue that HE systems typically comprise four distinct tiers: the central authorities; individual institutions; basic units and individuals. The central authorities include both governmental and quasi-autonomous bodies. Within individual universities are located several basic units. They are characterized as having academic responsibility for an identifiable course or group of courses, controlling their own operating budgets and exercising some element of choice in the recruitment of professional colleagues, and often also of students. The category 'individuals' incorporates both academic and non-academic staff, together with students.

This taxonomy may call for some modification in the light of the major recent changes noted above. In particular, the notion of a 'central authority' presupposes top-down control of universities by the state, while the trends are in practice contradictory. Alongside Neave's (1998) 'evaluative state', we have already remarked on a strong tendency for HE to be subject to market forces which are not necessarily in conformity with government policies. A more useful designation of activities at this level might be in terms of a loosely-defined national HE system, perhaps supplemented – in the light of the phenomenon of globalization – by an even more general level of HE worldwide. However this would still remain a very attenuated notion, given the major differences between provision in prosperous and penurious countries.

Along a different dimension, the chapters which follow identify various levels of cognitive activity, not only within broad disciplinary areas (see Chapter 2), but also in terms of individual disciplines (Chapter 3) and sub-disciplines and specialisms (Chapter 4). This pattern of cognitive features, especially at the level of disciplines and sub-disciplines, is matched by related social concerns in the academic community, reflecting the research interests of its members and, to a lesser extent, their teaching patterns as well. These are, though, subject to increasing pressures from marketization, developments in information technology and the range of other factors discussed above. The social concerns for academics can in their turn be seen as manifesting themselves at different levels, reflecting different intellectual and geographical boundaries: specialist and general international disciplinary affiliations, nationwide associations and more narrow departmentally-based groups.

These various frameworks – organizational, cognitive and social – can be seen to interact and at some points to interpenetrate, affecting the working lives of academics in different ways according to context. The importance of contextual considerations is often overlooked, but is – as subsequent chapters go on to argue – fundamental. Their significance is best brought out by the recognition that writings about HE, like academic activities themselves, are pitched at different levels of generality and specificity (Becher 1994).

At its most wide-ranging, HE research on what might be labelled the macro level focuses on system-wide issues, such as access studies and explorations of the labour market for graduates. Some of the enquiries in this genre offer international comparisons or focus on global phenomena. Because of their broad span, they have a tendency to homogenize their subject-matter and to filter out the uncomfortable exceptions that fail to match their generalizations.

An example can be found in the reference, earlier in this chapter, to 'Mode 2 knowledge', carrying the implication that traditional forms of knowledge generation are being phased out in favour of collective, applied transdisciplinary developments which take place mainly outside academia. Further reflection suggests, however, that such well-established areas of pure, monodisciplinary knowledge as anthropology, history, philosophy and the like are reasonably certain to survive under the assault of advanced technology. Even within scientific disciplines such as physics and biochemisty there remains considerable scepticism about the benefits gained from collaborative applied research compared with the serendipitous scientific discoveries that come from basic science (Henkel 2000: 201). Indeed one of the purposes of this book is to serve as a reminder of the diversity of knowledge forms and their associated knowledge communities, and hence to question the widespread tendency to assimilate them to the large-scale and headline-winning developments whose main home is in the applied sciences (see Chapter 8).

In contrast to these large-scale, generalizing studies, one can identify another set of enquiries directed at the micro level which focus on individual academics and students. Investigations of teaching approaches and learning experiences commonly have a home here. Other relevant findings have been remarked on earlier; for example, that research has shown managerialist policies to have imposed new and less favourable working conditions, reduced the scope of individual discretion and generally tended to deskill the members of the academic profession. Diversification too – as noted – has had an impact on individuals' qualifications for employment and for their subsequent promotion.

Intermediate between these two categories – enquiries that concentrate on global issues and those which direct themselves to individual concerns – lies a further group of studies located at what may be termed the meso level. These embody a distinctive set of social and cognitive considerations relating to academic communities clustered around common intellectual interests. Such communities can be studied from a number of different perspectives. In this book they are examined from a cultural standpoint, which is in its turn related to the social and cognitive contexts in which they operate.

To lay claim to this as being the distinctive approach adopted in the chapters which follow is not of course by implication to invalidate the other levels of research activity to which we have referred. It is rather to offer another source of understanding of a highly complex whole. The simile put forward by Allison (1971) makes the point in a telling way: much as nets of varying mesh trawl for different kinds of fish, so spectacles with contrasting lenses show up different aspects of the same field of vision. As noted in a different context in Chapter 4, one has to allow for a trade-off between comprehensiveness and specificity, between a broad view and a scrutiny in depth; each approach has its own particular advantages and limitations.

One point about the perspective adopted in the rest of the book remains to be underlined here: namely that it illustrates the need to pay closer attention than is often given to the differences between disciplinary – and in some cases sub-disciplinary – groups. That need has been increasingly recognized in relation to a diversity of aspects of HE, serving to emphasize that both theoretical understandings and practical policies cannot be assumed to relate equally to all academic contexts.

A variety of exemplars can be cited: for instance in relation to disciplinary differences in undergraduate teaching and learning (Hativa and Marincovich 1995; Ylijoki 2000); conventions in postgraduate education (Becher *et al.* 1994; Parry 1997); relations between teaching and research (Neumann 1996; Smeby 1998); aspects of staff development (Trowler and Knight 1999); perceptions of quality issues (Kekäle 2000); the concept of academic standards (Becher 1997); and approaches to departmental management (Kekäle 1998, 1999). In most cases, the identified contrasts between established cultural assumptions and practices can be seen to be overridden by uniform, undifferentiated policy requirements. In consequence such requirements can result in anomalous and insensitive impositions, which are liable to be tacitly, if not overtly, rejected by those called on to adopt them. A further development of this argument is to be found in Chapters 8 and 9.

Note

1. Scott (1998) usefully distinguishes internationalization from globalization. While the former is purposive and potentially more constrained geographically than the latter (being limited to Europe, for example), it is also more bounded in its scope. Globalization includes features that impact on all universities in multi-dimensional ways: for example environmental, conceptual and cultural.

2

Points of Departure

Relating tribes and territories

The central concern of the pages which follow is the relationship between the distinctive cultures within academic communities – academic tribes – and academic ideas – the territories across which they range. By 'cultures' we refer to sets of taken-for-granted values, attitudes and ways of behaving, which are articulated through and reinforced by recurrent practices among a group of people in a given context. Our primary focus in on practitioners in a dozen varied disciplines whose livelihood it is to work with ideas; the ideas are those that lend themselves to sustained exploration, and which form the subject matter of the disciplines in question.

The contention we advance, and here set out to substantiate, is that the ways in which particular groups of academics organize their professional lives are related in important ways to the intellectual tasks on which they are engaged. We argue that the ways in which academics engage with their subject matter, and the narratives they develop about this, are important structural factors in the formulation of disciplinary cultures. Together they represent features that lend coherence and relative permanence to academics' social practices, values and attitudes across time and places. Both disciplinary epistemology, understood as the 'actual' form and focus of knowledge within a discipline, and the phenomenology of that knowledge, the ideas and understandings that practitioners have about their discipline (and others), are important here. We shall be commenting on both in the following chapters.

In practice, academic cultures and disciplinary epistemology are inseparably intertwined. The flow of causation is not one way, rather the relationship is mutually infused: disciplinary knowledge forms are to a large extent constituted and instantiated socially. Meanwhile their constitution has a reciprocal effect on the cultures from which they spring. The relationship, then, involves a mutually dependent interplay of, on the one hand, the structural force of the epistemological character of disciplines that conditions culture and, on the other, the agentic capacity of individuals and groups for autonomous action, including interpretative acts.

In attempting to explore the characteristic features of their relationship it is nevertheless necessary to separate culture analytically from the epistemological properties of disciplines. We therefore seek to draw a distinction between the social aspects of knowledge communities on the one hand and the epistemological properties of knowledge forms on the other, and also to look closely at how the two influence one another.

We do not claim that the pattern is a simple one, or that the connections are unconditional. We acknowledge too that our focus here is on only one aspect of a complex web of causality and conditioning factors around the articulation of culture. Elsewhere one of us has identified a range of structural factors influencing academics' cultures (Trowler 1998a). In addition to epistemological factors these include: the patterns of educational ideologies found in any given university; the unique, pre-existing cultural configuration present within universities (including the organizational culture); and the 'profitability' (Levine 1980) attached to particular practices in given contexts. According to those analysts who subscribe to 'resource dependence theory' – for example, Slaughter and Leslie (1997) – the last is particularly important: the changes in funding of HE and in particular the decline in the unit of resources have brought about major changes in academic behaviour, changes in what faculty members do and how they allocate their time (1997: 112). Chapter 1 has tracked the changing nature of many structural features relevant to HE. Giddens (1984: xxxi, 17) notes that structures have the characteristics of both rules and resources. The former consist of normative elements and codes of signification while the latter comprise both authoritative and allocative aspects. In each case there have been important changes both to the status and significance of academic knowledge and changes to the power enjoyed by and resources available to academics across the world.

Importantly, too, the 'flow' of cultural currents into universities from their environment can have considerable influence on academic practices, values and attitudes. These currents include the norms, values and recurrent practices associated with, for example, 'Great Culture' (Alvesson 1993) (the characteristic national culture), and those associated with external structural features such as gender, ethnicity, social class and so on. Individuals entering new organizational settings inevitably import cultural patterns deriving from the wider environment and do not lose them simply because of the power of disciplinary epistemology.

The picture is made even more complex by the fact that culture cannot be simply 'read off' from structural location. Culture is both enacted and constructed, played out according to structurally-provided scripts as well as changed during that process. The academic, like all other social actors, is not a victim of circumstance, a 'homo sociologicus' (Dahrendorf 1968) completely driven by external forces but is at least partly empowered to reconstruct the cultural environment, both consciously and (more often) unconsciously.

Just how strong are the relative forces of social background, disciplinary epistemology, gender and the rest has been a matter of academic debate (see for example the contributions to the *European Journal of Education*, 25(3) 1990). This debate need not detain us here: our concern is to give sustained attention to one among a number of structural factors which have differential, and fluctuating, degrees of cultural influence.

We recognize then, the limits of any attempt to draw a one-to-one linkage between 'tribal cultures' and disciplinary territories. However our concern is to highlight a significant number of situations in which disciplinary practices can be reasonably closely matched with the characteristics of the relevant domains of enquiry and to explore the nature of this link.

In the process of identifying the interconnections between academic cultures and the nature of knowledge, a number of subsidiary themes are developed in the book. The first is about how knowledge itself can usefully be categorized and characterized for the purposes of the present argument. Other topics relate to the epistemological properties of disciplines, individually and collectively, and to their subsidiary specialisms; others again to the people who inhabit the academic world, their careers, their interactions, their taken-for-granted knowledge and attitudes and the rules that govern their behaviour.

The source material

The first edition of this book was based on data from interviews conducted by Tony Becher in the USA and England with 221 academics in 12 disciplines (see Appendix). We refer to this from here onwards as 'the initial study'. For this second edition we also draw on data from a study of a single university, 'NewU', and interviews with 24 newly appointed academics in England and Canada. We refer to these here as the 'NewU' and 'new academics' studies respectively. Wherever assertions or quotations remain unattributed in the text, they should be taken as based directly on the initial study.

The subject areas covered by the initial study represent a deliberately wide variety: biology, chemistry and physics are from the pure sciences; mechanical engineering and pharmacy are from applied science; economics and sociology are normally classified as social sciences; history and modern languages are located among the humanities; academic law may be described as a humanities-related profession; and geography and mathematics are not easily categorized, though the former is sometimes included among the social and the latter among the pure sciences.

We have also drawn extensively on the published – and more rarely the unpublished – writings of other researchers interested in this general area of enquiry. For this second edition we have particularly focused on integrating into the argument literature published since 1989, the publication date of the first edition. In so doing we have moved beyond the initial sample to comment on a broader range of disciplines and a more diverse set of institutions than those originally studied. The process of writing the new edition has also led to some refinement and development of the earlier argument.

The questions raised in the interviews for the initial study fell into five main categories. The first concerned the characteristics of the discipline: its overall nature and content, its internal and external boundaries, its degree of unity across specialisms, its nearest intellectual neighbours, the extent to which its profile varied from one country to another, and so on. The second group concerned epistemological issues: the role of theory, the importance of specialized techniques, the extent of quantification and modelling, the degree to which findings could be generalized, the way conclusions were established, and the like. The third concerned career patterns, including questions about the recruitment of new members and their induction into the discipline, how their specialisms were chosen, how they established independence and gained tenure, how much mobility there was between specialisms, and whether it was common to experience a 'mid-career crisis' in one's research. A fourth, closely related cluster of issues concentrated on reputations and rewards, such as the criteria for professional recognition, the existence and characteristics of disciplinary heroes, terms of praise and blame, and prizes and other marks of distinction. The fifth category explored questions about professional activity: the nature of communication patterns, forms and rates of publication, the structure of personal networks, competition and priority, plagiarism and sharp practice, grantsmanship and fashion, the extent of teamwork, and the incidence of jargon.

A final set of questions sought, without intruding too far into respondents' private lives, to explore their value systems: the extent of their involvement in their work, the aspects of their jobs that they considered particularly rewarding or unrewarding, the degree to which, as professionals, they were concerned with contemporary social and environmental issues, the wider benefits of their academic training, their stereotypes of fellow practitioners, and their stereotypes of practitioners in a variety of other disciplines.

The two new empirical research projects that inform the second edition were conducted by Paul Trowler between 1991 and 1998. The first was a 5-year ethnographic study of one English University, 'NewU', a medium-to-large unchartered (i.e. post 1992) institution. The research questions concerned academics' responses to changes of the sort that commentators had identified as damaging to academic life. The data collection methods involved 50 in-depth interviews with academics in 30 disciplinary or domain areas at or below Head of Department level, participant observation over a 5-year period and the use of secondary data, including other studies of the institution. This study is written up more fully in Trowler (1998a). The second was a study conducted by Trowler and Knight of 24 new academic appointees (NAAs) in five disciplines in ten Canadian and English universities, both chartered and unchartered. Again there were in-depth interviews with individuals, in some cases followed up by a second interview after around one year, as well as one extended focus group session with members of a single discipline in one institution. The research explored the experiences of organizational socialization and induction of NAAs into new settings, and the conclusions offered recommendations for better practice (Knight and Trowler 1999; Trowler and Knight 1999).

Academic cultures and structural location

The set of interviews for the initial study were conducted only with members of those departments that were viewed as reasonably prestigious within their disciplinary communities[1] on the ground that these people most clearly delineate and embody the central values of the discipline. As Clifford Geertz (1983), among others, has pointed out:

> Induction into the [disciplinary] community takes place at or near the top or center. But most people are not settled at or near the top or center but at some region lower down, further out . . . The majority of people follow a career pattern in which they are for several years at the perceived heart of things and then, in differing degrees and with different speeds are, in the jargon, 'downwardly mobile'.

Most academics at the time of the first set of interviews would have taken their own first and higher degrees in elite institutions, even if they later took up posts in non-elite ones. It was reasoned that the disciplinary values with which they were first inculcated would therefore be the values of the leading departments in their fields. Although these values might become modified by the demands of their present jobs, the definitive pattern would be the one found 'at the perceived heart of things'. So it seemed sensible to concentrate on the pacemakers rather than those who follow behind them.

However, we have subsequently come to revise these ideas. First, as we noted above, contextual factors can be a powerful means of moderating the impact of epistemology and epistemologically-related structural factors. Second, as we noted in Chapter 1, the nature of HE changed in fundamental ways between the mid-1980s and the late 1990s, particularly in the UK. While it was probably true in the 1950s, as David Riesman (1958) argues, that American HE institutions performed a 'snakelike procession' with lower status ones following the higher status ones just as the snake's body follows its head, this is much less the case today. A process of institutional diversification began during the 1980s across Europe (Teichler 1988). In the USA, the difference between doctoral-granting institutions and community colleges was already the difference between 'night and day' (Clark 1987a: 184). As a result, generalizations from data derived from elite academics in elite institutions have become increasingly tenuous.

Third, as well as system-wide diversification, institutions have become internally more diverse as the processes of subject parturition, dignification and programme affiliation take effect. The academic cultures among university staff in women's studies, business studies, fashion design and professions allied to medicine are in their nature and origins quite different from the sample of disciplines from which the original interviews for this study were drawn. In short, the multiple cultural configuration (Alvesson 1993) found within even elite universities is much more complex and diverse today than it was 15 years ago.

For these reasons, then, we consider it important for the links between academic tribal cultures and their disciplinary territories to use data and literature from a wider range of academic life than was originally the case in our consideration.

The interviews in the initial study were designed to encourage reasonably open-ended discussion about professional issues, but not specifically about the academic's role as a teacher. A limited number of respondents – particularly in the more vocationally oriented disciplines – did choose to talk about undergraduate courses and students, but the large majority preferred to focus on their activities as seekers after knowledge rather than as communicators of it.[2] The reason for this, it might be inferred, is that membership of the academic profession in elite departments is defined in terms of excellence in scholarship and originality in research, and not to any significant degree in terms of teaching capability. Again, extending the scope of the discussion for the new edition means giving more attention to pedagogical and other aspects of the academic's role.

Some landmarks in the argument

In the final chapter a systematic attempt is made to identify the linkages between the social and the cognitive – between academic tribes and the territories they inhabit. The patterns of interconnection are built up gradually throughout the text, rather than presented initially as a matter on which the reader is offered no evidential base to exercise his or her own critical judgement. However, it may be helpful to identify in advance some of the main considerations that support the concluding analysis, and to draw attention to some particular features which differentiate our argument from the accounts already advanced by others.

The first point to be established is how academic knowledge may usefully be categorized for the purposes of the study as a whole. The consideration of that issue occupies the concluding part of the present chapter, and provides a base from which to embark on a survey of the nature of disciplines and their constituent specialisms. It will be seen that the proposed classification is a well-established one, based on the two independent dimensions of hard and soft, pure and applied, knowledge.

The dimensions used to categorize the social features of knowledge communities are, however, less familiar. The first, which denotes the spectrum between convergent, tightly knit disciplinary configurations and those which are divergent and loosely knit, is first adumbrated in Chapter 4, but is developed further in the subsequent discussion. The second, marking the continuum from urban to rural modes of research activity, is introduced in

Chapter 6, as a prelude to the scrutiny of the distinctive patterns of communication associated with different types of academic networks.[3]

Another dichotomy worth highlighting at this point, in that it plays a significant, if sporadic, part in the discussion, is one between contextual imperatives and contextual associations. These opposing notions derive from the the antithesis between hard and soft knowledge areas. Contextual imperatives denote closely patterned sequences of explanation, with each new finding fitting neatly into place as the whole picture is pieced together. Contextual associations signify loosely knit clusters of ideas, with no clearly articulated framework of development. Both have clearly identifiable social correlates.

The characteristics attributable to the various levels of aggregation of knowledge – from broad subject groupings to small segments within specialized subdisciplinary areas – form another, and more important, subsidiary theme in the exposition. In particular, it transpired in the course of the initial study that specialisms display certain structural features which distinguish them from other specialisms within the same discipline, but which they share with comparable specialisms in other disciplines. As a result, the specialism rather than its parent discipline not only emerges as the fundamental unit of analysis but also comprises the domain in which the interrelationships between the cognitive and social aspects of the academic enterprise are most clearly manifested.

If the book as a whole has something new to say, it is perhaps because its theme straddles the little-explored border zone between the sociology of knowledge and social studies of science on the one hand and the study of HE on the other. The first has tended to concentrate almost exclusively on highly articulated areas of enquiry – the physical as against the biological sciences, physics as against chemistry, and high-energy physics as against more applied specialisms such as optics. It has had relatively little to say about technology, the social sciences or the humanities, except insofar as it represents them as less perfect manifestations of the orderly and relatively easily depicted ideal of hard pure knowledge. Writers on HE have focused largely on structural and organizational issues, playing down what Trow (1976a) has called the 'private life' of HE. Our own prime concern has been with the latter, and in particular with the range of disciplines and disciplinary communities outside as well as within the domain of 'big science'.

A fitting way to begin mapping this relatively uncharted territory is by recognizing the diversity and range of its topology and attempting to bring some order into the apparently chaotic configuration of features that constitute the landscape of academic knowledge.

The pieces of the patchwork

Knowledge has many metaphors. The image of a landscape is only one: another favoured candidate is that of a seamless cloak. Both, however, have implications of continuity and coherence, which bear poor comparison with the current state of human understanding. From the perspective of those engaged in its creation, knowledge would appear more closely comparable with a badly made patchwork quilt, some of whose constitutent scraps of material are only loosely tacked together, while others untidily overlap, and yet others seem inadvertently to have been omitted, leaving large and shapeless gaps in the fabric of the whole.

This claim may be readily illustrated from the accounts of witnesses who are themselves involved in the enterprise. The brief bulletins that follow on the current state of awareness in four different subject areas are based directly on the evidence of the initial set of interviews with researchers in each field in question. Their individual statements may not of course be representative, but, taken together, they indicate a series of idiosyncratic approaches towards the definition of relevant knowledge on the part of their own disciplinary groups. None matches closely the stereotype of hard pure knowledge adopted by many writers on the subject.

Let us start with biology: it is a field in which 'the living organism is the centre of gravity'; but 'the biological sciences are more wide-ranging than other scientific disciplines – and the extremes are further apart from one another'. Besides being 'very heterogeneous', biology is also 'an inexact science': 'the evidence is incomplete and scrappy, and in many cases the observations can't be repeated'. Although 'biologists are attracted by the idea of generalization, [they are] very conscious of the variability of the material with which they deal'; 'virtually every generalization is suspect'. In their turn, 'the variations in nature give rise to interpretation – there is a greater degree of subjectivity than most of us like to admit'. But even so, 'there is not much room for ideology . . . whatever your own beliefs, eventually someone will be able to demonstrate that results caused by personal bias are invalid'.

Mechanical engineering is also said by its proponents to be a 'very wide-ranging subject'. It is centrally concerned with 'the application of mechanical principles to technical devices', but it is about 'hardware for people' as well – and is thus 'concerned with economics, environment and the social situation'. Because it is 'a professional discipline . . . the problems are in a sense externally defined'. Moreover, 'the problems usually have no unique solutions'. Knowledge is cumulative, in the sense that 'it follows the development of understanding and technique'; but 'the relevance and implications of particular results are less clear than they are implicit'.

The core of sociology lies in 'exploring the action of social forces', and 'understanding the principles of change in society'. This involves 'looking for generalities', 'seeking causal explanations', and leads to a concern with 'the development of theory' and 'choices between hypotheses' – with 'knowledge that has explanatory power'. But the material for investigation is held to be too complex to allow for 'immutable social laws': there are 'very few axioms'. So a more realistic aim is to seek 'common patterns and processes in particular contexts'. There is a sense of 'progression in ideas' – 'both the subject-matter and the theoretical emphasis change over time'. Sociology is 'closer to history than to physics', in that 'it's more a matter of revising the existing corpus than building a new one'; of 'refutation and reformulation' – there is 'no sense of superseded knowledge'. The discipline embraces 'a spectrum from hard to soft data' – there are 'no tight, clear boundaries'. Theories are 'always contested – there are no consensual judgements'. But there are nonetheless 'perennial issues and problems', certain 'basic continuities and perennial concerns' which give the subject its definition and its shape.

In academic law, 'the centre of the subject is a body of rules'. The concern of its proponents is 'mainly with ordering a corpus of knowledge: it is a largely descriptive pursuit'. Law, one respondent observed, 'is the object, not the method of study – it can only be the method of practice'. There is a constantly changing body of material arising from new legislation – 'everything is always in a state of flux'. There is 'a tradition that law is value-free'; it is arguable that 'it is more resistant to ideology than some subjects'. Nevertheless, 'it leaves open the possibility of a critical, ideological function'. The subject allows 'room for shades of opinion', 'an absence of certainty, no clear-cut rules'. However, 'some aspects are uncontentious'; there are 'shared criteria of judgement'; 'a substantial consensus – at least until recently'; and 'validity in some areas within the existing norms'.

These very diverse accounts seem at first glance to point towards an unmanageable variety of knowledge forms. To be able to discuss them in any coherent manner, the next step must be to find a suitable means of grouping and classifying them.

Restrictions and paradigms

Taxonomies of knowledge fields have been generated in a wide variety of ways, and have yielded a multiplicity of different structures. Two examples are worth quoting at the outset, because of their particular contributions to the understanding of forms and communities of knowledge. The accounts of their originators (Pantin and Kuhn) share certain superficial similarities: both advance a simple, two-fold categorization; both are ostensibly concerned with the sciences to the exclusion of other disciplinary groups. However, it should be remarked that the basic distinctions that are made in each case can be extended to apply across the whole realm of academic knowledge, rather than being confined to one part of it; and that the import of the two is different in significant respects. Pantin's classification bears primarily on knowledge structures and relates to individual specialisms within disciplines, while Kuhn's is primarily concerned with academic communities and applies to the disciplinary rather than subdisciplinary level of research activity.

In marking the contrasts between what he calls the restricted and the unrestricted sciences, Pantin (1968) writes:

There is one real, and graded, distinction between sciences like the biologies and the physical sciences. The former are unrestricted sciences and their investigator must be prepared to follow their problems into any other science whatsoever. The physical sciences, as they are understood, are restricted in the field of phenomena to which they are devoted. They do not require the investigator to traverse all other sciences. But while this restriction is the basis of their success, because of the introduction of this restricted simplicity of their field we cannot necessarily take them or their methods as typical of all the sciences.

Earlier in the same chapter, he elaborates on the point:

The more we restrict the class of phenomena we observe and the number of its variables, the more far-reaching are the possible deductive consequences of our hypotheses. But in doing so, much of the grand variety of natural phenomena is systematically excluded from study. Very clever men [sic] are answering the relatively easy questions of the natural examination paper. In contrast, in biology such problems as 'What will be the ecological consequences of a general increase in nuclear radiation?' are so difficult that our answers seem paltry and emotional.

He does not attempt, in discussing the application of this dichotomy to 'the relations between the sciences', to draw out its implications to any significant extent (though Whitley (1977) argues that restricted sciences are also characterized by an esoteric theoretical structure and the need for elaborate technical facilities, while unrestricted fields are less theoretically specific). If he is less than clear about how current developments in unrestricted fields should be evaluated, and what directions future work should take, he offers no doubt that the more 'narrowly and specifically conceptual closure is made', the more clearly the domain boundaries are drawn.

The stratagem which Pantin's analysis exposes is that of defining out the messy problems in order to maintain the clarity and coherence of the physical sciences. To the extent that this is successful, one might say that the disciplines concerned depend on an artefactual definition of their boundaries. But it also has to be recognized that the territory so bounded has certain inherent characteristics that make such a definition possible (these are further explored below, in the process of marking the distinctions between hard and soft knowledge). In contrast, other areas of science – those which span 'the grand variety of natural phenomena', but also those which embrace practical applications – are less tidy. And in the social sciences and humanities many of the problems seem, as one historian interviewed in the initial study vividly put it, 'inherently lumpy'.

Kuhn is concerned with exploring a different distinction. His starting point (Kuhn 1962) was in the study of revolutionary phases in the development of physics, which led him to develop the notion of a paradigm. This is central to his differentiation of disciplinary groupings: on the one side the 'mature' sciences with clearly established paradigms, on the other those areas of research that are still at a pre-paradigmatic stage of development.

The contrast Kuhn marks is predominantly a social one: it is more akin to that between convergent, tightly knit and divergent, loosely knit academic communities than it is to that differentiating hard from soft knowledge domains. Its attraction to those who have subsequently adopted it seems, however, to have rested at least in part on the malleability of the underlying concept of a paradigm. The term is variously used and variously defined.[4] In some contexts it appears to denote the particular constellation of ideas and techniques, beliefs and values which serves to define a disciplinary culture (a sense that it is 'global, embracing all the shared commitments of a scientific group'; Kuhn 1977). In others, it is given the narrower sense of a 'disciplinary matrix', a compilation of the symbolic generalizations, models and exemplars that form 'the common possession of the practitioners of a professional discipline' (Kuhn 1977).

Clear and unambiguous paradigms denote disciplinary consensus; competing, formless, or non-existent ones are ascribed to communities in which there is a significant level of internal disagreement in both general ways of seeing the world and specific ways of tackling research issues. Scientific progress stems from working in a context in which there is close agreement on theories, methods of inquiry and the training of newcomers to the discipline. Where there is pluralism and dissension, as in many of the humanities and social sciences, systematic advances in knowledge must await the onset of maturity and the emergence of a developed paradigm. The implication here – which Kuhn does not develop in any detail – is that in the course of time preparadigmatic subjects will evolve towards mature paradigmatic status. As things now stand, there are a number of key distinctions, such as the demands for solutions to problems in the mature sciences to be unique, though this is not required or necessarily expected in other fields; the extent to which past knowledge is superseded, as against its maintaining some relevance over long periods of time; and the 'radically different value placed on innovation for innovation's sake' (Kuhn 1977).

It is tempting at this point to ask whether it is right to interpret Kuhn's analysis as suggesting that the differences in the degree of consensus which a disciplinary community is able to command are the result of no more than historical or social circumstance. We argue in this book that subtle interactions between disciplinary knowledge and the various social processes operating in and on academic cultures combine, for example, to enhance the development of consensus among physicists and hinder it among sociologists or linguists.

Knowledge as portrayed by the knower

Both Pantin and Kuhn base their taxonomies on the detached observation of how researchers operate in their exploration of different domains. From the standpoint of this study, another useful approach to categorizing and characterizing knowledge forms derives from an examination of how the actors themselves perceive the particular arenas in which they are engaged. This type of phenomenological analysis can be illustrated by the contributions of Biglan and Kolb.

Biglan (1973a) based his discussion of 'the characteristics of subject matter in different academic areas' on questionnaire data from academics. His sample was relatively small (168 faculty members at the University of Illinois and 54 at a small western college), but his findings were detailed. On the basis of the judgements he had solicited about similarities and differences among 36 subject areas, he was able to derive three main dimensions against which to map the responses: hard versus soft, pure versus applied and life system versus non-life system. He associates the first with 'the degree to which a paradigm exists' (though it would in our view be more aptly identified with Pantin's restricted-unrestricted dichotomy); the second is related to 'the degree of concern with application'; and the third serves to differentiate 'biological and social areas from those that deal with inanimate objects'. His mappings of subject fields onto pairs of these dimensions help to underline the diversity of epistemological characteristics of different academic disciplines. While the data suggest some close affinities between particular knowledge groups across any two of the three mappings, only relatively few (such as chemistry and physics or the various subspecialisms of engineering) form a stable cluster across the whole range.

Where Biglan – in common with other writers such as Lodahl and Gordon (1972) – concerned himself with how academics themselves perceive the characteristics of knowledge fields, using survey techniques, Kolb (1981) adopted a contrasting approach. His data were derived from students' learning strategies rather than from the judgements of faculty members and involved the application, not of a questionnaire, but of a psychometric test – the Kolb Learning Style Inventory (LSI). It would seem all the more remarkable that his findings were quite closely consistent with those of Biglan. Kolb set out to measure 'learning styles along two basic dimensions of abstract-concrete and active-reflective' (the former contrasting a bias towards conceptualization with a domination by immediate experience, and the latter a preference for active experimentation over detached observation). In a study of 800 practitioners and students of management, who came from a wide variety of disciplinary backgrounds, Kolb found that 'variations in learning style . . . were strongly associated with . . . undergraduate educational experience'. When the average LSI scores for various undergraduate majors were charted against the abstract–concrete and active–reflective axes, the subject mappings overlapped to a significant extent with Biglan's. To be more specific, using the latter's 'dimensions accounting for the most variance . . . hard-soft and pure-applied' (i.e. dropping the life system–non-life system category), Kolb was able to show that 'of the twelve disciplines common to the two studies, nine are in identical quadrants'. When the exercise was repeated on a much larger and wider database, the results were again 'highly consistent' between Kolb's classifications and Biglan's. Kolb concluded that:

the commonly accepted division of academic fields into two camps, the scientific and artistic, or abstract and concrete ... might be usefully enriched by the addition of a second dimension, namely active reflective or applied-basic. When academic fields are mapped on this two-dimensional space, a four-fold typology of disciplines emerges. In the abstract reflect-ive [hard pure] quadrant are clustered the *natural sciences and mathem-atics*, while the abstract-active [hard applied] quadrant includes the *science-based professions*, most notably the engineering fields. The concrete-active [soft applied] quadrant encompasses what might be called the *social professions*, such as education, social work, and law. The concrete-reflective quadrant [soft pure] includes the *humanities and social sciences*.

(1981, original emphasis)

The Kolb-Biglan classification of academic knowledge seems to us a particu-larly apposite one for the purposes of this enquiry, though we prefer Biglan's more familiar contrasts between hard and soft, pure and applied, to the more esoteric terminology used by Kolb. It has a number of advantages over its competitors. It is capable of making more subtle distinctions than are the unidimensional scales adopted by Kuhn, Pantin and many other writers, but is not so complex as to become unfunctional – a defect from which Whitley's (1984) scheme would appear to suffer. It is more directly related to established disciplinary groupings than are such abstract catego-rizations as that developed by Hirst (1974), but departs from the well-worn clustering of the natural sciences, social sciences and humanities to elide the division between the latter two and to include relevant areas of applica-tion. In contrast with the organizationally based taxonomy of Collins (1975), it directs attention to the epistemological properties of knowledge fields as much as to the social characteristics of research groups. Accordingly, it is the system we propose to adopt in the subsequent discussion.

Characteristics of subject matter

So far, the emphasis has been on categories rather than contents. While consideration has been given to the broad areas into which knowledge might conveniently be classified, relatively little has been said about the epistemological features of any given category. The overall framework within which characteristics will be assigned will be the one already identified, comprising four domains: hard pure, soft pure, hard applied and soft applied. Table 2.1 summarizes the characteristics of each of these categor-ies as they are portrayed in realist accounts; those that see disciplinary know-ledge as reflecting real-world differences in subject matter.

In this type of account, then, there are reasonably clear distinctions between the knowledge domains in terms of the following: characteristics

Table 2.1   Knowledge and disciplinary grouping (adapted from Becher 1994)

Disciplinary groupings	Nature of knowledge
Pure sciences (e.g. physics): 'hard-pure'	Cumulative; atomistic (crystalline/tree-like); concerned with universals, quantities, simplification; impersonal, value-free; clear criteria for knowledge verification and obsolescence; consensus over significant questions to address, now and in the future; results in discovery/explanation.
Humanities (e.g. history) and pure social sciences (e.g. anthropology): 'soft-pure'	Reiterative; holistic (organic/river-like); concerned with particulars, qualities, complication; personal, value-laden; dispute over criteria for knowledge verification and obsolescence; lack of consensus over significant questions to address; results in understanding/ interpretation.[5]
Technologies (e.g. mechanical engineering, clinical medicine): 'hard-applied'	Purposive; pragmatic (know-how via hard knowledge); concerned with mastery of physical environment; applies heuristic approaches; uses both qualitative and quantitative approaches; criteria for judgement are purposive, functional; results in products/techniques.
Applied social science (e.g. education, law, social administration): 'soft-applied'	Functional; utilitarian (know-how via soft knowledge); concerned with enhancement of [semi-] professional practice; uses case studies and case law to a large extent; results in protocols/procedures.

in the objects of enquiry; the nature of knowledge growth; the relationship between the researcher and knowledge; enquiry procedures; extent of truth claims and criteria for making them; the results of research. Such relatively clear delineations were at one time quite easy to find in the literature concerning or drawing on disciplinary differences. The realist approach is particularly evident in work that seeks to distinguish between disciplines for an applied purpose. Examples include Davidson's (1994) and Gregg's (1996) accounts of the responses to curricular modularization displayed in different disciplines in the UK, Kekäle's (1999) account of preferred leadership approaches across the disciplines and the description of different teaching approaches in Hativa and Marincovich (1995).

The result of using such broad-brush depictions and such stark delineations to depict the four knowledge domains must inevitably be closer to a painting in rough outline than to a fully formed and faithful likeness. Three particular caveats must be entered against the account that has been given. The first returns to the significance of social factors in the construction of disciplinary knowledge. The second concerns the effects of temporal change and the third the oversimplification of categories.

We have already noted that disciplines can be viewed from a realist or a phenomenological point of view: the one adopting a perspective that sees disciplinary knowledge as reflecting a discernible and stable reality, the other seeing it as essentially socially constructed: 'the personal map of knowledge which we all have in our heads' (Evans 1995: 253). We reject the relativism that wholehearted adoption of the latter position implies. Rather our view is that knowledge structures are mediated by social processes.

So far we have been primarily concerned with disciplinary epistemology in the abstract but at this point we need to remark on the role of the social in shaping the epistemological. Power is an important variable in this connection. Bernstein (1971) notes that both a discipline's classification (the extent to which its contents are delineated from those of other disciplines) and its framing (the extent to which there is an explicit and agreed content to be transmitted to students and the degree to which this transmission is under the control of academics) essentially reflect power relationships. A related issue is whether the discipline has a strong collection code (that is, where knowledge is seen as cumulative) rather than an integrated code (where it is agglomerative). A situation in which a discipline is highly classified, strongly framed and has a strong collection code is one in which academics are empowered.

For Bernstein, however, this is a social characteristic, not an epistemological one. Where academic power is under threat, for example in a highly market-oriented HE system or in lower-status institutions in a highly diversified one (Clark 1987b), what are superficially the same disciplines will take on different characteristics. Accordingly we concur that the location of an academic tribe within the flow of power relations will have important effects on the 'shape' of its disciplinary knowledge, as well as the obverse being the case:

> principles of power and social control are realized through educational knowledge codes, and through the codes they enter into, and shape, consciousness . . . [A] change of code involves fundamental changes in the classification and framing of knowledge and so changes in the structure and distribution of power and in principles of control. It is no wonder that deep-felt resistances are called out by the issue of educational codes.
>
> (Bernstein 1971: 54 and 63)

Related to this is the impact on epistemological forms of government and other agencies with the power to change the character of disciplines. Henkel reports that government and European policies have had important effects on the ways that disciplines work, re-shaping practices that had been developing in other directions as a result of epistemological drivers, among others. Examples include the mathematization of economics (a result of the Research Assessment Exercise) and the push towards collaborative activity and the division between research and teaching in the sciences: 'some [respondents] feared that a model of development appropriate to science was being imposed upon them without due regard for the differences between different fields of knowledge' (Henkel 2000: 135). One consequence of academics' increasing involvement in 'chasing the dollar' is that the dollar's involvement in shaping epistemological forms is becoming increasingly central (Henkel 2000: 202–4).

Social context is also important at a lower level of analysis than the HE system or the individual institution. Disciplinary narratives are also constructed by individual academics, and are influenced in part by the educational ideology to which they adhere. Thus engineering can be perceived as having a strong or a weak collection code, for example, depending on whether the academic concerned subscribes to a traditionalist or progressivist ideology (Trowler 1998a), and whether the discipline is seen as applied, professional, discipline or pure (Henkel 1987). Likewise English as a discipline may be perceived as having a strong or a weak collection code – as being primarily about appreciation and analysis of 'the canon' or as being closely related to social scientific concerns, depending on the academic (Evans 1993). Social context at the micro level is important in another sense too. Gilbert and Mulkay (1984) have shown that natural scientists construe their actions and beliefs in a context-dependent way using, promiscuously, both empiricist and non-empiricist repertoires. 'Science' is represented in different ways depending on the situation, including (we may infer) that of being interviewed by a social scientist (Knorr Cetina 1988). For these reasons, then, we need to take into account narratives, 'stories', about disciplinary epistemology as well as disciplinary knowledge itself.

Moving to our second qualification the steadily changing (and, in the long term, transient) nature of knowledge makes it difficult to claim that any attempt at categorizing it can be permanent and enduring. It is not only that what counts as present understanding obviously changes with the passage of time: as Hirst (1974) allows, it is also possible that quite new forms of knowledge could emerge and – one might add – existing ones become defunct, or drastically modified.[6] Taxonomies of the kind discussed in this chapter can do no more than take account, more or less effectively, of our existing state of intellectual awareness. Accordingly, they can at best be seen as convenient but contingent devices for ordering our understanding of what knowledge is like in all its various forms. Moreover the long-term trend appears to be one of fragmentation of the 'epistemic machinery', the different machineries of knowledge construction in the disciplines. Examining two hard-pure intellectual fields, Knorr Cetina (1999: 3) notes that:

Magnifying this aspect of science – not its production of knowledge but its epistemic machinery – reveals the fragmentation of contemporary science; it displays the different architectures of empirical approaches, specific constructions of the referent, particular ontologies of instruments, and different social machines . . . This *disunifies* the sciences; it runs counter to an assumption generally associated with the work of the Vienna Circle of more than fifty years ago, particularly the argument for the unity of science.

(Emphasis in original)

Where the focus is on the disciplines themselves rather than some object outside them with which they interact, such as modularized curricular structures or patterns of leadership, the differences between them are foregrounded and the categories begin to erode.

The usefulness of knowledge categorization systems has to be further qualified, finally, by noting that they do not comprise neat and regular pigeonholes; nor do they, in practice, contain perfectly formed and purebred pigeons. To put it more plainly, the boundaries between the hard/soft, pure/applied knowledge domains cannot be located with much precision, and even when they have been staked out, several of the established disciplines fail to fit comfortably within them. It is all very well to group together, say, the social sciences and humanities, as one more or less homogeneous category of soft pure knowledge; but to do so is to brush aside the evident differences between and within their constituent subjects. Economics, one might argue, is closer to a hard pure than a soft pure discipline, especially if contrasted with, for example, anthropology; and there are quite fundamental distinctions too in methods, concepts and forms of argument between history and psychology. Moreover, most individual subject areas themselves turn out on examination to contain a diversity of research styles and epistemological characteristics. Physical geography has to be placed on the hard, and human geography the soft, side of the dividing line between science and social science; some of the more theoretical aspects of engineering are purer in character than some of the more practical aspects of physics. To allocate disciplines to domains in the apparently straightforward way that Biglan (1973a, b) and Kolb (1981) have done – alongside the exponents of other taxonomic systems – may be acceptable at a broad general level of analysis, but could prove seriously misleading when subjected to closer and more detailed examination.

Classificatory exercises of this kind nevertheless serve a useful purpose. As Kolb (1981) points out, they 'cannot do justice to the complexity and variation of inquiry processes and knowledge structures in various disciplines', but they do 'identify useful dimensions for describing [disciplinary] variations'. They also help to show up continuities and interconnections that more minute and localized scrutiny could obscure, or at best, fail to bring to light. The Kolb-Biglan framework, as subsequent discussion will show, can provide a workmanlike set of categories and a useful basic terminology for exploring knowledge in all its variety (as evidenced in the diverse subject fields) and in all its particularity (as exemplified in their constituent specialisms).

Notes

1. The selection of departments in Britain was in most cases based on advice from members of the disciplines concerned in the University of Sussex.
2. Compare the observation by Sanford (1971) that: 'teachers at distinguished institutions are orientated not to their institutions but to their disciplines... Such professors, when they assemble informally or formally, almost never discuss teaching; this is not the 'shop' they talk.'
3. It is interesting to note that, although urban research (typically involving densely populated problem areas, close interaction, intense competition, high budgets and large teams) occupies a relatively small part of the whole scenario, it tends to be singled out for attention by most social scientists concerned with the study of research activity. This undue weight of concentration on one particular mode of enquiry may perhaps reflect the predominance accorded to the positivistic worldview, even by those who profess to be out of sympathy with it.
4. Masterman (1970) was able to distinguish no less than 21 different senses of the term in Kuhn's exposition.
5. The point has been aptly developed, in relation to history, by Weber (1977): 'essentially... the study of history is the re-reading of the past... in the beginning because one wants to discover it for oneself and assimilate it, and later because what one looks for (hence sees) in familiar territory may be quite different from what one has discerned before or learned from others.'

   In a different disciplinary context, Becker (1982) makes the closely related observation that, as a general rule: 'Sociology does not discover what no one ever knew before, in this differing from the natural sciences. Rather, good social science produces a deeper understanding of things that people are pretty much aware of.'
6. The candidates for mortality identified by respondents were all at the sub-disciplinary level: geometrical optics in physics as 'a subject that has died'; comparative anatomy in biology as 'played through'; the classification of finite groups in mathematics as 'pretty well moribund'; and human capital theory in economics, 'once a lively area, now virtually defunct'.

3

Academic Disciplines

The nature of a discipline

The concept of an academic discipline is not altogether straightforward, in that, as is true of many concepts, it allows room for some uncertainties of application. There may be doubts, for example, whether statistics is now sufficiently separate from its parent discipline, mathematics, to constitute a discipline on its own. The answer will depend on the extent to which leading academic institutions recognize the hiving off in terms of their organizational structures (whether, that is, they number statistics among their fully-fledged departments), and also on the degree to which a freestanding international community has emerged, with its own professional associations and specialist journals. In some of the typical instances of dispute, certain institutions may have decided to establish departments in a particular field but may find that the intellectual validity of those departments is under challenge from established academic opinion (as has happened in the case of black studies, viniculture and parapsychology). Disciplines are thus in part identified by the existence of relevant departments; but it does not follow that every department represents a discipline. International currency is an important criterion, as is a general though not sharply defined set of notions of academic credibility, intellectual substance, and appropriateness of subject matter. Despite such apparent complications, however, people with any interest and involvement in academic affairs seem to have little difficulty in understanding what a discipline is, or in taking a confident part in discussions about borderline or dubious cases.

Disciplines and organizational structures

One way of looking at disciplines is through a structural framework, noting how they are manifested in the basic organizational components of the HE system (e.g. Clark 1983; Evans 1995). Such a perspective tends to highlight one particular range of issues: the variation in how academic institutions elect to draw the map of knowledge; what operational distinctions need to be made between traditional established disciplines (such as history or physics) and interdisciplinary fields (urban studies, peace studies and the like); the organizational complexities of combining autonomous, self-generating units within a single managerial structure; the mechanisms for accommodating newly defined intellectual groupings and phasing out those that are no longer regarded as viable. For Ball and Lacey (1995: 95), studying subject departments in schools, 'subjects are not monoliths but . . . contextual realizations': what counts as English, maths or history will differ from department to department, or at least could have done so before the implementation of the national curriculum in the UK. This is a strong form of what might be called a situationally contingent approach to understanding disciplines: while it may have resonance with recent thinking in practice-based theorizing and situated learning theory (Lave and Wenger 1991; Lave 1993; Gherardi 2000), it arguably goes too far.

As we suggested in Chapter 2, there clearly are divisions within disciplines that are enacted across and within departments. The discipline of English in the UK is divided between critical theorists and Leavisites (Evans 1993). The equivalent split in the USA is between those concerned to dismantle disciplinary boundaries and focus on gender, class and ethnoracial formations on the one hand and the National Association of Scholars on the other, whose concern is with excellence and the appreciation of the greats (Saldivar 1997). Sociology meanwhile is split between 'pomos' (postmodernists) and the rest. Such divisions are conditioned by larger structural factors, particularly educational ideologies, and so conform to more regular patterns than would be the case if they were entirely contingent on their organizational context.

We have already addressed the issue of the extent to which the attitudes, activities and cognitive styles of groups of academics representing a particular discipline are bound up with the characteristics and structures of the knowledge domains with which such groups are professionally concerned. We have argued that the two are so mutually interdependent that it is difficult to untangle them and impossible to determine any single direction of influence between them. We concur, then, with Knorr Cetina (1999) who, in discussing epistemic cultures, argues that what she calls 'epistemic machineries' are imbricated in unique cultural mileux, especially in terms of their symbolic dimensions but, at the same time, the practices associated with those machineries inform in important ways the cultures within which they operate:

I take the position that signification and the behavioral text of practice cannot be separated, and that views of culture that ignore the conduct of experience are just as limited as the views of practice that squeeze symbols out of the picture.

(Knorr Cetina 1999: 10–11)

Even so, if one is to examine the nature of the interconnections, a distinction must be made – at least in theoretical terms – between forms of knowledge and knowledge communities. That contrast is explored in detail in Chapter 9, though it crops up on a number of occasions in the intervening discussion.

Global disciplines: unity and diversity

While it is convenient in some contexts to represent disciplines as clearly distinguishable and reasonably stable entities, in Chapter 2 we acknowledged that they are subject to both historical and geographical variation. The changing nature of knowledge domains over time has its impact on the identities and cultural characteristics of disciplines. Apart from the traumas of the birth of new disciplinary groupings, the death of old ones, or the occasionally dramatic metamorphosis of those in middle life, the process of steady evolution has its own recognizable consequences. Not only are relatively fast-moving fields such as biochemistry noticeably more sophisticated and more specialized than they were a decade or two ago: even the apparently more reflective and conservative subjects (e.g. history or modern languages) have undergone significant long-term changes. Taking history as an example, Burton Clark (1996b: 420) notes that substantive disciplinary growth has been a remarkable feature of the past three decades and one aspect of this, subject dispersion, has meant that history as a discipline has been constantly spreading its wings to cover 'more eras, locales and activities'. But, as Toulmin (1972) remarks, 'each discipline, though mutable, normally displays a recognizable continuity', its differentiation over time is seldom such as to obliterate all significant resemblance.

The same is true of changes in spatial location. Here, Toulmin draws attention to the 'differences of emphasis in the characteristic judgements of different research centres'. On a localized scale, Ruscio (1987) has sensitively explored the 'subtle, intricate interaction' between 'the various disciplines and . . . the many institutions, each with its own culture'. He uses the biological analogy of a genotype and a phenotype: 'The genotype represents the fundamental instructions to the organism and its potential for survival and growth; the phenotype represents the actual manifestation of that potential in a particular physical setting.' His study shows the phenotypical variations to be substantial, but he is confident that one can nonetheless identify genotypical 'cultures endemic to each discipline'.

Ruscio's study was confined to universities and colleges in the USA. But even if one takes a more global perspective, namely that of the cross-national manifestations of disciplinary cultures, there are noticeable similarities as well as discernible differences. Some of the variations stem from identifiable features of a particular society, such as the structure of its education system, or its level of economic development. Others, however, would seem more broadly to reflect national traits and traditions: 'Great Culture'.

Among relevant sources in the published literature, Alvesson's (1993) work theorizes well the relevance of Great Culture as it impinges on practices, values and attitudes in organizations, including universities. Meanwhile Hofstede's writing (1980, 1994) is best known in this field in relation to intercultural practices, though not specifically in relation to academic work. In terms of nationally distinctive disciplinary approaches and practices, Podgorecki (1997) finds some significant variations in practice and approach between Canada, China, Poland, the United Kingdom and the USA. These developed as national cultures filtered through organizational context, creating distinctive approaches in each case.

Within the initial sample of academic disciplines, the respondents in physics felt able to talk about 'typical French papers', or to contend that 'run-of-the-mill physics in Russia is very different from its counterpart in Britain'. National stereotypes of a conventional (and relatively crude) kind were evoked. For example, one academic engineer remarked that:

> the French use what might be called an absolute approach, beginning with a highly mathematical exploration of the feasibility of each problem; US engineers adopt a comparative approach, starting straight in on solutions and looking at the relative merits and demerits of different ones.

Another referred to the 'heavy-handed' nature of German mechanical engineering. Among the historians, who in their turn identified 'different national habits of mind', one remarked that:

> History is not and cannot be culture free. There is a national way of looking at things. Even if you take a strong and clearly defined ideology such as Marxism, the English Marxist historian differs from the German Marxist historian, and both in their turn differ from the Russian.

Significantly, however, the same respondent added that 'even if it contains different ideologies and cultures, there is nevertheless a definable world of historians'. Similarly, 'there are different national profiles, but economics is an international discipline in the sense that economists in one country can understand what economists in another country are talking about'.

No one who writes or speaks of national differences seems to want to deny that strong resemblances persist between different branches of the same family.[1]

Tribalism and tradition

Despite their temporal shifts of character and their institutional and national diversity, we may appropriately conceive of disciplines as having recognizable identities and particular cultural attributes. We shall need next to consider the forms that such identities and attributes may take.

In a characteristic piece of reminiscence, Evelyn Waugh (1956) wrote of pre-war English aristocratic society as:

divided into spheres of influence among hereditary magnates . . . the grandees avoided one another unless they were closely related. They met on state occasions and on the racecourse. They did not frequent one another's houses. You might find almost anyone in a ducal castle – convalescent, penurious cousins, advisory experts, sycophants, gigolos and plain blackmailers. The one thing you could be sure of not finding was a concourse of other dukes. English society, it seemed to me, was a complex of tribes, each with its chief and elders and witch-doctors and braves, each with its own dialect and deity, each strongly xenophobic.

The tribal aspects of academia are not too far removed from this, as a crowd of witnesses attests. Among them, Clark (1963) writes:

It is around the disciplines that faculty subcultures increasingly form. As the work and the points of view grow more specialised, men [sic] in different disciplines have fewer things in common, in their background and in their daily problems. They have less impulse to interact with one another and less ability to do so . . . Men of the sociological tribe rarely visit the land of the physicists and have little idea what they do over there. If the sociologists were to step into the building occupied by the English department, they would encounter the cold stares if not the slingshots of the hostile natives . . . the disciplines exist as separate estates, with distinctive subcultures.

However (to continue the metaphor) academic tribes do send out raiding parties from time to time. Clark (1993: 275), citing Harold Perkin, notes that historians frequently become 'licensed rustlers' who poach stock and purloin crops from neighbours. The same is true of sociologists and other disciplinary tribes (Becher *et al.* 1994: 77). Sometimes, of course, friendly relations may be established to mutual benefit, as descriptions of temporary alliances in Mode 2-type knowledge structures indicate. However the process of sub-disciplinary specialization constitutes a countervailing trend, in which particular segments of disciplines – especially those undergoing a process of divergence – dig their wells deeper and deeper and can in some cases 'press against the overall culture of the discipline [and] . . . threaten its unity' (Becher 1990: 333).

An individual's sense of belonging to his or her academic tribe is manifested in a variety of ways:

The culture of the discipline includes idols: the pictures on the walls and dustjackets of books kept in view are of Albert Einstein and Max Planck and Robert Oppenheimer in the office of the physicist and of Max Weber and Karl Marx and Emile Durkheim in the office of the sociologist.

(Clark 1980)

It also involves artefacts – a chemist's desk is prone to display three-dimensional models of complex molecular structures, an anthropologist's walls are commonly adorned with colourful tapestries and enlarged photographic prints of beautiful black people, while a mathematician may boast no more than a chalkboard scribbled over with algebraic symbols.[2]

It is, however, through the medium of language that some of the more fundamental distinctions emerge. A detailed analysis of disciplinary discourse (such as those attempted by Bazerman 1981, or Becher 1987b) can help not only to bring out characteristic cultural features of disciplines but also to highlight various aspects of the knowledge domains to which they relate. It is possible by this means to discern differences in the modes in which arguments are generated, developed, expressed and reported, and to tease out the epistemological implications of the ways in which others' work is evaluated.

On the latter point, Geertz (1983) remarks that 'the terms through which the devotees of a scholarly pursuit represent their aims, judgements, justifications, and so on, seem to me to take one a long way, when properly understood, toward grasping what that pursuit is all about'. The initial research data bring out some of the connections between the terms of appraisal that are widely used in a particular discipline and the nature of the relevant knowledge field. That historians will commend a piece of work as 'masterly', and will be ready to single out the quality of 'good craftsmanship' (features that are rarely identified in other disciplines), suggests a particular emphasis on gaining command of, and shaping into an aesthetically pleasing, purposeful and well-articulated product, a body of miscellaneous and formless raw material. The high premium placed on 'elegant', 'economical', 'productive' and 'powerful' solutions to mathematical and physical problems points towards a knowledge field in which it is possible to identify structural simplicity, reducing explanation to essentials, and where, in a close network of interconnected phenomena, certain discoveries hold within them the means of generating many others. The epithets 'persuasive', 'thought provoking' and 'stimulating', seemingly more common in sociology than elsewhere, suggest a particular concern with the quality of the analysis itself and with its effects on the audience, as against its substantive content. In similar vein, one might note that among physicists, 'accurate' and 'rigorous' are double-edged tributes, since no physics worthy of the name should lack either property; while in both history and sociology to use the word 'biased' is 'to betray one's naivete', in that every interpretation must have this feature to some degree.[3]

More generally, the professional language and literature of a disciplinary group play a key role in establishing its cultural identity. This is clearly so when they embody a particular symbolism of their own (as in mathematics and theoretical physics), or a significant number of specialized terms (as in many of the biological and social sciences), placing them to a greater or lesser degree beyond the reach of an uninitiated audience. But in more subtle ways the exclusion also operates in those disciplines (such as history and, perhaps, to a decreasing extent, literary studies) that pride themselves on not being 'jargon-ridden', since the communication here nonetheless creates what linguists would call its own register – a particular set of favoured terms, sentence structures and logical syntax – which it is not easy for an outsider to imitate.

The tribes of academe, one might argue, define their own identities and defend their own patches of intellectual ground by employing a variety of devices geared to the exclusion of illegal immigrants. Some, as we have noted, are manifest in physical form ('the building occupied by the English department', in Clark's words); others emerge in the particularities of membership and constitution (Waugh's 'complex of tribes, each with its chief and elders and witch-doctors and braves'). Alongside these structural features of disciplinary communities, exercising an even more powerful integrating force, are their more explicitly cultural elements: their traditions, customs and practices, transmitted knowledge, beliefs, morals and rules of conduct, as well as their linguistic and symbolic forms of communication and the meanings they share. To be admitted to membership of a particular sector of the academic profession involves not only a sufficient level of technical proficiency in one's intellectual trade but also a proper measure of loyalty to one's collegial group and of adherence to its norms. An appreciation of how an individual is inducted into the disciplinary culture is important to the understanding of that culture.

Disciplinary socialization

In its very nature, being a member of a disciplinary community involves a sense of identity and personal commitment, a 'way of being in the world', a matter of taking on 'a cultural frame that defines a great part of one's life' (Geertz 1983). Traditionally for a would-be academic the process of developing that identity and commitment may well begin as an undergraduate, but is likely to be at its most intense at the postgraduate stage, culminating in the award of a doctorate and, for a few, the first offer of employment as a faculty member. In recent times, reflecting the incidence of disciplinary dignification and the vocationalization of HE (see Chapter 1), the paths leading to academic life have become more numerous and have their origins in many different places. Academics are now quite likely to have a background in the professions, the arts or commerce and to have completed their doctorate later in life, if at all. Thus the teacher educators interviewed by Potts (1997) brought to the academy 'the influence of their past careers [in schools which] did not disappear' (Potts 1997: 224).

This diversification of entry routes gives even greater significance to recent thinking on organizational and disciplinary socialization than would be the case in a more stable environment. Influenced by postmodernist thinking on the one hand and neo-Vygotskyist approaches on the other, depictions of this process now stress the fact that individuals construct rather than simply adopt a particular 'way of being', a personal and professional identity, set of values, attitudes, taken-for-granted knowledge and recurrent practices. This goes beyond the notion of 'counter-socialization' (Gross 1975), which merely suggests that new recruits can change the organization as well as being changed themselves. Constructivist approaches influenced by postmodernism tend to stress the role of individual agency in identity and cultural construction (Tierney 1997; Trowler and Knight 1999), while culturalist 'situated practice' approaches place more emphasis on context-specific socialization and learning within 'communities' of practice (Lave and Wenger 1991; Guile and Young 1998; Trowler and Knight 2000). The former stresses the role of the individual in both taking and making social reality while the latter shifts the focus to the community, adopting a systemic, collective perspective. Here the power and role of individuals is de-emphasized and their historical and social context is placed in the analytical foreground (Engeström 2000).

However, the creative power of individuals should not be overstressed. Disciplinary socialization involves a number of different elements that are structural in nature, conditioning this accommodative process. Among them, Taylor (1976) singles out the power of the discipline's own ideology, built up of 'heroic myths'. Illustrating this with particular reference to geography, he remarks that:

> other disciplines are portrayed as involving specialist 'blinkers' or not fully appreciating the importance of the spatial dimension. In contrast there is the myth of the geographer as 'the great synthesiser', the 'foreman' who combines the individually futile ideas of the blind labouring specialists.

Representations of this kind, Taylor adds, need little empirical evidence; they are 'vast generalisations which have the basic role of creating an overall purpose and cohesion' out of what appears in practice as a highly disparate activity.

Other common components in a disciplinary ideology would include 'specially reconstructed histories', involving a judicious selection from past events, and a careful choice of folk heroes (as Taylor wryly remarks, 'Most other disciplines would be surprised at geographical claims concerning Immanuel Kant and Sir Francis Galton for instance'). These legendary aspects of a disciplinary culture have, incidentally, a wider role: they serve not only as part of the machinery of socialization, but also as weapons to be deployed in the course of internal disputes and controversies – a point to which we return in Chapter 6.

Myths and legends are, however, only part of what Bourdieu (1979) has termed the 'cultural capital', which one can inherit in acquiring the membership of a disciplinary community. At a more mundane level, novices are initiated into folkloric discourses and codes of practice and conventions that condition the way they see the world and interact with it. A telling example of how this 'hidden curriculum' operates, even at the undergraduate level, is provided by Snyder's (1971) analysis of intellectual and social life among engineering students at MIT. Becker *et al.* (1961), in a seminal study which has spawned relatively little follow-up work (but see Jefferys and Elston 1989; Cribb and Bignold 1999) offer a further illustration in the context of a medical school, showing in fascinating detail how professional attitudes and values are gradually shaped through the interaction of students with one another, with their instructors, and with their work. The key here is the interaction, not simply the transmission of values, attitudes, stories, myths and largely taken-for-granted ways of doing things. As McDermott and Varenne (1995) express the processual character of socialization:

> Life in culture is polyphonous and multivocalic; it is made of the voices of many, each one brought to life and made significant by the other, only sometimes by being the same, more often by being different, more dramatically by being contradictory. Culture is not so much a product of sharing, as a product of people hammering each other into shape with the well-constructed tools already available. We need to think of culture as this process of hammering a world.
>
> (McDermott and Varenne 1995: 326, quoted in Tierney 1997: 6)

One of Potts's Australian academic respondents illustrates this well:

> I don't know if the college has changed me but my colleagues have changed me . . . I have changed considerably since I have been here . . . We have a . . . highly intellectual, capable, competent group here, many of whom have challenged me intellectually to a great extent. And I think not only have I had to re-think my own value system but I've actually found my own value system, changing, adapting, being more flexible as a result of having people challenge me . . .
>
> (Potts 1997: 101–2)

A rich source of observations on how socialization takes place among doctoral students is provided by Gerholm (1985), who takes as his unifying theme the notion of 'tacit knowledge'. Introducing his analysis, Gerholm observes:

> Any person entering a new group with the ambition of becoming a full-fledged, competent member has to learn to comply with its fundamental cultural rules. This applies also to academic departments. To function smoothly within the group of teachers, fellow students and secretaries, the student needs a considerable amount of know-how. Most of it will be acquired slowly through the interaction with others and without anyone ever making a deliberate effort to teach the newcomer the rules of the game. Nonetheless, failure to comply with these implicit rules will undoubtedly affect the student's standing within the group.

He goes on to distinguish the technical aspects of such knowledge from its personal elements:

a graduate student, as part of his or her socialisation into an academic discipline, will come into contact with two main categories of tacit knowledge. One of them is the knowledge that has grown out of long experience in the discipline. It is a practical, almost subconscious, knowledge or competence that the department elite fully masters. The most important ingredient is the knowledge and command of the repertoire of scientific discourses. The other category of tacit knowledge is generated by the students themselves as they try to make sense of what they are experiencing in the graduate studies program. Like the former type, it is likely to be used as a guide for action. And for an understanding of what goes on in Academia they are both of great importance.

The first category, as Rorty (1979) has pointed out, calls among other things for an ability to recognize 'what counts as a relevant contribution, what counts as answering a question, what counts as having a good argument for that answer or a good criticism of it'. Within the language domain of a given discipline, Gerholm suggests that there are more subtle nuances: the official, 'front stage' style of research reports and other formal communications; the more domestic genre adopted in 'internal settings, such as local seminars'; and the type of 'back stage' discourse in which research students engage among themselves. Membership of a disciplinary community in its fullest sense involves 'the ability to define the situation correctly and to use the type of discourse required by that very situation'.

Complementing this external, communally defined component of tacit knowledge, the graduate student also has to acquire his or her own sense of what the disciplinary values comprise. It is not enough to recognize, and be seen to subscribe to, the official norms, such as those enumerated by Merton (1973) in relation to academic scientists:[4]

> for every [such] institutional norm . . . one can find at least one counternorm prescribing a diametrically opposed line of action. Scientific findings, for example, should be part of the public domain and thus rapidly communicated to whomever might be interested. But we all know that many findings are being kept secret for some time in order not to give other scientists a clue which they might use to get ahead.

In addition to the *de jure* rules of conduct (which Gerholm likens to 'a scientific version of the Ten Commandments'), a career-minded academic must become familiar with 'the more Machiavellian rules of conduct' that exist de facto within any academic community. And much as one must learn which linguistic repertoire it is fitting to adopt in a particular situation, one also has to acquire 'the *savoir faire* which consists in knowing how to handle these conflicting rules, when to invoke one and perhaps practise the other'.

Gerholm provides two entertaining instances of this dualism. In the first he contrasts the high-minded sentiments voiced by Evans-Pritchard (1951) about the makings of an anthropologist – 'intuitive powers which not all possess'; love of scholarship; imaginative insight; and 'the literary skill necessary to translate a foreign culture into the language of one's own' – with the more earthy advice proffered by the same authority to a student departing on fieldwork: 'Take quinine, play it by ear, and stay away from the women.' As his second example, he quotes a study by Kleinman (1983) of graduate students in sociology, sharply contrasting the public emphasis on 'collective identification' with a covert pressure towards individuation. At the inaugural cheese and wine party for the department's new recruits, the standard conversation-starter is 'What's your field of interest?' Even at this early stage, it is implied, each novitiate ought to have developed a distinctive research concern. Collaboration, or even talking shop with other students, is subtly discouraged. As one student reported, 'it is pretty much assumed that at this level you work by yourself'. Insofar as students talk to one another about sociology, their conversation is based on departmental gossip rather than on substantive intellectual issues; their time together is spent more in social than in academic activity.[5]

The initial empirical enquiry was directed at a broader, more general level than the studies quoted here. In an indirect way, they do confirm, however, the efficiency of the initiation process into academic life. Interviews with research students yielded few distinctive issues when compared with those put forward by their seniors: the pattern of responses from the two groups was along broadly the same lines. Given that nearly all the postgraduates were in their final year, one might infer that they had already reached an accommodation with the cultures of their chosen academic communities.

Some relevant writings

So far, we have been concerned with the general characteristics of disciplinary cultures – their unifying features, cultural correlates and initiation processes. Little has yet been offered in the way of concrete exemplification of what a disciplinary community is like. There are, however, difficulties in attempting to characterize the nature of any particular academic tribe to any satisfactory degree of depth. A likeness, to be at least recognizable if not revealing, must involve not only painstaking observation but the detailed refinement of what is seen and its communication in accessible form. Not many of those seeking to depict one or other aspect of academic life have attempted to offer such portrayals: and among the occasionally rich delineations that do exist, few, if any, lend themselves to easy reproduction. To scale down and simplify is to change the art form from portraiture to caricature.

A treatment of this theme, then, must depend on a number of distinct strategies, each more or less unsatisfactory. The most ambitious among them would be (continuing the pictorial analogy) to assemble an exhibition of full-length canvases of notable subjects – the drawback here being the demands it must make of its audience in both time and attention. Another possibility would be to abandon the attempt to assemble first-hand material, but instead to compile a catalogue directing those interested to the separate locations of some of the relevant published works. Neither of these strategies is of course exclusive of others, such as representatives of disciplinary cultures in terms of stereotypes.

The first entails the presentation of contrasting cases in enough detail to gain a sense of what their respective cultures comprise. Evans (1988, 1990, 1993) offers, for the general reader as much as for the connoisseur, a superb example of how two particular disciplinary cultures, those of modern languages and English literature, can be displayed in all their aspects.

An alternative strategy for tackling the ethnography of academic tribal groups – the compilation of a catalogue of works relevant to the topic – is likely to prove less satisfactory in some respects than the presentation of full-length portrayals, in that it places squarely on the reader the burden of seeking out and scanning through an inevitably heterogeneous mass of material. However, it does offer the advantage of pointing anyone who is sufficiently motivated to a series of original expositions, as against mediating them at second hand. In the bibliographical exercise that follows, we have done no more than set out, with the occasional comment or annotation, a list of some of the publications that happen to have caught our eyes during the course of preparing this book. Many of the references relate to the 12 disciplines in the initial interview sample, though we include some that were studied in the two later data-collection rounds.

Physics, and in particular the glamorous subfield of high-energy physics, has undoubtedly been the most popular area for study. The more substantial treatments include those by Gaston (1973), Pickering (1984) and Traweek (1982), though there are many other studies using physics as a basis of comparison with other disciplines, or as a vehicle for advancing some particular thesis. The other scientific disciplines are poorly attended to in comparison: in chemistry, for example, the substantial study by Strauss and Rainwater (1962) relates to the wider profession of industrial and government-employed chemists and has little to say about the discipline as such. Among writings on the theme of mathematics, Startup (1980) has contributed a useful but somewhat pedestrian review article. Fisher (1973), though ostensibly concerned with mathematicians in general, bases his argument for the most part on a detailed study of 15 mathematicians working on one particular, and highly specialized, topic. Wilder (1981) approaches the subject matter of mathematics as a cultural system, tracing its evolution and the cultural forces which have dominated it, but has little to say about its practitioners. Hardy's (1941) apologia, though a classic of its kind, offers an unashamedly personal interpretation.

Among the social sciences and humanities, economists appear to have a strongly hagiographical bent. While there are few if any analyses of economics as a disciplinary community, there are numerous writings on the lives and works of eminent individuals. Blaug (1985, 1986) provides the prime example in his potted biographies of the 100 best economists before Keynes, and the 100 best economists after. On a more modest scale, Klamer (1984) deferentially records his conversations with the nobility among the new classical macroeconomists. An attractive intellectual history of anthropology is to be found in Kuper (1975). Sociological writers on sociology, whom one might expect to have taken a reflexive interest in the workings of their own collective enterprise, seem in practice to have been surprisingly reticent on the subject, daunted, perhaps, by the prospect of a destructively critical audience. Platt (1976) offers an admirable, and highly readable, study of the process of social research, which illuminates a number of aspects of the working lives of professional sociologists. For the most part, however, writings in this category take the form of descriptive accounts of research practice, prescriptive discussions of methods of enquiry and historical treatments of the way the discipline has developed. Historians, in their turn, offer a fairly prolific choice of historiographical works, and of quasi-philosophical or methodological disquisitions on the nature of 'the historian's craft', but have little to say about themselves as an academic community, or about the social and cultural aspects of the discipline itself.[6] And although, as Evans (1983) points out, academics in the modern language field 'constitute a fairly well-defined professional group', in sociological and political terms 'Modern languages is uncharted territory' – or at least was so, until the publication of his masterly account, referred to above (Evans 1988).

Among the initial sample of 12 disciplines, academic law represents the social, and engineering and pharmacy the science-based, professions. The almost total neglect of these areas, in terms of any documentation of their cultures, may be connected with the fact that they are far from easy to demarcate from their surrounding domains of professional practice. Thus, for example, the (now dated) account of engineers offered by Gerstl and Hutton (1966) deals almost exclusively with the professional socialization of practitioners, allowing academic engineers no more than a few lines of text. The same is true of the briefer but more up-to-date discussion of pharmacy by Holloway *et al.* (1986). In the case of law, with the exception of an interesting discussion by Campbell and Wiles (1976), the attempt at a literature search drew a complete blank.

As a postscript, it is perhaps worth remarking on a small category of writings by insiders on the habits and customs of their own tribal groups. Typically, such writings take an allegorical form and adopt a self-consciously jocular tone: they convey an impression of archness and of occasionally rather laboured humour. Nonetheless, as with other examples of conscious self-parody, they offer a number of revealing insights. Works in this genre include Leijonhufvud (1973) on economists, Jones (1980) on sociologists and Ziman (1973) on high-energy physicists. The first of these is both the wittiest and the most meaty. A flavour of it is conveyed by the author's comments on the initiation process:

The young Econ, or 'grad', is not admitted to adulthood until he [sic] has made a 'modl' exhibiting a degree of workmanship acceptable to the elders of the 'dept' in which he serves his apprenticeship. Adulthood is conferred in an intricate ceremony the particulars of which vary from village to village. In the more important villages, furthermore (the practice in some outlying villages is obscure), the young adult must continue to demonstrate his ability at manufacturing these artefacts. If he fails to do so, he is turned out of the 'dept' to perish in the wilderness.

Jones's (1980) study of 'The Nacirema Tsigoloicos' includes a reference to the same topic:

This process [initiation] begins when the neophyte enters a Tsigoloicos temple, whereby he more or less withdraws from the profane world; the subsequent trials, which sometimes take many years, involve a series of severe ritual abstinences, including the eating of impure foods, fasting, loss of sleep, infrequent bathing etc. – all under the eyes of the old men of the clan, who serve him as godfathers.

Some complicating factors

In considering the status of these narratives about disciplinary tribes we need to return to the point raised in the previous chapter about the complex structural conditioning of academic cultures and the issue of agency. Their effects are far too subtle and complex to be adquately depicted even in careful ethnographic studies, which are anyway inevitably coloured by the standpoint of the observer.

This point is best illustrated by a reference – to be elaborated in more detail later in the book – to the impact of a social structural factor on the disciplinary communities: gender. Like any other tribal social formation, academic tribes have internal divisions of power, status and labour organised on a basis which is not only meritocratic. Social structural factors play an important part in conditioning the shape of these internal divisions and central among which is gender. While any caricature will occlude the more subtle features of the object caricatured, the fact that the highly gendered nature of the academic tribes is often lost in stereotypical descriptions of disciplines leads one to agree with feminist writers that there is a form of 'gender blindness' in operation (Wormald 1985; Coffey and Acker 1991).

In reality gender divisions ought to be readily visible, as is evident from the accounts of female tribal members. Writing as a sociologist Rosemary Deem (1996) recounts how her path to a professorship was throughout conditioned by her gender. When she set out 30 years previously sociology was (and still is) divided into three tiers of different status: theoretical, empirical and applied. The lowest status, applied, fields were the ones to which the women were predominantly allocated and in which they continued to labour, though Deem found an opportunity to engage in middle-status empirical research. In other academic areas women are also typically found doing the low status, unrewarded work, often reflecting gender roles in the wider society. An example is caring for others as personal tutors (Acker and Feuerverger 1996; Cotterill and Waterhouse 1996, 1998; Letherby 1996; Barnes-Powell and Letherby 1998) or being involved in teaching as opposed to research (Deem, 1996). Meanwhile there remains inequality of opportunity in a range of other areas: such as the possibility of gaining research funding and of working towards a PhD rather than an MPhil.

The fact that female academics are more poorly rewarded in terms of pay and other official recognition than their male colleagues is very well documented. The HESA individual staff return for the UK, 1997–8, shows that:

- only around 10 per cent of professors are women
- 30 per cent of females researchers were on the lowest researcher grade and 0.15 per cent on the highest, compared with 20 per cent and 0.6 per cent for males
- out of the total number of posts at each level, women occupied the following percentages:
  senior lecturers/readers (chartered universities) and principal lecturers (unchartered): 20 per cent
  lowest grade lecturers: 35.6 per cent

Using HESA figures for 1997–8 UK, the lecturers' union, NATFHE, found that British women academics earn significantly less per year than their male counterparts in equivalent grades (Swain 1999: 64) with the gap varying between £1400 and £4300 depending on the subject (MacLeod 2000a). Differentials varied from institution to institution also, with very wide ones for example at the London Business School and much narrower ones at Thames Valley University.

In the USA a 1998 report by the American Association of University Professors (Benjamin 1999) showed that between 1975 and 1988, salary disparities between genders increased in almost all types of institution and employment rank. Between 1988 and 1998 there was a decline in almost all cases in these disparities, yet they remained substantial and were still greater in 1998 than in 1975 for 50 per cent of the categories of institution and academic rank. This was seen to be in part a result of the influx of women academics into HE, most of whom would have started towards the bottom of the professional ladder (Benjamin 1999).

Structural factors such as gender do not however impinge on tribal cultures in an unalloyed way. The nature of the disciplinary landscape as well as the organizational context will affect the nature and extent of their influence. Thomas (1990) notes that disciplines are permeated with connotative codes, that is they carry meanings, images and tacit assumptions that often involve taken-for-granted ideas about gender identities. They are not culturally neutral: areas of study are widely held to embody beliefs about masculinity and femininity. Thus, a woman specializing in a discipline with a masculine gender identity such as physics has to address a situation in which she (unlike a male physicist) has a dual identity, one part of which challenges widely available ideas about gender roles. The subject matter of applied social studies and social work departments, on the other hand, is 'traditionally defined as a women's profession associated with voluntary work and the "labour of love . . ."' (Dominelli 1998: 42). While they do not face the 'dual identity' problem in these areas, women are identified as being in low status occupations both within the university and outside it. Even in these disciplines, moreover, the leaders are still likely to be men: a 1994 AUPSW survey found that 12 per cent of professors in social work were women. This inequality affords men in a feminized discipline some immunity from the 'dual identity' problem that women face in an analogous situation.

According to Dominelli (1998) women in feminized disciplines in a male-dominated institution are liable to incur low status and other disadvantages because: 'men dominate in the upper echelons of the academy, men's agendas will once again determine the parameters within which social work will be evaluated and may mean that the discipline . . . will lose out' (p. 42). However, this is to over-generalize. Any university institutional context will have its own particular 'institutional logic' (Raffe *et al.* 1994) including a specific 'gender regime' (Connell 1987), which will make it more, or less, hospitable for women and for disciplines with a female gender identity.

Knowledge communities, then, are defined and reinforced by 'the nurturance of myth, the identification of unifying symbols, the canonisation of exemplars, and the formation of guilds' (Dill 1992), but as we have suggested, their boundaries are simultaneously blurred and weakened by a rival set of pressures. This does not of course invalidate the exercise of identifying the distinctive cultural characteristics of individual disciplines: it merely underlines the fact that such an exercise depends on the adoption of a particular frame of reference, more specific than that relating to knowledge fields, but still sufficiently broad and general to obscure several important qualifications. We shall go on to consider some of these as they emerge in the examination of internal and external subject boundaries. To lead on to that topic, it would seem appropriate to quote an observation from Gaff and Wilson's 1971 sample survey of faculty values and attitudes in American colleges:

> There are significant differences between faculty members in different fields of study on such aspects of culture as educational values, teaching orientation, and life style. These differences seem sufficiently great to [constitute] distinct faculty cultures . . . This is not to say that these cultures are discrete; indeed, there are areas of overlap on every item and every scale. [Moreover] the analysis . . . suggests that there are significant subcultural differences as well.

Notes

1. One of the geographers interviewed in the initial study brought out clearly why this was so. He took off his shelves a list of faculty members, and demonstrated that in most departments their higher degrees were gained in leading institutions in a variety of countries – the mixture of academic backgrounds was highly cosmopolitan. And as he pointed out, the international composition of many disciplinary communities is further reinforced by mutual visits and by specialist conferences, which bring together people from a diversity of national backgrounds. (Indirect evidence suggests that this characteristic is less prominent in non-elite departments: however, we have already argued in this chapter that it is the elite who set the defining disciplinary values.)
2. Tony Becher is indebted to Tomas Gerholm for this ethnographic observation (personal communication).
3. It is clear, in the context of such remarks, that no sanction is given to bias in the sense of distortion or lack of attention to contrary evidence.
4. The four principal norms of scientific conduct, according to Merton (1973), are universalism (the need for truth claims to be subject to 'pre-established impersonal criteria'), communism (the common ownership of scientific findings – to which 'secrecy is the antithesis'), disinterestedness (as exemplified less in individual conduct than in institutional procedures), and organized scepticism ('the temporary suspension of judgement and the detached scrutiny of beliefs'). His account has been much quoted, but also much criticized. A well-argued disputation of his thesis is provided by Mulkay (1969); other critiques include those of Barnes and Dolby (1970) and Rothman (1972).
5. The same tendency towards gossip rather than shop talk is reflected in the practice of historians, and is in marked contrast with that of physicists. Here is one of many instances in which the social and cognitive aspects of a discipline reflect one another (see Chapter 7 for a more detailed discussion of individualistic and collaborative enquiry).
6. Exceptions to this generalization include Church (1973, 1976, 1978) and, in the context of nineteenth-century academic life, Rothblatt (1968).

4
Overlaps, Boundaries and Specialisms

Adjoining territories

It was noticeable, though not unexpected, that the respondents in the initial study had no difficulty in enumerating the disciplines which were more or less closely related to their own, and that there was very little disagreement between their views on the matter. It seems natural enough to think of knowledge and its properties and relationships in terms of landscapes, and to saturate epistemological discussion with spatial metaphors: fields and frontiers; pioneering, exploration, false trails; charts and landmarks.[1] So enquiries about neighbouring areas of knowledge almost invariably produced clear and detailed conceptual maps (and even, in the case of one geographer interviewed, a neat pencil-and-paper sketch of his discipline and its adjoining territories). Thus, for example, economics was said to have one common frontier with mathematics and another with political science; some trade relations with history and sociology; and a lesser measure of shared ground with psychology, philosophy and law. Biology was portrayed as being bounded on the one side by mathematics and the physical sciences (especially physics, chemistry and physical geography) and on the other by the human sciences (in particular by psychology, anthropology and human geography). In this vein the catalogue continued across all 12 of the disciplines intially studied.

Within the published literature, too, one may come across instances of similar mapping exercises. Thus Buchanan (1966) confirms the areas of 'spillout' and 'spillin' identified by respondents in economics, but adds some further if less direct connections with engineering and physical sciences; and Mikesell (1969), confining his attention to human as against physical geography, notes its varying degrees of contiguity with anthropology, sociology, political science, economics, demography, psychology, history and area studies, again closely reaffirming the testimony of the geographers interviewed in the initial study.

However, the process of locating a discipline in relation to its neighbours is in itself of limited interest, and should be seen as no more than a preliminary to other more fundamental issues. Boundaries, after all, do not exist merely as lines on a map: they denote territorial possessions that can be encroached on, colonized and reallocated. The boundary between sociology and linguistics provides an example: sociology's 'linguistic turn' in the 1980s brought at least part of the former discipline much closer in methods and concerns to the latter. Disciplinary classification is, then, not cast in stone but is, as we noted in Chapter 2, socially constituted. However, some borders are so strongly defended as to be virtually impenetrable; others are weakly guarded and open to incoming and outgoing traffic: but in general a considerable amount of poaching goes on across all disciplinary borders.

The nature of the divisions between disciplines, one might contend, varies with the nature of the disciplines concerned: some borders allow a greater latitude than others. Disciplinary communities that are convergent and tightly knit in terms of their fundamental ideologies, their common values, their shared judgements of quality, their awareness of belonging to a unique tradition and the level of their agreement about what counts as appropriate disciplinary content and how it should be organized (the extent of disciplinary 'framing': Bernstein 1971) – in short, their sense of nationhood – are likely to occupy intellectual territories with well-defined external boundaries. What is more, when the patriotic feelings within a discipline run high, deviations from the common cultural norms will be penalized and attempts to modify them from the outside will be rejected. Any systematic questioning of the accepted disciplinary ideology will be seen as heresy and may be punished by expulsion; any infiltration of alien values and practices will be appropriately dealt with, either by direct resistance or by tacit incorporation into the prevailing framework of thinking. Thus, within economics, those who question the basic axioms of the subject are liable to find themselves cast into a wilderness of their own; deviants in other marginal fields, such as the statistical areas of mathematics, may be cut off and left to form an independent and self-sufficient community.

The inverse is true of disciplinary groups that are divergent and loosely knit, that is where the constituent members lack a clear sense of mutual cohesion and identity. In their case the cognitive border zones with other subject fields are liable to be ragged and ill-defined, and hence not so easy to defend. It may indeed at times begin to seem as if there is, in Whitley's (1984) terms, no 'central core which firmly controls intellectual boundaries and reputations'.[2] Geography appears to be a case in point. Its practitioners readily absorb ideas and techniques from neighbouring intellectual territories, and even identify themselves with other academic professions than their own (through publications in their journals, attendance at their conferences and membership of their communication networks). Academic pharmacists share some of the same centrifugal tendencies, often preferring to see themselves primarily as members of more clearly identified and more prestigious knowledge fields such as pharmacology, biochemistry, or one of the relevant branches of chemistry. Scholars in modern languages are less inclined to form allegiances outside their own broad subject area, but many of those who specialize in literary criticism are hospitable to itinerant theories from psychology, sociology or structural anthropology.

Once again, one can observe connections here between the social and cognitive aspects of knowledge. Impermeable boundaries are in general a concomitant of tightly knit, convergent disciplinary communities and an indicator of the stability and coherence of the intellectual fields they inhabit. Permeable boundaries are associated with loosely knit, divergent academic groups and signal a more fragmented, less stable and comparatively open-ended epistemological structure. But it should be noted that the correlation is not a perfect one (we return in Chapter 9 to consider some significant exceptions to it).

Areas of common ground

It often happens that adjoining disciplinary groups lay claim to the same pieces of intellectual territory. This does not necessarily entail a conflict between them. In some cases, depending on the nature of the claimants and the disposition of the no man's land, it may involve a straightforward division of interest; in others it may mark a growing unification of ideas and approaches.

As Toulmin (1972) has pointed out, 'any particular type of object can fall within the domains of several different sciences', depending on what questions are asked about it. He instances the behaviour of a muscle fibre, which can fall within the spheres of interest of biochemistry, electrophysiology, pathology and thermodynamics, and may also be made a topic for, say, quantum mechanical or psychological investigation.

What demarcates one disciplinary perspective from another in a theme or topic which they share may vary between a distinction in style or emphasis, a division of labour or a difference in conceptual framework. Examples of the first are provided by Megill (1987) and Barry (1981). Focusing on 'the philosophy/history frontier', Megill contends that:

> philosophers, in their writing, are inclined to consider at great length matters that historians will pass over quickly, and vice versa. Judged as philosophy, works of history are likely to seem weak. Judged as history, works of philosophy are likely to seem irrelevant.

In similar but more detailed terms, Barry contemplates 'the relation between the kind of theoretical works on politics that gets done by people in political science departments and the kind of thing that people in philosophy departments do when they turn their attention to politics'. Here, he suggests:

> the most noticeable difference is that philosophers tend to be short on background and political scientists long on padding . . . 'Background' and 'padding' both refer to contextual information: the difference lies

in the use made of it. To have a good background in a theoretical subject is, I take it, to have a firm grasp on the relevant empirical phenomena associated with it, and also to be on top of the theoretical literature concerned with it . . . Padding, by contrast, is the presentation of factual material or the rehearsal of previous opinions or old controversies to make up for the fact that the author personally has relatively little originality to contribute to the subject.

Other cases clearly display a separation of intellectual spoils, the task of exploration being divided by common agreement between the interested parties. The interview data from the initial study contain a number of examples. To take a case in point, one of the informants, a physical chemist, began by observing that the scientific background of physicists is based on deductive solutions, whereas that of chemists is based on induction. This distinction, he suggested, pervades the practice and marks the common boundary of the two disciplines. Physics is limited in range: when a problem turns out to be too hard, the physicist marks it down as 'dirty' and abandons it to the chemist. If the chemist also finds it too hard, he or she passes it on to the biologist, who adopts a phenomenological, rather than an inductive or deductive approach. However, this tidy division of effort is disappearing as more physicists begin to tackle problems previously left for the chemists, while the chemists are now encroaching on the biologists' share of the pickings.

The third way in which territorial rights are divided up among rival interest groups – by distinctions in conceptual framework – is not entirely separable from the other two (i.e. contrasts in style or emphasis, and the division of intellectual labour), but goes beyond them to encompass more fundamental and far-reaching disciplinary variations. A cogently argued analysis by Yates (1985) highlights a dichotomy between anthropologists and sociologists. Even when they are studying essentially the same phenomena, crucial differences emerge. Sociologists 'seem obsessed with methodology and scientific status while anthropologists seem more relaxed on those issues'. To the anthropologist, 'fieldwork is not meant to be about data, it is about experience'; the method of inquiry is 'an internal process, itself inseparable from the experience in which it is realized'. In sociology, to the contrary, 'unpredictable subjective qualities are detrimental to the [researcher's] role as an instrument of science, especially as a recorder of what is actually there'. One might say that 'in social anthropology relationships are data, whereas in [sociology] relationships produce data'. Summing up, Yates concludes that for sociologists, 'methodology is external and technical and related to the possibility of objective knowledge', whereas for anthropologists 'methodology is the internal apprehension of relationships and their transformation through sets of cultural meanings . . . what is of significance is competence of introspection'.

But the sharing of ground, as already remarked, can lead to convergence rather than a separation of interests. In his comparison of 'historical sociology' and 'theoretical history', Jones (1976) begins, as Yates does, by marking the epistemological contrasts between the two fields. He berates, with equal vigour, history for its failure to theorize and sociology for 'the vague and shifting character of much of its knowledge, its proneness to passing theoretical fashions and the triteness of some of its laws'. Nonetheless, the two are, he maintains, more intimately related than superficial appearances suggest. At base, 'they are only different aspects of a single concern: the construction of a historical science'.[3]

On a grander and more sweeping scale, Geertz (1980) identifies a 'culture shift', a 'refiguration of social thought' bringing the humanities and social sciences closer together in their intellectual kinship:

> What we are seeing is not just another redrawing of the cultural map – the moving of a few disputed borders, the marking of some more picturesque mountain lakes – but an alteration of the principles of mapping. Something is happening to the way we think about the way we think.

Geertz characterizes this as 'a turn ... by an important section of social scientists, from physical process analogies to symbolic form ones', and illustrates his argument by referring to the growing use of comparisons between society and 'a serious game, a sidewalk drama, or a behavioural text'. This change in 'the instruments of reasoning' has 'disequilibriating implications' for social scientists and humanists alike. The 'social technologist notion of what a social scientist is ... the specialist without spirit dispensing policy nostrums' is now brought into question; but 'the cultural watchdog notion of what a humanist is ... the lectern sage dispensing approved judgements' is by the same process being systematically undermined.

The cause of unification

Geertz and Jones, together with those who argue along similar lines, appear content to uncover intellectual similarities that already exist or to discern disciplinary mergers which lie in store over the horizon. There are, however, others who adopt a more activist stance, seeking positively to promote unification rather than passively to identify it: to break down boundaries, not only to diminish their significance. Their calls to arms are of some interest, in that they lead on to a consideration of whether there are systematic connections between disciplines, and if so what form they take – from the espousal of one kind of cause to the investigation of another.

The contrast drawn by Barry (1981) between philosophers' and political scientists' approaches to the same question has already been mentioned. He goes on to suggest that the differences are counterproductive, demanding a change in 'organizationally induced incentives ... ways in which the political philosophers and the political theorists can move toward one another without jeopardizing their positions in their own departments'.

The structural reforms he outlines are thus directed towards 'a great increase in the amount of organizational boundary crossing'.

Campbell (1969) is more ambitious, espousing as his goal the achievement of 'a comprehensive, integrated multiscience'. The major obstacle in the way of achieving this goal is 'the ethnocentrism of disciplines', the internal dynamics that favour the growth of what is regarded as the disciplinary core and allow the relative atrophy of its peripheral or marginal elements.

What is of particular interest in the present context about Campbell's argument is that, as in Barry's case, his diagnosis of what he sees as our present intellectual malaise, as well as his suggested remedies, are organizational rather than epistemological. The blame can, he contends, be laid firmly at the door of disciplinarily- and departmentally-based structures: the 'tribalism or nationalism or ingroup partisanship' that acts as a powerful centrifuge, promoting an artificial alienation and distance between even closely-related specialities on either side of a boundary. Thus, 'centrality becomes reinterpreted as common root, trunk and fountain head when initially it meant only remoteness from the boundaries of other departments'.

Campbell's analysis leads him to assert that the 'present organization of content into departments is highly arbitrary, a product in large part of historical accident' (one might, incidentally, wish to make the same charge against nationhood). Writing in the same volume – devoted to the theme of interdisciplinarity in the social sciences – Wax (1969) adopts a closely similar stance. The attempt, he suggests:

> to structure the social-scientific disciplines into a set of mutually exclusive and exhaustive enterprises . . . is not so much impossible as it is destructive. For, from the viewpoint of a systematic and logical division of scientific labor, the very existence of the disciplines or sciences that are taken to constitute the social or behavioural sciences makes but little sense. Sociology, anthropology and their siblings are not the outgrowths of a systematic division of social-scientific labor, but are instead the arbitrary consequences of particular social processes . . . social scientists must become far more conscious of the arbitrariness, deliberate bias and ethnocentricity of their critical assumptions.[4]

Elaborating on his theme, Wax argues that the problem is not so much that 'the social sciences are chaotically organized and that the various disciplines are professional rivals for the same subject areas . . . each studying the same subject matter, while giving different labels to their activities', but rather that 'the gaps among our disciplines are much too large'. The prime need, then, must be to bridge or fill in these gaps, a goal that Campbell endorses and one whose realization, he believes, has to be based on promoting 'collective comprehensiveness through overlapping patterns of unique narrowness' – on creating 'a continuous texture of narrow specialties which overlap with other narrow specialties', as against 'trying to fill these gaps by training scholars who have mastered two or more disciplines'.

Disciplines under the microscope

With this move, Campbell deftly shifts the focus of attention and the locus of analysis from disciplines to specialisms. It may be worth pausing briefly to review the steps that have led from the macroscopic view of knowledge to the microscopic one which now presents itself.

Chapter 2, it may be recalled, concerned itself in part with the delineation of broad epistemological categories. In Chapter 3, the framework was narrowed to allow for the evident disciplinary variations within such categories. Once it is conceded, however, that disciplines comprise an untidy level of analysis in certain respects, in that the boundaries between them are constantly shifting and sometimes poorly demarcated, and that there are numerous apparent gaps and overlaps in their pattern of coverage of knowledge domains, it becomes necessary to introduce a yet more finely meshed set of explanatory concepts. Much as disciplines have to be invoked to accommodate the anomalies within broadly defined fields of knowledge, specialist areas or segments seem to offer the most appropriate analytic currency to account for the complex internal and external relationships that are made manifest in any close scrutiny of disciplines themselves.

In their replacement of discipline-based categories by those of specialisms, Campbell and Wax manage to convey a sense of movement from the superficial to the fundamental. The heart of the academic enterprise, the true basic unit of intellectual organization, is the specialist field; it is, they believe, within its narrow but profound matrix that the closest contact is achieved between human understanding and the realm of epistemological reality it seeks to explore.

Two further points need to be considered before we move on to a more detailed discussion of the specialisms that fragment the internal structure of disciplines as well as those which straddle their boundaries. First, there has been noticeably little mention in all this of the views of natural scientists, humanists or those in professionally oriented fields: nearly all those who have been quoted in the discussion so far are social scientists. That may be because of a greater tendency for the latter to concern themselves with the social aspects of knowledge; or perhaps because academics in other knowledge domains take it more for granted that they have interests in common and areas of overlapping coverage with their disciplinary neighbours. But that such a blurring of boundaries also occurs in fields outside the social sciences cannot be in dispute. For every statement, such as the one by Buchanan (1966) that 'it is easier for an economist working with non-market decisions to communicate with a positive political scientist, game theorist or organizational theory psychologist than it is for him [sic] to communicate with a growth-model macro-economist with whom he scarcely finds any common ground', it is possible to point to comparable assertions in the initial interview data from informants in other knowledge domains. Thus, one respondent, a chemist, spoke of the 'strong connections with physics' that characterized the elementary chemical reactions which he was studying at the molecular level; another, a mechanical engineer, remarked: 'I have more in common with the mathematicians who study fluid mechanics that I have with other engineers who study combustion – though combustion is my main research topic'.

Second, in marking the transition from a concern with disciplines to an emphasis on specialisms, one can note an accompanying elaboration of the metaphors it seems natural and appropriate to use. To be sure, it is still possible to talk of boundaries and border disputes; but there is also a strong tendency to invoke another and rather different family of concepts. Campbell's (1969) ideal of 'a comprehensive social science, or other multiscience' calls for what he terms a 'fish-scale model' in which specialist research areas overlap like the scales on a fish, so bringing about 'a collective communication, a collective competence and breadth'. Polanyi (1962) envisages 'a chain of mutual appreciation . . . the whole of science [as] covered by chains and networks of overlapping neighbourhoods . . . the consensual chains which link [each individual] to all the others'. Crane (1972), in her turn, observes that each specialist field 'appears to be related to a few others, but in such a way that all fields are interlocked in a kind of honeycomb structure'. And so in this convergence of scales, chains and honeycombs, it becomes possible to contemplate the vision of a return from the incohate to the coherent, from fragmentation to wholeness: *e pluribus unum.*

The notion of a specialism

It is not only at their borders that disciplines can prove a troublesome unit of analysis. When one begins to look closely into their epistemological structures, it becomes apparent that most of them embrace a wide range of subspecialisms, some with one set of features and others with different sets. There is no single method of enquiry, no standard verification procedure, no definitive set of concepts that uniquely characterizes each particular discipline. It is in some contexts more meaningful to speak about the identifiable and coherent properties of subsidiary areas within one disciplinary domain or another. Once this change of emphasis is adopted it becomes possible (as we see in later chapters) to recognize between subspecialisms certain patterns of similarity and difference that cut right across disciplinary boundaries.

The move from the arena of disciplines to that of specialisms calls for a corresponding shift in perception. One aspect of the change is brought out by Crane (1972), generalizing from her close study of communication among academics to society at large:

> Instead of seeing society as a collection of clearly defined interest groups, [it] must be reconceptualized as a complex network of groups of interacting individuals whose membership and communication patterns are seldom confined to one such group alone.[5]

There are two features particularly worth noting in this view of collective life under the microscope. The first is that the complexity, like that of an active biological culture, is inevitable and inexorable: the individual cells subdivide and recombine, seek to defend their integrity while changing their shape and disposition, as if this constant process were a necessary part of survival. Ruscio (1985) writes of specialization as 'an iron law [that] controls the progress of science and similarly the academic profession'. He adds some useful reminders of why this is so:

> There are epistemological reasons: the sheer volume of knowledge and its rapid expansion compel a scientist to carve out his own niche of expertise. There are also sociological reasons: Academics achieve status within the profession by advancing knowledge, a dynamic that requires precise contributions. Institutions of higher education themselves compete for status, reinforcing the individual's motivation.

The second feature is a consequence of the first: it is that there is little to be found here of the relative constancy and stability of the disciplines themselves. Once inside the framework of academic specialties, one can only clutch at the metaphysics of Heraclitus: all is in a state of constant flux.

A specific illustration of this shifting, kaleidoscopic process was given by one respondent, a mathematician, in his remark that the Mathematical Reviews Index – an important bibliographical tool within the discipline – has found it necessary to change its classification system in more or less drastic ways at least once a decade. The notion of specialisms as elements whose only constant feature is their lack of constancy is reinforced and extended by Bucher and Strauss (1961) in their study of medical specialization. Stressing the heterogeneity of professional groupings, and the divergence of interests between them, they develop a 'process model', which entails 'the ideal of . . . loose amalgamations of segments pursuing different objectives in different manners and more or less delicately held together under a common name at a particular period in history'.

This last comment suggests a nominalism, which the incohateness of pattern makes it tempting to adopt: specialisms, it might seem, can only be defined in terms of the labels with which groups of people choose to identify themselves at any given time.[6] To make matters worse, specialist fields may, like disciplines, themselves be represented as subject to internal fragmentation. Thus Gaston (1972) observes of high-energy physics that 'differentiation is not only within the same discipline but within the same speciality'. Bucher and Strauss (1961), in developing their process model, elect to refer to the 'groupings which emerge within a profession' as 'segments', adding in parentheses that:

> Specialties might be thought of as major segments, except that a close look at a specialty betrays its claim to unity, revealing that specialties, too, usually contain segments, and, if they ever did have

common definitions along all lines of professional identity, it was probably at a very special, and early, period in their development.

Later in the same paper they refer to 'the different organizations of work activities that can be found within single specialties', and comment that 'while specialties organize around unique missions, as time goes on segmental missions may develop within the fold'.

One is reminded of the physicists' unending quest for the ultimate particle of matter, in which it seems that every new candidate turns out itself to be a composite; or of the more commonplace conception that 'big fleas have little fleas upon their backs to bite 'em; little fleas have lesser fleas, and so ad infinitum'. It is perhaps scarcely surprising in the circumstances that Whitley (1984) argues that, especially in weakly co-ordinated disciplines with a high degree of 'task uncertainty', it is 'difficult to establish ... the division of the field into separate yet interdependent specialisms'.

The looseness and untidiness of the terminology reflects that of the situation to which it applies. As a rough approximation, it might be said that disciplines take institutional shape in departments, though changes in the latter will tend to lag behind shifts in the former. As Evans notes:

> [Discipline] can be enacted and negotiated in various ways: the international 'invisible college', individuals exchanging preprints and reprints, conferences, workshops ... But the most concrete and permanent enactment is the department; this is where a *discipline* becomes an institutional *subject*. The match between discipline and subject is always imperfect; this can cause practical difficulties when, for example, the (discipline-based) categories of research selectivity do not fit the way the subject is ordered in a particular department.
>
> (Evans 1995: 253–4, original emphasis)

Specialisms, by contrast, are less formally recognizable in terms of organized professional groupings, dedicated journals and bibliographical categories. However, some specialisms cover such a broad span of knowledge that it becomes useful or necessary to subdivide them (Mulkay 1977, notes a possible classification of solid-state physics into 'twenty-seven relatively distinct fields of investigation'). Such subspecialisms are harder to identify, being variously associated with 'social circles', 'networks', 'invisible colleges' and other comparable notions, and may vary considerably in character and scope, being attributed to active research populations of anything from half a dozen (Roberts 1970) to around 200 (Price and Beaver 1966).

To compound the complexity of the problem we can observe that disciplines are multi-dimensional in character. At its most obvious a discipline has an object of study (music, medicine, history), though this will vary according to sub-discipline and may shift over time, as has happened in anthropology. Moreover the object of the discipline may be more or less contentious: in the study of English literature, for example, there is disagreement over whether the object of study is the body of literature or the sociological issues to which it gives rise (Bergonzi 1990).

The second dimension is disciplinary stance. Here the differences are concerned with intention: whether the discipline is concerned with knowing or with doing, and if it is concerned with knowing, then what form that might take: illumination; critical awareness; factual accuracy and so on. As Squires reminds us, in some contexts knowledge can be no more than a metaphor (Squires 1990). There can moreover be sub-disciplinary differences in stance, as in different areas of law. As elsewhere this can give rise to conflict: different groups of researchers in the area of educational policy approach the subject with quite different sets of intentions, for example, so that Ozga describes the field as 'contested terrain' (Ozga 2000).

The third dimension is disciplinary mode. Here a discipline may be 'normal' in the Kuhnian (1962) sense, or reflexive. If its mode is normal then there is a 'working acceptance of current assumptions and procedures' (Squires 1990: 56); if reflexive, the discipline turns to ask questions of itself. Again, modal status will vary according to sub-discipline and might be the basis of disciplinary schisms. On the latter point, Kuhn observes that disciplinary revolutions do not occur through persuasion but rather through the natural process of replacement.

Two further conceptual categories have already been discussed: classification and frame: the degree of 'boundedness' from other disciplinary areas and the extent to which there is agreement and control over content among specialists in an field of enquiry. We discuss these in more detail elsewhere in this book, suffice it to say here that, like the others, they too vary within the discipline and over time.

In addition to these there are yet other contextual dimensions. Gilbert and Mulkay (1984) contend that the way natural scientists construe their actions and beliefs about the discipline is context-dependent in that they use, alternately, empiricist and contingent repertoires. Thus we need to take further into account discursive context and interpretive form, that is the situations in which text about disciplines is being produced and its effects on the character of that text and the way it is interpreted.

Some social considerations

The social and the cognitive aspects of the specialization process are interdependent, although some writers tend to emphasize the former at the expense of the latter. Thus, Griffith and Mullins (1972) write about 'some members of a scientific speciality' as 'small, coherent, activist groups . . . that subsequently had major impacts on their "home" disciplines'. To quote Bucher and Strauss (1961) again, in amplification of this:

> Professional identity may be thought of as analogous to the ideology of
> a political movement; in this sense, segments have ideology. We have

seen that they have missions. They also tend to develop a brotherhood of colleagues, leadership, organizational forms and vehicles, and tactics for implementing their position . . . [But] it must be pointed out that not all segments display the character of a social movement. Some lack organised activities, while others are so inchoate that they appear more as a kind of backwash of the profession than as true segments.

The contrast noted by Griffith and Mullins (1972) between 'a loose communication network' and one with 'high levels of communication and organization' is one of many which can be drawn in the attempt to analyse the process of specialization. The first, in which group members have many contacts outside – 'suggesting that scientists work in and influence more than one speciality' – is, they contend, characteristic of Kuhnian 'normal science'. The second, highly organized type of group typifies 'revolutionary science' ('groups that are in the process of formulating a radical conceptual reorganization within their field . . . convinced that they [are] achieving the overthrow of a major position within their discipline or making a major revision in methodology'). However, in modification of this claim, Griffith in an earlier paper with Miller (1970) pointed out that 'the use of special methodology might spread through or even define a speciality within the literature without creating a highly coherent group or any sense of being at a major research front'; and, more generally, 'a research literature may be the product of a coherent group in continual contact or of individuals operating almost completely independently of one another'.

As an aside at this point, it could be argued that knowledge is likely to be rendered, in Campbell's terms, more cohesive and less fragmented by the activity of loosely knit specialist groups, since it is they who promote communication across the boundaries of specialisms. In contrast, closely knit groups might be claimed to contribute more to the overall advancement of knowledge, particularly if they are associated with major intellectual revolutions that succeed.

Conceptual revolutions cannot, however, be legislated for – like accidents, they just happen (though a combination of circumstances can serve to prevent them). There is a risk, too, that they may go wrong and in doing so create a pathology of their own – that of in-breeding within the group concerned. Griffith and Miller (1970) observe that 'the focusing of the group's attention on a single series of phenomena and the development of a distinctive scientific style results in a considerable restriction of the range of information regarded as relevant', and a 'virtual indifference to the work of others'. Ruscio (1985) refers to specialized groups that become separated from other subfields within their own discipline, and quotes a political scientist he interviewed as saying that close identity in research 'should not be seen as something that's putting everybody in communication with one another; it's not that kind of thing at all. Instead, what's happening is that very distinct groups of communicators are growing up.' Crane (1972) writes of circumstances in which the operational definitions given by techniques cannot be reconciled, so that narrow fields cannot merge into broader ones. There is in consequence little intercommunication: 'little concern for theory or for the implication of ideas for other groups . . . Gimmicks develop, often in the form of a procedure, equipment or task which is then mechanically repeated.'

Some cognitive considerations

Specialization does not however have to be regarded as a predominantly social process. It is easy to sympathize with Chubin's (1976) complaint that sociologists of science – who have contributed a major part of the writings on the topic – have underemphasized the extent to which 'intellectual, cognitive or problem content can generate different kinds of structure'.[7] By taking 'social structure as an antecedent of specialties – that is, as impelling a convergence of interest on a research problem or set of problems', they seemingly deny 'the possibility that intellectual events and the relations they engender give rise to a social structure that we treat as a specialty'.

It would be wrong to play down the importance of social factors in deter-mining the characteristics of a specialized knowledge field. Indeed, it will be necessary to develop further the analysis of networks, along with the role of intellectual fashion, in the exploration of some of the main mechanisms of academic life in Chapter 5, and the question of career motivation in Chapter 7. However, it is also as well to recall, with Elzinga (1987a), that 'differentiation is certainly more than just the result of a social and micropolitical process in the world of higher education'.

To restore the balance, we ought to begin by noting that it is in the domain of hard pure knowledge, as it was defined in Chapter 2, that spe-cialization is apparently at its most intense. Hard pure areas seem to exert an almost hypnotic effect, allowing many attempts at analysis to ignore the fact that specialization also occurs in hard applied fields (as the study by Bucher and Strauss (1961), makes plain) and in soft pure and soft applied contexts as well. It is perhaps the linear, cumulative and atomistic character of hard pure knowledge that creates a natural arena for specialization and a natural target for the study of intellectual networks of communication. But while closely focused areas of shared interest and their associated inter-est groups are a less predominant feature of other epistemological cat-egories, they are nonetheless readily to be found, and they have a good many of the same characteristics as specialisms in the hard sciences.

One may indeed discern a similar spectrum within the social science disciplines, the humanities, and the technical and social professions, from loosely knit confederations to closely cohesive segments. Close-knit groups are often clustered around 'a distinctively different theory or a new or modified research methodology in opposition to a clearly established posi-tion' (Griffith and Mullins 1972); looser ones are commonly based on a shared area of content or a shared field of professional practice. The most noticeable disciplinary difference lies in the response to radically new ideas. In closely articulated, hard pure, knowledge areas, revolutionary theories may have the effect of overthrowing and replacing the current orthodoxy (Kuhn 1962); in other domains (because, one might say, there is no clear orthodoxy to replace), they tend rather to be absorbed into the more organic, amorphous conceptual structures, which are in their very nature not readily amenable to being superseded.

Types of specialization

It is important for some purposes to recognize that specialisms fall into distinct logical categories. Law (1976) marks them in straightforward and readily understandable terms as theory-based, technique- or methods-based and subject matter specialities. The last of the three is perhaps the most familiar, in that it designates a particular area of knowledge (tax law, say, within legal studies) or set of problems (algebraic geometry, say, within mathematics) on which research activity is focused. The definition of a specialism of this kind can of course be more or less precise: an academic may in some contexts identify himself or herself as concerned with classical drama and in others as being a student of the late Elizabethan theatre, or as interested in a particular playwright or even as working on a particular play. But the reference here is to the object of study rather than to the mode of investigation employed or the perspective that is adopted.

Methods-based specialisms (Law gives crystallography as an example) introduce another dimension, in that 'methodological differences can cut across specialty – and even professional – lines with specialists sharing techniques with members of other specialties which they do not share with their fellows' (Bucher and Strauss 1961). Moreover, someone armed with a suitable technique may invade a number of subject specialisms in turn and use it to produce novel results; a process which, with an illuminating difference of metaphor, physicists tend to describe as 'skimming the cream' and chemists as 'turning the handle'.

Theory-based specialities may be broader still, in that they derive from sometimes quite general ways of looking at the world. The richest of them are capable of being carried across disciplinary boundaries to attract followers in a diversity of fields. For example, catastrophe theory, stemming from topology, has helped to clarify a variety of problems in the biological and social sciences; structuralism, with its origins in linguistics, has made inroads into anthropology, sociology and literary criticism. Espousing a theory – as against choosing a subject field or learning to apply a technique – can have ideological as well as straightforwardly cognitive implications, with the result that those with conflicting theoretical stances may show much the same mutual antagonism as the adherents of rival political creeds.

The three types of specialism are not necessarily separated in practice, in that a given subject area may be closely associated with a particular method, some methods are a natural accompaniment to particular theories, and certain theories are in their turn confined to specific bodies of subject matter. Nonetheless, the category in which a specialism is located can make a considerable difference to the types of things one can say about it.

To put some flesh on these bare logical bones, it may be useful to draw on a few examples from outside the overworked domain of the natural sciences. For historians, the Annales school has represented not merely a methodological break, but a new theoretical conception of what should count as acceptable evidence and where the boundaries of historical subject matter should be drawn. The oral history movement, in contrast, has to be seen as a predominantly methodological specialism, even if – in its nature – it is currently confined to the subject field of modern history. Within economics, monetarism is a theory-based specialism, econometrics is defined in terms of technique, and labour economics is a subject field. Modern languages also encompasses all three types of specialism: deconstruction among the theoretical approaches, practical criticism as a methodology, and language, period and genre as dimensions of subject matter. Among the professions, Bucher and Strauss (1961) remind us that, 'Within a core specialty like internal medicine there are many different kinds of practice ranging from that of a 'family doctor' to highly specialized consultation'; but more 'profound divisions . . . frequently arise around the exploitation of a method or technique, like radiology'.

Frames of reference

In the discussion so far, disciplines and specialisms have appeared as competing forms of analysis. The disadvantages of attempting to chart knowledge fields in terms of disciplines were emphasized by Geertz and others, who noted their overlapping boundaries and their conceptual congruences, and by advocates of interdisciplinary enquiry, such as Campbell, who charged them with a failure to tackle important interstitial areas of enquiry. But an alternative account in terms of specialisms was seen not to be entirely satisfactory either; at least in part because of imprecisions in their definition and instabilities in their inherent characteristics. Whitley (1984) further reinforces the causes for complaint:

> Taking the immediate specialism to be the basic unit of intellectual and social organization . . . creates substantial problems . . . First, it is not always very clear how these are to be identified across the sciences . . . Second, the present high degree of intellectual specialization is historically specific and thus temporal comparisons would be difficult to carry out. Third, they are often highly fluid and changeable so that comparisons of their structure and operations as relatively stable work organizations is [sic] fraught with obstacles. Finally,

because the degree of specialization and intensification of the division of labour varies across the sciences . . .

Even so, it is difficult not to agree with Chubin (1976) that ' "specialty" is a viable concept whose various representations capture better than conventional units of analysis, especially "discipline", the process and structure of research'.

Perhaps, in the end, there is no need to postulate an irreconcilable rivalry between the macro and the micro – between broad knowledge fields at the one extreme, narrow specialisms at the other, and disciplines poised uneasily between the two. Particle physics does not have a monopoly of scientific truth that renders the study of astronomy invalid. Alternative frames of reference only serve to emphasize different aspects of the same reality, allowing a trade-off between comprehensiveness and specificity. To see the whole is to see it in breadth, but without access to the particular vision: to see the part is to see it in depth, but in the absence of the general overview.

Notes

1. 'That our epistemological metaphors are (at least partially) culturally specific, and that our knowledge of knowledge is therefore (at least partially) culturally constrained' is argued by Salmond (1982) in an interesting comparison of contemporary Western with traditional Maori conceptions of knowledge. The latter represent knowledge not in spatial terms, but as a shared and valued possession, a source of power and wealth, analogous in some ways with Bourdieu's notion of 'cultural capital'.
2. In another context, he distinguishes fields in which 'how the core is separated from peripheral, or "deviant" areas is of critical concern' from those where the matter is given lesser importance. Thus, the physicists' 'policing of intellectual boundaries and fears of "pollution" from "applied" issues are as marked as those of economists, especially in European countries, and are a strong contrast to the more relaxed attitudes of chemists' (Whitley 1984).
3. The intellectual links between historians and sociologists were a particular subject of discussion by both disciplinary groups in the 1970s and '80s. The *British Journal of Sociology* 17(3) (1976) has other relevant articles besides that by Jones (see also Erikson 1970, Smith 1982, and, for a more extensive and thoroughgoing analysis, Burke 1980).
4. In the course of passionate argument the occasional rhetorical flourish can be forgiven. The accusation of arbitrariness, however, goes too far for comfort. While the institutionalization of disciplines into departments might be said to distort the way in which they develop, the cognitive distinctions between disciplines are in many cases too fundamental to attribute to mere historical accident. Some territories may be demarcated by political artifice (as the 49th parallel sets apart Canada from the USA); but other divisions follow the lie of the land (as the Himalayan range disjoins India from Tibet).
5. The analogy with nationhood remains as close here as elsewhere. Drawing on a quite different intellectual tradition, the historian Eugene Weber (1977)

writes in strikingly similar terms about the emergence of France as a distinct national entity:

> Perhaps ... the nation is a complex of collective bodies, all in process of perpetual change and in a constantly varying relationship with one another. The static view of the nation as a precise entity that having once been forged is thereafter stable ... is thus replaced by a Bergsonian model of continual interaction much closer to what actually went on.

6. A nominalist stance neatly rules out a whole range of bothersome epistemological questions. But against this attraction must be offset the misleading nature of the claim that inventing labels is the only issue at stake, i.e. that there is no point in asking what those labels are meant to be tied to. In terms of the metaphor of knowledge production, a claim to a specialism is a claim to a distinct product, and one which is saleable and useful. It can of course be questioned on the (social) grounds that no one else is interested enough to buy it; but it can also be denied on the (epistemological) grounds that the product is not new, does not stand up to critical testing, and does not serve any cognitive purpose.

7. A trap into which Chubin, on his own admission, falls in the later part of the same article.

5

Aspects of Community Life

The quest for recognition

The discussion up to this point has focused, in one way or another, on knowledge territories, and in particular on their internal and external boundaries. Sociological phenomena have been seen as connected to epistemological characteristics in important ways. In the present chapter and the two that follow it, the thrust is in a converse direction: the emphasis is more on the characteristics of the academic tribes than on the territories they inhabit. We shall concentrate on key features of intellectual communities and consider how the various forms of knowledge may be related to them.

Social and cognitive perspectives are not in contradiction with one another; nor is either in conflict with the underlying theme of the argument, that forms and communities of knowledge are interdependent in many important respects. The change is one of perspective, not of the object in view. It is necessary to make it because certain features can be more clearly seen through the lens of social observation than through that of cognitive scrutiny. In marking this new departure, an appropriate starting point will be to explore the patterns of work in academia: to try to see what makes the whole thing tick.

It is a common finding of studies of what motivates academic researchers that what moves them is primarily factors intrinsic to the discipline itself, particularly the desire to develop a reputation in the field and to contribute significantly to it. As the study reported by Henkel found, professional aspirations and academic identity were intimately bound together:

> The ideal science career was to continue in research throughout. A biochemist, asked about what was most important to him, replied that it was to continue to be active in research. This was critical for his sense of identity. He would be very disappointed if he stopped being active in this way at any time before he was due to retire.
>
> (Henkel 2000: 183)

Similarly in the USA, the HERI study of faculty (Sax *et al.* 1999) found that the desire to become an authority in one's own field was ranked important or essential by around 50 per cent of academics in HE institutions generally with much higher percentages in research universities. It consistently ranked above the significance of being well off financially, though lower than a number of motherhood and apple pie statements such as 'being a good colleague'. This aspiration, as our research data underline, is not confined to the sciences alone but manifests itself across the whole range of academic disciplines. Thus, an engineer could speak of 'a major incentive in the feeling that you are recognized in your field', and modern linguists and economists alike would comment on the crucial steps to be taken in establishing 'a scholarly reputation'.

Knorr Cetina (1982), writing on 'the scientist as an economic reasoner', emphasizes that what is at stake in the academic's 'preoccupation with value . . . , is not the value of some product, but the value of the scientists themselves'. The outcome of one's work, whatever tangible form it may take, is not an end in itself but a means to the end of one's own professional achievement. What counts towards success in an academic career may vary from one field to another. In the technical professions, such as medicine or engineering, a name can be made by discovering or inventing a product (prime examples would be penicillin and the jet engine); in the social professions, such as law, it is possible to become an eminent academic consultant without having had to write a great deal. But for the most part, in leading academic circles, credit is earned through the publication of one's research findings; excellence in teaching counts for little towards recognition by established colleagues in the same field.[1] It is precisely this issue that the British Institute for Learning and Teaching (ILT), established in 1999, seeks to address:

> It is widely held that teaching in HE takes second place to research in terms of its standing and recognition. As stated in the Dearing report *'one current barrier is that staff perceive national and institutional policies as actively encouraging and recognising excellence in research, but not teaching'*. Therefore, a first useful function of the ILT would be to attempt *to redress the balance between teaching and research* by providing a national focus for teaching.
>
> (ILT 1999, para 5, original emphasis)

According to Finkelstein *et al.*'s study in the USA most faculty, both new and experienced, agree that teaching rather than research should be the main promotion and tenure criterion (Finkelstein *et al.* 1998: 86–7), although this is less true of men than women. Other data, however, suggest that there has been a steadily increasing stress on the primacy of research over decades (Carnegie Foundation for the Advancement of Teaching 1989; Russell 1992; Milem *et al.* 2000). Likewise in Australia, while the majority of academic staff believe that proficiency in teaching should be the primary promotion criterion, most acknowledge that in practice it is only the fifth most important factor to be considered (McInnis 2000). Adams (1998: 424), comparing three decades of surveys of Australian academics concurs, noting that faculty 'have been disinclined to believe the rhetoric emanating from university administrations that good teaching is valued and is considered favourably in promotion applications' (see also Ballantyne *et al.* 1999). Milem *et al.* (2000) concur that the academic reward structure is largely responsible for a shift in academics' time and priorities towards research in all types of American HE institutions. They report that this has been at the expense of time spent interacting with students outside the classroom.

A consequence of the emphasis on research reputation is the academic's concern to establish and to safeguard his or her rights to intellectual property (Ravetz 1971). As one of the informants explained: 'You get a sense of possessiveness about an idea, and automatically feel you have to defend it.' Powerful taboos exist against plagiarism. Taking and using other people's ideas without acknowledging them is regarded as no better than theft of a more material kind: it can lead to the ruin not only of one's reputation but of one's whole career. Even the inadvertent repetition of previous findings is frowned on: you need to know what the people who came before you have said, and you only make a fool of yourself by unwittingly saying it again and claiming it as a new insight. The legitimate counterpart is the process of paying a tax on intellectual borrowing, in the form of the citation of relevant sources – though that has a variety of other functions, as we see in Chapter 6.

There were some among the junior academics interviewed in the initial study who were unclear whether a good reputation was more strongly determined by quantity than by quality of published writing, a finding confirmed by Boice's study of newly recruited academics in the USA (Boice 1992). However, the more senior and established academics generally took the view that it was quality that counted.[2]

In the UK the funding councils' research assessment exercise (RAE) has had important implications for the priority given to research and the research work of academic staff. It has also helped shape understandings of what counts in research terms. A report on the impact of the RAE for HEFCE, the English funding body, by Ian McNay (1997) suggested that there were concerns among HE representatives from whom he gathered data that the RAE had the following effects on academic staff cultures:

- because of the assessment criteria, the already high status of theoretical areas of research is enhanced. This has consequences in terms of gender equity given that, as we have already noted, there is a tendency for women academics to be involved in lower status research (see pages 54–5)
- RAE assessment panels are setting research agendas and thus generating externalist rather than internalist epistemological changes within disciplines: other funding agencies are having a comparable effect
- the division formalised by the RAE between 'research-active' staff and others in many institutions has had the effect of fragmenting the profession. This is described in McNay's executive summary as 'possibly the most traumatic

HR [human resources] effect linked to the RAE . . . Obviously, pressure on individuals – whether designated research active or not – is increased when funds are limited and distribution is increasingly selective'.

(HEFCE 1997: 13)

Martin and Irvine (1992) lend evidence to support the last concern. They show how the emphasis on the 'bid and deliver' model of research funding generally in the UK and elsewhere is influencing the shape of academic enquiries, and argue that teaching work was being casualized to release permanent staff to do research. Similarly the research into higher education reforms reported by Henkel (2000) found that the RAE has had a number of effects on institutional practices, values and attitudes. Generally the significance of research has been raised and responsibility for academic development in universities has been centralized with research becoming an institutional rather than individual concern. In some cases heads of department have become more interventionist in terms of monitoring, and chasing, the research output of colleagues. This research too concluded that the effect of the exercise on relations between academics had been deleterious, particularly in the sciences, as this comment from a respondent suggests:

> [The RAE] had a divisive effect, a polarisation between researchers and teachers, in the sense that it requires individuals to have a very strong portfolio of research . . . As in other places, we have to identify those people whom we think likely to meet [the RAE] criteria and reduce their teaching loads, with the inevitable consequence that others have still higher teaching loads and 'cannot dabble in research, as they might have done in the past'.
>
> (respondent n4bc5, quoted in Henkel 2000: 128)

Such a policy almost inevitably led to resentment among those effectively designated 'teaching only' staff.

The way to get on

While publication constitutes the formal and explicit criterion for recognition, there is (here as elsewhere) an informal and tacit dimension which also has to be taken into account. However important quality may be, it is not only what you write but who you are and where you come from that counts. In her study of 'productivity and recognition', Crane (1965) observes that:

> in terms of his [sic] chances of obtaining recognition, a scientist gained more from affiliation with a major university than from high productivity or from his sponsor's prestige, probably because the major university provided better opportunities for contacts with eminent scientists in the same discipline.

Reskin (1977) reaches a similar conclusion. Moreover, as Cole (1978) remarks, a scientist who acquires a position in a highly ranked department may experience a rise in the perceived quality of his or her work. Cole was able to detect no significant differences here in the way in which the reward systems operated across the five disciplines he studied (three in the natural and two in the social sciences; see above). Hargens and Hagstrom (1967), in a study of patronage versus open competition among American academic scientists, identify (for fairly obvious reasons) the prestige of an individual's doctoral institution as a more important factor than research productivity in early career advancement. Among economists, Oromaner (1983) suggests that there is a tendency to cite articles by those from prestigious institutions, while Lightfield (1971), in his study of social scientists, contends that recognition is affected by the status rank of both the doctoral department and the present academic location. Without any prompting, one of the informants in the initial study (an academic lawyer) made a precisely similar point: 'Of two equally bright people, one might have a better reputation than the other. That will almost certainly have something to do with the institutions where they got their degrees and the institutions they teach at now.'

On the question of sponsorship as a source of career advancement, most of those interviewed, regardless of discipline, took the same line. It could be useful to have a well-regarded patron in applying for one's first appointment or two: but after that, one was expected to be judged by one's own efforts.[3] As one historian remarked, 'the best scholars tend to attract the best students . . . if you are a protege of one of these leading figures, you may well have some advantage in getting your first job – though seldom beyond that'. The biologists also allowed some scope for patronage, and one observed that 'some research supervisors have an extensive range of contacts, which helps them to place their students – traces of the old boy network still remain, though it is less strong than it once was'. On the whole, the scholarly population has become too large, too diffuse to allow for the survival of a once-powerful patronage system.[4]

The academic study of law in Britain seems to be the one interesting exception (the American scene is very different in this respect), perhaps because its related professional community, and the Bar in particular, still depends to a considerable extent on close informal contacts and personal recommendation. Thus one of the legal informants averred that 'there is preferment and sycophancy in some law schools – if you want to get on you have to have a mentor, work in his [sic] areas of interest and follow up the leads he gives you'. Another (from a different institution) spoke of the world of academic law as 'bitchy and sycophantic, with a certain amount of mild corruption in the form of preferment'.

Another aspect of acquiring a reputation is not easily detected in studies (such as those already quoted) that rely largely on bibliographical analysis. It comes out quite strongly in the competitive environment of hard pure knowledge domains, though it seems more muted elsewhere. A number of biologists made the point with characteristic clarity: 'There is a large element of public relations involved'; 'you have to make yourself known, to sell yourself at meetings'; 'you have to put your work across to the right people'; 'few people get there by pure talent, though you do have to be able as well'; 'you get an FRS not only on the basis of what you know, but of who you know'. Reif (1961) writes of the need for physicists:

> to create, either through personal contact or through published work, a favourable impression among as many key scientists as possible. Professional mobility of the scientist depends . . . in an essential way on the reputation he [sic] has acquired among prominent people in his field.

By way of confirmation, one of the US physicists informants, speaking half-admiringly of a colleague who had 'made it', remarked 'he's not that smart, but he's very tough and good at promoting himself'.

Once again there is a gender dimension to this discussion. This has already been highlighted by the language used by the writers, which in many ways reflects the reality on the ground. Where the mechanisms for 'getting on' involve (literally) an 'old boys' network', in other words a system of sponsored rather than contest mobility (Turner 1960), male-dominated patronage rather than meritocratic progression, then inequality of opportunity is ingrained in the system, most obviously in terms of gender but also in respect to other aspects of social difference. Ann Brooks' research in New Zealand and the UK (1997: 38) suggests that for many academic women it is in precisely the area of 'appointments, promotions and membership of committees making both' that control by male academics is most clearly discernible. She quotes several respondents who confirm the importance of an old boys' network in promotion to chairs in particular, especially in the higher status institutions. As noted above, the nature of the institution is an important variable in this, as is the position from which an academic embarks on the process of self-advancement. The very opportunity to be involved in more transparent 'contest' models of promotion is open mainly to those who already have full-time permanent posts: and these are more likely to be men. As Brooks puts it:

> Academic women found in research posts are generally appointed on a contractual basis . . . They are not part of, and do not experience, a career structure and promotion opportunities similar to those of lecturers. These groups do not have access to the process of appraisal which could assist them in their professional development. Thus academic women are differentially located within the culture of the academy.
> (Brooks 1997: 43)

However, even where there is a good deal of transparency there may remain points in the recruitment and promotion process that are 'murky', as Evans (1995) puts it, and where backstage deals become more important than front-of-stage deliberations. In the initial phases of the academic appointment process, for example, the tasks of job-creation and the drawing

up of long and short-lists, including the assessment of references, are usually done backstage (Evans 1995: 255–61). At other points the process tends
to be conducted more openly, particularly in defining the job specifica-
tions, and assessing candidates' presentations and their interview performances. That is to say conformity to equal opportunity procedures and
adherence to a contest model may vary over the course of the whole
appointment process as a whole.

Pecking orders, elites and the Matthew effect

One of the striking features of academic life is that nearly everything is
graded in more or less subtle ways. Leading researchers are quite clear
about the most prestigious journals in their discipline, about which there is
virtual unanimity: though because the consensus is usually tacit it can give
rise to difficulties for those new to research when the status of their 'output'
is assessed in terms of how it is disseminated (Gerver 1997: 18). Established
academics are also willing, when pressed, to list institutions and departments in order of intellectual precedence; there is a constant process of
implicit and explicit ranking of individuals (the outstanding scholar, the
student with the 'first class mind', and, more often by implication or omission, those who are less well regarded).

There is moreover a prestige that attaches to some subjects in particular,[5]
and in some areas even a rough pecking order between the component
specialisms. Physicists consider themselves, and are regarded by others, as
better than the common crowd; historians are accepted to be a cut above
geographers; economists look down on sociologists; and so the catalogue
continues. Roughly speaking, hard knowledge domains are regarded more
highly than soft ones, and pure than applied. Within what might be called,
in sociological parlance, the more stratified disciplines (those with clearly
marked internal status distinctions), certain fields of activity are seen as
prestigious and others as less so. In general, theoreticians are reckoned to
have to deal with the most difficult intellectual tasks. Thus Gaston (1973)
remarks that in high-energy physics, 'recognition is, first, a function of
scientific productivity and, second, a function of the type of [sub-specialism].
Theorists are recognized more than experimentalists for their research.'
Again, among the respondents in the initial study, mathematical economists were considered the *crème de la crème* within the discipline; 'messy'
areas such as labour economics were generally given a low rating. But the
orders of priority here are susceptible to conflicting criteria (the more
applied fields often attract the largest share of the grants), and subject to
intellectual fashion.

In non-elite university settings factors other than disciplinary specialism and
other audiences become important in conferring status and self-esteem.
Clark (1997: 29) found that in middle-level institutions in the USA 'professors often spoke of their relationship with students as the thing they value

most. Students begin to replace peers as the audience of first resort.' The shift in priorities became more marked in community colleges:

> In a setting that is distinctly opposed to disciplinary definitions of quality and excellence, pleasures and rewards have to lie in the task of working with poorly prepared students who pour in through the open door. For example . . . 'We are not sitting here on our high horses looking to publish'.
>
> (Clark 1997: 29)

In non-elite universities in the UK the situation is more complex. Internal diversity with regard to the engagement with research means that different sets of value systems, and so status structures, are at work. Professional roles and academic identities also interact with educational ideologies, though in ways that display reasonably regular patterns. Thus in the NewU study an academic lawyer not engaged in research situated in a department with only an emerging research profile articulated a student-centred ideological position, what Trowler (1998a) calls progressivism, close to the position articulated by Clark's respondents in community colleges. However, a respondent in cultural studies in the same university, articulating a traditionalist ideological position, adopted a stance towards status and rewards close to that seen in high-status research universities.

Discussion of disciplinary pecking orders in research settings can open up a host of intriguing issues. Why, for instance, do historians, sociologists, lawyers and mechanical engineers apparently find it difficult to rank their specialisms while mathematicians and pharmacists are at least able to do so to a limited extent? What is it that makes people by and large accord chemists a higher status than biologists? Such questions, which are ostensibly about knowledge communities, are (as has already been implied) to do with epistemology as well: with the nature and precision of criteria for judging merit; with the degree of elegance of the intellectual field; with the extent to which it lends itself to abstract thinking, responds to mathematical modelling or provides the apparently rigorous basis for policy-making. Such considerations will be taken up again in Chapter 9. For our present purposes, however, it is necessary to return to the question of institutional and personal prestige.

The standing of a particular department is determined in part by the status of its parent institution, and also in part by the reputation of its individual members. But the relationships here are reciprocal, in that an institution's standing is made up in large part of the reputations of its constituent departments, which themselves condition the regard in which their individual members are held. The ascription of status is thus a delicate and complex business; this does not, however, appear to inhibit the pervasive process of evaluating intellectual worth.

One outcome of this constant exercise of discriminative judgement is the creation of elites and the marking down of those who are not among the front runners. Aldous Huxley once wrote of 'A million million spermatozoa,/All of them alive:/Out of their cataclysm but one poor Noah/Dare hope to survive.' A less dramatic version of the same syndrome can be seen across the whole range of academic communities. Selectivity is at its most ruthless in hard pure domains, where the pyramid has a broad base and a sharp pinnacle. Mulkay (1976) argues that a small elite of scientists enjoys a disproportionate share of grant resources and peer recognition; Gaston (1973) observes that there is a relatively small number of scientists at the centre of the information network; and 'most work by average scientists is hardly ever acknowledged, much less rewarded with citations and prizes'. A number of bibliographical studies (e.g. Price 1963) have shown that, taking the science community as a whole, a sizeable proportion of individuals publish no more than one or two papers throughout their careers; of those papers that are published, a significant number (Price 1965, Gustin 1973) are never cited, and some, one might conjecture, will be read by only a handful of people.

The gulf between fame and anonymity is progressively widened by the operation of what Merton (1973), invoking a well-known passage in the first of the Four Gospels, called the Matthew principle: 'To those that have shall be given, and from those that have not shall be taken even that which they have.' Mulkay (1977) refers to 'a self-reinforcing elite structure' and adds that 'The more eminent a scientist becomes the more visible he [sic] appears to his colleagues and the greater the credit he receives for his research contributions.' As a biologist informant in the initial study remarked, 'It's a cumulative process. Once you earn a name for yourself, it acts as a magnet: you get invitations to join societies, give papers and take up offices', or as Professor of management science Peter Checkland said at his 1997 exaugural lecture at Lancaster University: 'you know when you've arrived when the invitation to speak says that the foundation will reimburse your expenses'. Boice's study in the USA (1992) found that academics who are productive in their early careers are likely to remain so, while those who are not are unlikely to become so: the evidence that success breeds success spans the disciplines.

The 'Matthew principle' is a particularly appropriate name for the effect under discussion here in that it posits an agency with the power both to give and to take away. The multiple agents at work involved include leading academics, tribal elders in different disciplines and government and its agencies. As far as the latter is concerned, current policies – in the UK at least – have had the effect of enhancing the Matthew principle. Before the nominal abolition of the binary divide in 1992, polytechnics in the UK were excluded from research assessment exercises and hence from research funding. Despite their last-minute inclusion in 1992 and in subsequent such exercises they still receive only a small proportion of total research funding. The trend seems to be further to reinforce the Matthew effect: in 1992 those assessed at grade 2 received some funding, whereas in 1996 they did not. As Henkel (2000: 131) points out, the effect of receiving a low assessement score in the sciences is to further reduce the chances of getting funding for collaborative research with industry and so to reinforce the downward spiral. It seems likely that future exercises will continue this trend, repudiating the principle that aspiring new entrants to the research community should be nurtured rather than strangled at birth.

Leading academics, gatekeepers and the exercise of power

Even among those who reach elite status during their professional careers, there are few who achieve recognition as great academics. Perhaps true eminence is hard to judge except retrospectively: many cases have been known of pygmies turning into giants over time. It is also possible to speculate, as Griffith and Small (1983) have done, whether there is some difference between hard and soft knowledge areas in the ease with which ability is recognized and commonly acknowledged. They suggest that 'softer' clusters are more likely to be dominated by the work of only one or two people – the 'few ancestral spirits', in Jones's (1980) spoof account of American sociologists, who 'are endowed with extraordinarily creative powers . . . a very few of [whose] inscriptions are sometimes said to embody all the sacredness diffused throughout the whole clan'. It is certainly in the hard pure knowledge areas, where significant discoveries are easy to identify, and where criteria of merit are less open to wide interpretation and dispute, that prizes and other public symbols of recognition abound, and that eponymy is commonplace ('Fermat's last theorem'; 'Maxwell's equations'; 'Halley's comet'; 'Darwin's finches').

It stands to reason that the personal qualities which go to make up greatness are as many and diverse as the disciplines within which it is achieved, and as the people who inhabit them. Attempts to define genius, or even to pinpoint exceptional creativity, have met with only the modest success that attends most speculative psychological investigation. However, there are certain social and cognitive features that appear to distinguish major from minor intellectual contributions. One of these is range of applicability. 'Prestige accrues predominantly to those whose discoveries prove fruitful as a basis for further work by other scientists' (Reif 1961); people who, according to the biologists interviewed, had changed the shape of the discipline in some significant way. Another is breadth of reference. Crane's (1972) analysis of invisible colleges suggests that it is the most productive scientists who have the highest number of professional ties outside their own specialism; and it became clear from discussions with historians that those who seek greatness must be 'more than narrow scholars'. In the disciplinary groups in which the same people's names kept cropping up in the course of the initial interviews (Sauer, for example, among American geographers, or Kahn-Freund among English academic lawyers), they were singled out for their 'broad, philosophical view of the subject', their 'range of knowledge, breadth of education and concern'.[6]

The achievement of a measure of eminence in one's lifetime brings with it a potentiality for the exercise of power. As one informant, a sociologist, remarked, 'Power resides in the membership of salary and promotion committees: people suddenly realise that they are being judged by their seniors'; another added, 'rank counts when it is a question of getting references for jobs – you are subtly confronted by the need for support from your superiors'. Whitley (1969) comments that 'Power in the sciences is seen as an adjunct of prestige' entailing one's appointment to key positions such as journal editors and referees. Mulkay (1977) develops the point:

> Because judgements of the highest quality can only be made by men [sic] who are already eminent, those at the top of the various informal scientific hierarchies exercise great influence over the standards operative within their fields. And those scientists who wish to advance their careers and to produce results which are accepted as significant contributions to knowledge must comply with the standards set by these leaders.

A certain element of continuity is built into this judgemental process, in that 'as a result of their academic training, editorial readers respond to certain aspects of methodology, theoretical orientation and mode of expression in the writings of those who have received similar training' (Crane 1967).

The role of 'gatekeeper' – the person that determines who is allowed into a particular community and who remains excluded – is a significant one in terms of the development of knowledge fields. 'Generally', Cole (1983) points out, 'the stars of a particular discipline occupy the main gatekeeping roles. By their acts as gatekeepers and evaluators, they determine what work is considered good and what is unimportant.' A prime example emerged from the interviews with mathematicians, when it became apparent that one distinguished member of the discipline in Britain had played a key part in all the significant appointments to his field over several years, and had also had considerable influence on the promotion pattern in neighbouring specialisms. Whitley (1984) remarks that the significance of gatekeeping may vary between subject fields:

> Anglo-Saxon sociology and economics, for instance, differ greatly in the influence a relatively small number of intellectual leaders are able to exert over research strategies and significance criteria . . . Generally, the more concentrated is control over the major communication media, the easier it is for a small elite to set standards and direct strategies.

This qualification seems plausible in the light of the differences that have already been noted (see especially Chapters 2 and 4) between distinct knowledge forms and communities. The more closely defined and better-defended the boundaries are between hard specialisms, and the more tightly knit the groups associated with them, the easier it is to maintain the integrity of received doctrines by the ostracism or expulsion of internal dissidents and the refusal to provide entry permits to outsiders with dubious credentials. Yet traces of the gatekeeping function may be found even in epistemologically soft areas whose associated specialist groups are loosely knit. In history, one informant spoke of the need to 'defer to the elders of the tribe', and another remarked that it was at least a matter of courtesy, if not of expediency, when one wanted to enter a new specialism, to write to one or more of the leading experts for initial advice and guidance.

Peer review and the process of validation

Although particular weight is given to the pronouncements of the more eminent academics in any community, they are not alone in shaping its values and standards. The responsibility for quality control in research has traditionally been a collective one, distributed across the whole membership of a given group; except in the strongly hierarchical subject areas, leadership is only granted on sufferance, and those who are accorded it have to continue to justify themselves as especially competent and active exponents of their discipline or specialism. The right of any member of a particular field to criticize the work of any other member, regardless of their relative status, is strongly defended in principle even where it is only weakly exercised in practice. This right rests on a procedure that is commonly termed peer group judgement or peer review.

The notion of an academic peer group is not clearly defined. It has some affinities with a specialist network, some with an 'invisible college' and some with a wider disciplinary community, though the contexts in which the term 'peer group' is used differ from those in which the other labels are commonly found. It is related to the exercise of a number of key evaluative functions (Zuckerman and Merton 1971) performed by suitably selected members of a body of reasonably close colleagues. It forms the basis of the grant-awarding process in the case of many research funding bodies (proposals are typically sent out to two or more independent referees with appropriate expertise), and is also used in assessing articles submitted for journal publication and in determining eligibility for the membership of learned societies. Senior members of the peer group may be invited to act as external examiners for degree awards, to participate in the process of appointment to senior posts, and to offer comments on candidates for promotion within an institution.

The principle of mutual judgement by informed specialists seems well-founded, in that only those with a mastery of a particular field are capable of making an authoritative appraisal within it.[7] In terms of research activity, as Mulkay (1977) argues:

> trustworthy assessments of the quality of a given piece of work can only be made by those who are working on the same or similar problems and who are known to be capable of producing results of at least the same level of quality. There can be no separate formal hierarchy of control in scientific research. All participants, as they use, modify or

disregard the results communicated to them, are continually engaged in judging the adequacy and value of their colleagues' work. As a result of those judgements, recognition is allocated and reputations are created; not only for individual researchers, but also for research groups, university departments and research journals.

Peer review, it may be said, serves to maintain overall standards as well as to recognize individual excellence.

Like many useful social mechanisms, however, the peer group has its drawbacks. The indictments are as numerous as they are varied. One fairly obvious one was noted earlier: that those who have already earned reputations tend to be consistently favoured at the expense of those who have not.[8] Another is that in the more highly specialized areas, the scope for informed and impartial judgement is limited – the selection of referees may have to be made from those whose professional acquaintance with the field is only indirect (and whose judgements will in that sense be amateur), or from the few people with shared expertise who may wish to protect their own standing against rival claims.

A third common and predictable set of complaints arises from the fallibility of human judgement. The failure of experts to agree is commonplace, in this as in other spheres, and especially so at 'the research frontier' where 'getting a research grant depends to a significant extent on chance'; though, perhaps reassuringly, 'the great bulk of disagreement . . . is probably a result of real and legitimate differences of opinion among experts' (Cole *et al.* 1981). It should be noted that Cole's later research identifies less difference in this respect between the natural sciences and the social sciences than has usually been assumed: they have 'similar [that is, comparatively low] levels of consensus at the research frontier' (Cole 1983).

Cole, who has made a particular study of peer review procedures, argues that leaving aside questions of reliability – that is, consistency of judgement – their validity must also be suspect, in that they often fail to predict the winners:

> In one subject we studied, algebra, . . . people whose proposals [for grants to the National Science Foundation] were declined actually turned out to be on average slightly more productive than those whose proposals were accepted. Although there may be some discoveries which are immediately judged to be significant and do indeed turn out to be highly significant, for most science it is not clear to participants, when work is produced, whether it will turn out to be important. Although we have always assumed that this is true for the social sciences, [a number of studies] suggest that it is also true for the natural sciences.
> (Cole 1983)

We have already quoted (p. 6) the UK Quality Assurance Agency's view that the 'shared assumptions and informal networks and procedures' which underpin peer review are no longer appropriate or acceptable in a 'mass'

HE system, and no doubt the authors of that text shared at least some of the concerns articulated above. As we indicated in Chapter 1, the trend across the world is for the 'evaluative state' to become centrally involved in assessing the quality of all dimensions of university work, including both teaching and research. The future of relatively informal arrangements for peer review seems uncertain, particularly in the area of teaching, learning and assessment. The QAA, for example, employs accredited 'academic reviewers' for its quality assessment exercises and is concerned to establish the boundaries between these and external examiners. In their report on its trials of a new system of subject review the QAA states:

> Several academic reviewers indicated in their comments that a clear distinction could be made between the roles of academic reviewers and external examiners: academic reviewers would be considering student work to gain an *overview* of standards being achieved, rather than to consider the achievements of individual students. It was also suggested that external examiners would continue, where appropriate, to act as 'critical friends', a role which should be denied to academic reviewers.
>
> (QAA 1999)

It may be remarked that, apart from its congenital weaknesses, peer review tends to operate unevenly between different knowledge fields: 'Disciplines vary in the extent to which articles by authors from diverse intellectual backgrounds are selected for publication in their principal journals' (Crane 1967). Soft areas with relatively permeable boundaries are in their nature more tolerant of divergence than those whose subject matter is hard and whose boundaries are closely defined. It was commonplace among respondents[9] that different speciality groups within the same disciplines adopted different standards of academic rigour: the variations between disciplines in this respect were acknowledged to be endemic (and often held to be related to their ranking in the intellectual pecking order).

Where the system shows signs of breaking down, it does so in different ways according to the knowledge domain in question. The venial sin of 'sloppy refereeing' seems most prevalent in mathematics, where it can be particularly difficult and time-consuming to enter into someone else's frame of reference and follow the train of reasoning within it (in contrast, respondents in some more loosely organized disciplines remarked on the importance accorded to meticulous evaluation procedures). One of the mathematical informants condoned the fact that 'people don't take enough care to check papers for accuracy', remarking that 'there is no reward system built in for that kind of work'. Another observed that 'people used to be more conscientious in the old days, when they weren't so pressed for time', but commented that the comparatively slipshod current practice was not damaging to the subject in the long run, since any important errors would eventually get known – it merely demanded 'more vigilance from the general mathematical public: and in any case it is the author who cares most passionately about not making mistakes'.

The last comment, incidentally, underlines an interesting disjunction between supposition and actuality. Perhaps because of the insistence of positivist philosophers of science that the validity (or falsity) of an empirical proposition ought, at least in principle, to be tested by replication of the supporting experimental procedures, it seems to be widely supposed outside the natural science community that this is indeed the normal practice. However, the data from the initial study are unequivocal in confirming Thagaard's (1987) contention that:

> Replication of previous findings is seldom performed because replications are difficult to publish. Publication of papers requires presentation of new aspects. One way to meet both the demands for new findings and for verification of new results is to work on similar projects, which usually implies the same design.

In effect, validation by the peer group, even in the universalistic world of hard pure knowledge, is less a matter of the careful, repetitious checking of one another's results than of a seemingly more haphazard process: assuming that people's findings are correct and building on them until something is clearly seen to have gone wrong, at which point some credit may be given for tracking down the original error. 'There is almost always', one of the respondents in the intial study remarked, 'a deeper reason to replicate – it isn't something people do in the normal run.'

The very notion of validation has (as the discussion in Chapter 2 attempted to make plain) to be translated into different terms in the particularistic, interpretive domain of soft pure knowledge – which demands some form of 'authenticity' – from those adopted in the contrasting domains of hard applied and soft applied knowledge, where the respective requirements might be identified as functional efficiency and procedural utility. The peer groups concerned with establishing standards in these diverse knowledge areas are thus faced with dissimilar tasks. It is not surprising that they have to tackle them in distinctive ways, and that breakdowns in procedure may be traced to different sources of weakness in the system.

When the hard scientists – pure as well as applied – in the initial study referred on occasion to unethical refereeing, they frequently had in view cases of sharp practice or plagiarism. Their stories, mythical or personally experienced, related to eminent referees who had caused others' submissions to be rejected or long delayed, and who had then proceeded themselves to publish suspiciously similar findings. In soft knowledge domains, this form of corruption is uncommon, because few people are working on the same issues, and even if they are, their interpretations of them are very rarely identical. On the other hand, there is more room in such fields for the venting of personal preferences or antipathies. Any member of the peer group may be open to the accusation of 'log rolling' for friends and proteges (by treating their efforts more kindly than they deserve) or of 'doing down' enemies and rivals (by unduly harsh criticisms of their work). The deliberate freezing-out of contributions that are seen as in some way threatening (usually because they purport to undermine an established ideology or school of thought) is not confined to any one knowledge area, manifesting itself from time to time with comparable partiality in every kind of discipline.

The limitations of the exercise of peer judgement are easier to discern in the more or less publicly accessible arena of book reviewing or the refereeing of journal articles – where opinions are at least open to being challenged or appealed against – than in the closed world of making appointments and promotions, approving grant proposals, according honours or awarding prizes. Here the only recourse against the suspicion of unfairness is to try one's luck at another time or in another place, with the attendant risk that one or more of the same unfavourable referees will be employed. Where the achievement of a coveted goal is open to strong competition from people in a diversity of fields, the problem of making a just choice is all the worse. Faced with an array of well-supported, highly qualified candidates from disciplines whose standards are not easily comparable with one another, the temptation to lapse from the niceties of intellectual judgement to the coarser pursuit of political bargaining can become intense, as many of those who have been involved in such situations may be prepared in their unguarded moments to acknowledge.

Taking the long view, however, such complaints about the peer review process may be of no great import. They serve a useful purpose in signalling familiar pitfalls to be guarded against or in suggesting modest reforms in current practice,[10] but they cannot be allowed to constitute a major indictment against the system as a whole. Most of those who advocate parliamentary democracy as a method of government are prepared to acknowledge its manifold weaknesses: their defence of it rests on the claim that there is no preferable substitute. So too, it can be argued, the exercise of peer group judgement must be tolerated, for all its admitted faults, because no one, and certainly not the QAA, has yet come up with an approach to academic evaluation that would not be discernibly worse.

Networks and social circles

The concept of a peer group has affinities with that of a network, as may be seen from the following comment by Crane (1972): 'Behind the seemingly impersonal structure of scientific knowledge, there is a vast interpersonal network that screens new ideas in terms of a central theme or paradigm, permitting some a wide audience and consigning many to oblivion.'

That a network also has a close relationship with the notion of a specialist area or segment may be seen by relating some of the observations in Chapter 4 to this statement by Mulkay (1977):

Research networks are amorphous social groupings which, partly due to migration . . . and partly due to overlapping membership . . . are in a state of constant flux. At any one time the research community as a whole, as well as particular disciplines and specialties within it, is composed of numerous networks at various stages of formation, growth and decline.

An attempt to locate a tidy pattern in both sets of relationships might go something like this. A general distinction can be made (Becher and Kogan 1992) between what individuals or groups of individuals do – which may be termed their operational mode – and what their values, aspirations and loyalties are – which may be labelled their normative mode. The two modes are interdependent, in that significant changes in one will tend to be reflected in changes in the other. The peer group represents the academic community in its normative mode, where its predominant concern is with establishing standards, assessing merit and evaluating reputations. The network represents its operational mode, in which the focus is on the development and communication of knowledge as such. The interconnections may be seen in the way in which knowledge development is tested against professional norms (screened, in Crane's words, 'in terms of a central theme or paradigm') and the comparable way in which reputation may affect the collective identification and communication of 'new ideas'.

The distinction between norms and operations has a different frame of reference from that between the social and the cognitive aspects of academic life, though a shadowy connection may be discerned between them. It is in terms of this second dichotomy that networks and segments are related. It was suggested in Chapter 4 that the term segment might be seen in cognitive terms to signify divisions in knowledge at the microscopic level, whether or not such divisions fell within disciplinary domains or straddled the boundaries between them. The term network may be reserved to designate the corresponding social divisions: 'amorphous social groupings', as Mulkay describes them, of which 'the research community . . . is composed'.

A useful analogy, in attempting to characterize networks in more detailed terms, is that of a 'social circle' (developed by Crane 1969a, 1972). The parallel is a neat one, in that social circles are 'amorphous', 'overlapping' and 'in a state of constant flux'. They are centred on, and drawn around, both individuals and groups. That is, they can be defined in both personal and interpersonal terms – one may speak for some purposes of 'X's social circle', and for others of 'the social circle to which X belongs'. They also allow for pluralism, in that an individual may be said to belong to more than one such group. The attributes of social circles may vary. They may be large or small, active or moribund, important, colourful and exciting or insignificant, drab and mundane. They may be cliquey or open, and the relationships between members may be close or relatively distant, somewhere on the spectrum from best friends to nodding acquaintances. And they may be seen to be 'at various stages of formation, growth and decline'.[11]

The abundant research literature on the theme has three noticeable features. The first will by now seem familiar: it focuses largely (though not exclusively, as we shall see later) on the hard pure domain of the natural sciences. The second is its tendency to concentrate on the high life, on those active, glamorous situations in which interesting things are always happening, at the expense of those that follow the everyday routines of what Kuhn (1962) calls 'normal science'. The third characteristic of network studies is that they more or less consistently adopt the group as against the individual perspective, which sometimes has the effect of reifying the concept into an independent, substantive entity, divorced from the consideration of membership and, as Chubin (1976) complains, careless of the question of intellectual content. In contrast, the data from the initial study, being drawn more widely from a scatter of disciplines, tend to emphasize everyday circumstances as against contexts of high intellectual excitement, and to reflect the individual's standpoint rather than that of the group as a whole. The two approaches turn out in the event to be complementary to, rather than contradictory of, one another. The ensuing discussion will deal briefly with both.

To start with the material from the initial interviews, one phenomenon is clearly evident in the testimony from members of virtually every discipline; namely, the existence of an inner and an outer circle of professional acquaintance. The outer circle is in many cases quite large in compass, numbering somewhere between 100 and 400 people, with a norm of about 200. Its members comprise those colleagues with whose names and work one is more or less familiar – the distant intellectual relatives and passing professional friends one might occasionally meet and greet at conferences, those who might appear on one's mailing lists for offprints or publisher's notices. The inner circle is usually surprisingly small, ranging from half a dozen to a score, with a dozen as a fairly common average. The bonds here are tighter and more resilient, singling out those colleagues with whom one has a direct affinity and a closely shared interest; those critical friends to whom one would send draft papers for comment and whose own drafts one would take some trouble to read; the kind of people one would go to for assistance over a knotty problem, advice on research tactics, or support at times of intellectual adversity, and whom one would expect to help in one's turn.[12]

The size of the outer circle shows some variation from one type of specialism to another, with practitioners in socially well-organized, cognitively hard knowledge fields (physics in particular) often claiming large numbers, and those in loosely organized soft areas (social geography, say, or minority languages) usually quoting smaller ones.[13] The inner circle, however, seems to reflect no such cognitive contrasts. Variations in size here seem more a function of individual gregariousness than of subject field. Rather than reflecting a curiously uniform property of knowledge in all its different manifestations – the ability to be neatly parcelled up into small units capable of accommodating some 20 active researchers at most – the incidence of such small groupings seems more likely to arise from the difficulty academics have in sustaining more than a limited number of close affinities. Links of the intense kind in question are demanding as well as rewarding:

they take time to develop and sustain. Moreover, there is usually a limit to the extent to which one is prepared to confide in others about one's own half-formed ideas, or to be receptive to theirs.

Previous researches into academic networks give some indirect support to this contrast between inner and outer circles, though they do not address it directly. Thus Crane (1972) quotes Roberts's contention that groups could be as small as half a dozen (Roberts 1970), but attributes this to low paradigm development in the humanities; and Mullins (1973a) ascribes the size of 'clusters' – a 'minimum core of 13 to 15 active students, teachers and researchers' – to a particular phase in the cycle of growth of coherent intellectual groups.

A more commonly noted contrast in network research is that between open and closed groups. Mullins (1968) and Knorr Cetina (1982) are among those who focus on the incidence of informal contacts across group boundaries. The first author, however, in a joint paper with Griffith (Griffith and Mullins 1972) also discerns certain highly coherent groups that develop their own enclosed and private worlds: 'these groups generate "tribal folklore" and customs, including distinctive lifestyles, mock ceremonies and awards, special ingroup roles, and even, on occasion, a group sport'. Close cohesion is generally seen to be more common in 'revolutionary' than in 'normal' contexts. Those who are united in an attempt to contest the prevailing orthodoxies, or to strike out in a novel direction, tend to show a higher level of interaction and a more intense pattern of communication than those who are engaged on central problems demanding accepted modes of practice in areas in which the appropriateness of the subject matter, methods and theories are not in dispute (we return to a more detailed consideration of this point in Chapter 6).

Case histories of particular networks, understandably enough, tend to focus on the interesting exceptions to everyday routine. They are not confined to groups in the hard sciences, though these remain the dominant focus. Thus, alongside Knorr Cetina's (1999) careful scrutiny of laboratory cultures in high energy physics and molecular biology, there is a comparable exploration by Evans (1993) into the English discipline and the networks that permeate it.

Studies along these lines commonly represent the evolution of their research grouping as falling into three or four phases. Mullins, one of the front runners in such research, labels them as 'normal', 'network', 'cluster' and 'specialty', giving them somewhat surprisingly precise definitions, sizes of membership (Mullins 1973a, 1973b) and collective lifespans ('10 to 15 years is typical'; Griffith and Mullins 1972). Leaving aside the first of these, which can be taken simply as the characteristic form of loose network underpinning most academic activity, the remaining stages are usually identified in terms of (1) a disorganized, spontaneous growth of interest in a new development, as a result of which a network begins to coalesce and its defining doctrines to crystallize; (2) a more systematic structure of communication, recruitment and training, during which small internal interest groups appear and external boundaries become more firmly staked out; and (3) a stage at which the area becomes institutionalized, the excitement dies down and routine sets in. In the end, 'the penalty of success . . . is the death of the group as a distinct social and intellectual entity' (Griffith and Mullins 1972); 'growth turns imperceptibly into decline as recruitment falls away and as established members of the network move elsewhere into problem areas in the process of formation' (Mulkay 1977). The process can be aborted at any stage. Where a particular area of intellectual development proves to be less promising than it initially seemed, support ebbs away and the network dies a premature death – though here, as elsewhere, a rump of the highly committed converts may remain to pursue their unfashionable concerns in what will by that point have become an intellectual backwater.

However, this account of the life-cycle of research groupings needs to be modified in the light of research funding councils' adoption of more dirigiste policies during the 1990s, at least in the UK. Henkel (2000) notes that the ESRC promoted a shift in favour of team research in that decade. In common with other research councils, its funding policies were increasingly organized around collaborative programmes so that by 2000 less than 40 per cent of its allocations were made to individuals in what is called the responsive mode. Such policies will interfere with the natural cycle of birth and death in collaborative research groupings as well as with the shape and characteristics of the groups themselves.

Understandably, the internationalization and globalization of HE, discussed in Chapter 1, has important implications for the networks in which academics are involved. Scott (1998) identifies three important processes in academic staff networking at this level: the international flow of staff; the internationalization of collaboration between institutions; and the internationalization of the flow of ideas. None of them are new, but all have been invigorated by technological and economic change as well as by changes in HE itself.

The first, staff flows, spans the range from permanent relocation to brief visits, the latter now becoming predominant, but with the research universities of the USA provides the prime destination for the former. Scott discerns a class system of sorts at work in terms of international travel, with elite scholars and the 'management class' more able than run-of-the-mill academics to take advantage of new opportunities for travel.

The second, collaboration, typically involves bi-partisan arrangements and, increasingly often, multiple-partner regional or global agreements. These may be directed towards a political goal (for example the development of the HE systems of Latin American countries, as in the EU's Alfa programme). Alternatively they may offer a response to a perceived threat (as in the case of the British government's call in 2000 for consortial bids from universities and private sector companies to develop collaborative 'e-universities' – designed to counter perceived incursions into domestic markets by virtual universities abroad).

Scott's third category, the flow of ideas in relation to the humanities natural and social sciences has always been international. He notes that while the 'hardware' of big science may need to be increasingly concentrated, the balance is shifting in favour of the 'software' in that it can readily be produced in a variety of locations. There is moreover a pattern in the dispersion of software production, an unequal division of academic labour, 'with the truly creative paradigm-busting science being done in North America (and, to a lesser extent, Europe) and routine science subcontracted to outworkers in the Indian subcontinent, Latin America and so on.' (Scott 1998: 120). The patterns of internationalization and globalization of academic networking are thus increasingly conditioned by social structural factors and economic considerations.

The influence of fashion

Every one of the 12 disciplines covered by the intial study appeared to be subject to fashion (or, as one sociologist preferred to call it, 'paradigm choice or shift'). Some informants considered this a healthy feature of their academic community, allowing scope for individuals to move in new directions and ensuring that ideas did not stagnate. Others took a less positive view, deploring the tendency of some colleagues to 'behave like a flock of lemmings' in pursuit of novelty, noting the adverse effects on the systematic development of the field, and commenting on the consequent overpopulation in some areas at the expense of underpopulation in others. One of the chemists interviewed summed up a common worry: that susceptibility to fashion served to create 'a cyclical pattern of glut and scarcity'. Another remarked on the 'tendency to flock into new areas while other fields become comparatively neglected'.

The term itself, as some respondents noted, is value-laden, in that the same research activity might be represented as 'a mere fad' by those who disapproved of it, where those in favour would describe it as 'a hot area', and hence as rightly attracting new recruits.[14] Crane (1969b) attempts a neutral account in her observation that: 'The key factor in fashion is that similar perceptions of an area come to be shared by large numbers of scientists due to a process of social validation occurring in a rapidly expanding communication network.'

Recruitment to meet the need for expansion 'depends upon the number of scientists in related areas who are capable in terms of training of moving into [a new field]'. It tends to stem from three main groups of academics. The first consists of those who are highly mobile by temperament and profession: people who eschew fixed loyalties to a single line of research and are eager to seek out novel ideas as they begin to appear over the horizon. The second is the group of individuals who, at any given time, have become disenchanted with their current line of research – usually because it is, or they themselves are, apparently going stale – and who are therefore looking out for promising fresh departures. The third group comprises the novitiates to the discipline, the research students who arrive with no fixed loyalties, keen to make their mark in areas which have not yet been heavily worked over, and susceptible to recruitment and proselytization by seniors wanting to attract a following into a new area of development.

Fashion takes a particularly intense form in those hard pure areas in which it appears relatively easy to identify promising new issues (see Chapter 2). Ruscio (1985) reports one of the biologists he interviewed as saying:

> a lot of people who have been trained in molecular biology ... jump around from one biological system to another. Some of these people are more technologists than biologists who operate with a question in mind and then take their systems and techniques to answer that question. I call it the bandwagon effect: they work on one problem and then something else turns up and a whole bunch will switch over to that and then over to the next one that comes up.

Mulkay (1972) documents the comparable practice, in hot areas of physics, of 'skimming the cream' and 'moving on', a theme that was also frequently touched on in the interviews with physicists (one of whom likened the associated groups of intellectual predators to 'shoals of piranha fish').

In most instances of fashion, the race is to the swift. Those who lag behind the trendsetters and opinion leaders often end up with the skimmed milk:

> in many cases a major proportion of the innovative work is completed before the field has begun to acquire a significant proportion of its eventual membership ... opportunities for making a notable scientific contribution and the chances of receiving an unusual amount of professional recognition decline very quickly.
>
> (Mulkay 1977)

It is not only in the natural sciences that fashion holds sway, though it takes distinctive forms in other knowledge fields. Soft pure areas, where new issues are not sharply defined in terms of the existing state of enquiry, allow the exercise of a more eclectic choice, perhaps 'promoted by foundations' or by 'the activities of elites or special interest groups', in contrast with those domains in which the selection of problems is made 'on the basis of strong theoretical imperatives' (Crane 1969b). Applied disciplines are different again. Here fashions tend to follow the demonstration (or at least the plausible claim) of success with novel techniques or procedures, sometimes with the backing of an associated theory but at other times on a straightforwardly heuristic basis.

Some types of development are more amenable to fashion than others. This may well be because, as Crane (1969a) argues, the acceptability of a new idea is affected by 'the amount of cognitive reorganization required to integrate the new information with previous knowledge'. As the Ruscio quotation above suggests, the extension of existing ideas and methods into a new subject field offers an attractive hostage to fashion. Methodological innovations, provided they are reasonably straightforward and do not demand a substantial amount of special training, are also relatively easy to take up. Significant changes in theoretical orientation and requirements to adopt complex new techniques (the use of computers in engineering design, say, or the earlier introduction of electron microscopy into biological research) are another matter, in that they demand a major reinvestment of time and effort, a theme that we explore further in considering the reactions of academics in general to innovative ideas.

Fashion, then, is a pervasive aspect of academic life, taking a variety of shapes and sizes. It may appear, as an eminent cell biologist once observed, in the guise of a mink coat, expensive and difficult to carry off, or in the form of a chainstore outfit, so cheap and simple as to be accessible to anyone who wants to go for it (Fell 1960). However, it owes its prevalence in the context of HE less to frivolity than to a concern on the part of many academics to find a rapid and effective way of enhancing their own reputations. And it needs to be remembered that there is a cognitive price to pay for most such social self-improvement: namely, the need to show that one has succeeded in some discernible way in advancing the cause of learning.

Reactions to innovative ideas

Among the paradoxes that abound in academia, one of the most curious is the apparent coexistence of radical chic with entrenched conservatism. Many respondents who complained about their discipline's susceptibility to fashion were equally ready to assert – within the compass of the same interview, if not in the same breath – that the jealous guardianship of the status quo, especially among the more senior of their colleagues, acted as a barrier against promising innovations. This conflict between tradition and change is enshrined in the title of Kuhn's (1977) essay on the subject (which is also the title of the book in which it appears): *The Essential Tension.*

Resistance to innovative ideas in their discipline is inborn among academic communities, as can be clearly shown by the length of time it often takes for a major insight or discovery to gain general acceptance. Merton (1973) canonizes the phenomenon as 'organized scepticism', one of his four basic norms of scientific behaviour, and Mulkay (1969), although critical of the norms themselves, does not dispute the contention that such a tendency exists. One among many instances is provided by Duncan (1974), in his account of how the seminal ideas of one geographer, Hagerstrand, after years of being disparaged or ignored, eventually succeeded in promoting a new approach to the discipline. Barber's (1961) general treatment of the subject offers other examples, in the process of suggesting why it is that new findings are only reluctantly conceded.

On this point, the explanations are various. Kuhn (1962) puts it down to a concern to maintain an existing paradigm, even in the face of conflicting evidence. Cole (1983) claims to have found 'many examples' of the contention that:

> If the experimental results do not fit the predictions made from the theory, the theory is not assumed to be incorrect. Rather, the scientist will assume that there was something wrong in the experimental techniques and that a proper experiment will bring about results which do indeed fit the theoretical expectations.

Boissevain (1974) adds two further considerations: besides 'the logical momentum of a scientific theory', he identifies 'the social climate . . . and the considerable power differentials inherent in all scientific communities' as factors 'which contribute to the persistence of all paradigms once they become dominant'.

Mulkay (1977) contests Kuhn's suggestion that major scientific advances typically demand a conceptual revolution, maintaining that 'although uncompromising intellectual resistance does occur . . . it is by no means as pervasive as Kuhn suggests'. He concedes, however, that 'a closed orthodoxy may be more probable' in highly socialized, socially isolated and intellectually distinct areas, and that 'intellectual control may be more likely in networks with a stable elite', a view echoed by Whitley (1984):

> Radical intellectual change – such as is implied by the term 'revolution' – is improbable where work goals and procedures are relatively uniform and stable and the hierarchy of problems and areas is reproduced and controlled by a strong authority structure.

In fields 'lacking strong paradigms', Collins (1975) offers a markedly different interpretation of resistance to intellectual change, seeing it as a wish 'to keep the organization decentralized and thus relatively egalitarian. The development of any theory that would change this situation . . . involves a power struggle of a particular sort.'

Such accounts appear to ignore one straightforward motive – which emerged consistently during the initial interviews – for standing out against new ideas. In many fields it takes time and trouble to acquire the necessary expertise to make a significant research contribution. People who have spent some years – to take only two of several examples given by the respondents – building up the vocabulary and conceptual structure demanded of a specialism in mathematics such as homotopy theory, or undergoing training in Freudian psychoanalysis in order to use it as an approach to literary criticism, understandably see themselves as being committed to a sizeable intellectual investment. And as with investments of a more familiar kind, there is a consequent wish to capitalize on them, recouping in collegial credit the efforts spent in laborious endeavour. A new development that threatens seriously to undermine the value of one's existing intellectual shareholding is unlikely to be welcomed with much enthusiasm.

It was noted in the earlier discussion of intellectual fashion that some forms of innovation are more readily acceptable than others; particularly so, perhaps, where they do not entail the costly process of abandoning existing assets and reinvesting in new ones. In soft pure areas where the internal boundaries are weak and movement across them relatively uninhibited, new theories are liable to succeed one another with disconcerting rapidity. Opposition to intellectual change is relatively low, too, 'when ideas from one area are being applied to another area that has not been active previously' (Crane 1972). Analogously, 'because new areas have, by definition, not been conceptualized before, their discovery will not normally generate intellectual resistance' (Mulkay 1977).

The familiar contest of the Young Turks against the Old Guard can also readily be explained in such terms. Those who have as yet made no major intellectual commitments have little to lose by investing in potentially high-risk, high-profit commodities; those who already have a substantial blue chip portfolio tend to see the emergence of rival markets as a threat rather than a promise.[15] The market metaphor has a certain appropriateness here, in that a persuasive analysis along these general lines was first put forward by a distinguished economist, Harry Johnson.

Johnson's (1971) thesis involves the identification of 'the social and intellectual conditions that make a revolution or counter-revolution possible'. The precondition is 'the existence of an established orthodoxy which is clearly inconsistent with the most salient facts . . . yet is sufficiently confident of its intellectual power to attempt to explain those facts, and in its efforts to do so exposes its incompetence in a ludicrous fashion'. Against this background, Johnson argues, a revolutionary theory must depend for its success on five main characteristics. First, it has to 'attack the central proposition of conservative orthodoxy . . . with a new but academically acceptable analysis that reverse[s] the proposition'. Next, it has 'to appear to be new, yet absorb as much as possible of the valid . . . components of existing orthodox theory'. Third, it must be 'so difficult to understand that senior academic colleagues would find it neither easy nor worthwhile to study', hard enough to 'challenge the intellectual interest of younger colleagues and students but actually easy enough for them to master adequately with a sufficient investment of intellectual endeavour', thus allowing youthful iconoclasm 'quickly [to] earn its just reward . . . by the demolition of the intellectual pretensions of its academic seniors and predecessors'. The fourth and fifth requirements are, respectively, that it should offer 'a new methodology more appealing than those currently available', with 'a high degree of apparent empirical relevance', and that it should provide 'a new and important empirical relationship'.

These are stringent demands, which not all accredited revolutions, even within hard pure fields, let alone those outside, would be able to meet. Nonetheless, Johnson's analysis presents a sharply delineated picture of the type of struggle that characterizes a major generation gap within a particular academic community, relating social to cognitive considerations in an appropriately subtle way. Taylor (1976) shows it to be broadly applicable to the controversy over quantitative geography in the 1960s and early 1970s,[16] adding some useful observations about how such controversies may eventually be resolved.

Taylor argues that 'the traditionalist must overcome the disrespect of the young by using one of two strategies – he [sic] must either banish the heretics or else integrate everybody into a new unity'. Proponents of 'the hardline view' opt for confrontation, seeking to show that the new proposals fall outside the proper scope of the discipline and should be regarded as intellectually invalid, or at best as forming the basis of a separate enterprise. This claim may well be supported by a judicious re-presentation of the history and traditional values of the disciplinary community in question. The alternative course is one of conciliation: 'a very common general strategy in all types of social communities outside the academic world . . . the incorporation of the "avant-garde" into the establishment'. That, however, may not be the end of the story. Both Johnson and Taylor remind us that revolution may breed counter-revolution. The Keynesian revolution, attacking the prevailing economic orthodoxy, was succeeded by the monetarist attack on Keynesianism; and in geography, 'as the establishment, or at least part of it, quantifiers [once the reformists] have to take their turn in coming under attack from new young geographers'.

The revolutionary and the normal

It is easy to be carried away into imagining that all academic life shares this quality of high intellectual theatre. But major revolutions, it needs to be recalled, represent the grand opera of the scholarly community, much of whose everyday entertainment falls within the more humble genre of improvised street theatre. 'In mature fields with accumulated resources', Bourdieu (1981) contends, 'great periodic revolutions' give way to 'countless small permanent revolutions'. Change is for the most part small-scale, steady and persistent.

Nonetheless, among the relatively elite groups in which most research into academic cultures has been conducted (including the initial study on which much of this book is based), professional life is never entirely static. If one wishes to acquire and maintain a reputation, it is essential to keep up with, and indeed to contribute to, new developments in one's field. Such new developments are a feature not only of highly active academic areas but also of those in which a less hectic pattern of life prevails. Academia offers an environment in which progress and development, not stability, is the normal expectation.

For those in non-elite settings change is also the norm, but here, like the goals of these institutions themselves (Clark 1987a) the dimensions of change are multiple. Respondents from public universities in the North American HERI study (Sax *et al.* 1999) were more likely to report change in a number of dimensions of professional life than their colleagues in private universities. At the low status site of Trowler's research, NewU, nearly all the respondents remarked on the pressures created by institutional, rather than disciplinary change:

> I feel like I've never got to grips with CATS and it's been changed. We've got progression next week and at the moment I haven't got a clue what I'm going to say to the students.
>
> (respondent 39)

> In this place there's a change every five minutes ... it leaves you in a whirl ... [Tom] Peters [the author of *Thriving on Chaos*] has got a lot to answer for.
>
> (respondent 15) (quoted in Trowler 1998a: 24)

The basic mechanisms explored in this chapter can be seen as ways of living with intellectual change: its promotion through the reputational system, its concentration through differential recognition and the gatekeeping process, its evaluation through peer review, its promulgation through networking, its amplification through fashion, its containment through resistance, and its apotheosis through revolution. But the final and perhaps the most important point to be made about these various aspects of collective academic life is that they are projections into a particular environment of understandable, everyday social phenomena. To paraphrase the conclusion of Taylor's (1976) study, they are not the product of cool, rational analysis by objective intellectuals living in a social vacuum, but fairly predictable arrangements adopted by a set of people who happen to operate in a certain kind of community.

Notes

1. Among some notable exceptions are people whose ideas are developed largely in seminars and lectures, but given public recognition by their disciples. An example would be H.P. Grice, an Oxford philosopher who published little, but who was widely respected by those he taught and others who knew him professionally for the originality and clarity of his views.
2. To adapt the often-quoted words of Mandy Rice-Davis, 'Well they would, wouldn't they?' It is unlikely that those who had made the grade would want to suggest that they did so by the sheer width of the library shelving their works took up.
3. Cole's (1978) quantitatively based study reached the same conclusion in respect of the natural and social sciences: that sponsorship is primarily important in initial employment, but that it has little effect on later job acquisition.
4. Sheldon Rothblatt (personal communication) has a characteristically pertinent comment to make on this point:

   > At one time it was possible to see this [the replacement of personal connections by reputational systems in determining academic worth] as a gain, since the academic circles were relatively closed and club-like and it was difficult for outsiders to break in. The elite institutions dominated the hiring network, and recommendations for positions were discussed

by closed circuit. But given the number of ways in which reputational systems are created and manipulated, it hardly appears that we have advanced at all.

5. By way of illustration, one of the initial study's respondents, a chemist, referred to 'a hierarchy of arrogance ... Physics represents the hardest, most abstract reasoning – people know they're smart. Chemists feel defensive in relation to physicists, but superior in relation to biologists.' Another, an economist, remarked wryly, 'it's part of the status hierarchy that we don't talk to people who have to deal with reality'.

6. Compare Ruscio's (1986) findings, on independent evidence, that 'A highly regarded peer is broad and well-read and able to bring knowledge from other disciplines to broaden the perspective within his [sic] own', and that 'Landmark contributions' come from people who 'are not drowned by a particular orthodoxy but having chosen a problem look at it from a number of points of view'.

7. Trevor Pateman (personal communication) has pointed out that the notion of a peer group has its origins in the eighteenth century, when encyclopaedism and the amateur tradition were giving way to specialized professional knowledge. The idea of authority as derived from expertise is raised by Condorcet in the 1780s in his arguments against Mesmer's doctrine of animal magnetism (Darnton 1968), and the theme is developed at greater length in Lewis (1849). Bazerman (1987) confirms that 'in the middle of the eighteenth century, referees were introduced to maintain professional interests and quality' in the Royal Society's *Transactions*.

8. Cole *et al.* (1977) state:

    Scientists with an established track record, many scientific publications, a high frequency of citations, a record of having received grants from the NSF [US National Science Foundation] and ties to prestigious academic departments have a higher probability of receiving NSF grants than other applicants do. Nevertheless, the granting process is actually quite open ... the scientific enterprise is an exceedingly equitable, although highly stratified social institution.

9. The research literature appears somewhat confused on this point (see the comments on differential rejection rates of journal articles across disciplines in Zuckerman and Merton 1971, and Hargens 1975). But Ruscio's (1986) study supports the findings presented here: 'In a discipline where there is disagreement about the legitimacy of one approach or another and where it is hard to know who is doing path breaking work across the fields, the solution is to allow each subfield to set its own standards.'

10. For example, 'blind refereeing', in which the author's identity is not made known to the referee, even though it may sometimes be inferred.

11. An analogy along a different dimension is prompted by work in the field of applied linguistics. The notion of a 'discourse community', as elaborated by Swales (1988), has six defining features: common, public goals; a recognized set of mechanisms for intercommunication between members (in Swales's terms, a 'forum'); an existing process of information exchange; particular genres that 'articulate the operations' of the community; a shared and specialized terminology; and 'a critical mass of members' with relevant expertise in both content and discourse. Although the concept embraces a wide range of activities – Swales cites philatelists specializing in the postal history of Hong Kong and a

local society of birdwatchers as two examples – it is clearly applicable also to specialized academic networks.

12. Members of the inner circle are not necessarily to be found within one's own department: when they are, they rarely exceed one or two in number. The geographical scatter of membership is often very wide.

13. It also, not surprisingly, seems to vary with the stage of academic career. Doctoral students have not usually managed to build up as wide a circle of professional acquaintances as have established, active researchers, though they will usually have identified those working on closely similar topics, both through the literature and through the contact networks of senior colleagues.

14. An essentially similar point is made by Barber (1968) and Crane (1969b).

15. The point is developed in greater detail in Boissevain (1974):

> the 'young Turks' . . . advance new theories not only because they have not been fully socialized into the rules of the dominant paradigm, and are hence particularly likely to see that those rules no longer define a playable game . . . [but also] because they seek recognition. They are trying to gain status in a competitive community, to advance higher from their position at the bottom of the scientific totem-pole. In terms of the culture prevailing in all scientific communities, one way of doing this is to demonstrate the inadequacy of an existing theory and, if possible, to advance a new, more adequate, theory.

He goes on to argue that:

> The outsiders attack with one of the few power resources not monopolized by their rivals: ideas. Hence the seeds of change are always present in the structural asymmetry between those with more power and those with less power. Those with more power try to maintain the asymmetry, and hence their superordinate position, sometimes even innovating to accomplish this end. They defend the status quo. Those with less power try to reduce the gap by pointing out anomalies.

16. See also Goodson (1983) for a discussion of the emergence of 'the new geography'.

6

Patterns of Communication

The life-blood of academia

Communication is central to the academic enterprise. The validity of that claim is readily established, in that both the promotion of knowledge (the main cognitive concern) and the establishment of reputation (the key social consideration) are necessarily dependent on it. A fresh insight, a new discovery, a novel invention, unless made available to others in the public domain, will remain no more than a piece of private intellectual property, fated to accompany its owner to the grave. That owner in turn, unless he or she is able both to establish first ownership and to relinquish possession to others, will be given no credit for its origination.

The claim can be yet more strongly advanced. Social interaction, communication of all sorts and the partly socially constructed nature of disciplines that is associated with them are the forces that bind together the sociological and the epistemological, giving shape and substance to the links between knowledge forms and knowledge communities. The reward system and the communication system are closely interconnected (Gaston 1972); certain key epistemological distinctions may only emerge through a study of the structure of communication (Griffith and Small 1983); communication patterns reflect the characteristics of the field of enquiry as well as those of the relevant research community (Griffith and Miller 1970); and social interaction can lead to mutually understood values, attitudes and taken-for-granted practices (Trowler *et al.* 2001). Clearly the development and use of new communication technologies will both reflect and affect disciplinary communication patterns: we comment further on them later in this chapter.

A study of patterns of communication is accordingly important enough to deserve consideration in its own right. A beginning might best be made with an issue that has emerged from the enquiry as a key to the explanation of a number of otherwise unconnected and apparently random phenomena: namely, the density of population in a given specialism and the related scope and tractability of its component problems.

Population density

The original interviews with physicists first drew attention to the notion of 'the people-to-problem ratio'. In some specialist fields, it became clear that the number of issues currently being pursued was relatively small, though the number of people in pursuit of them might be quite substantial. At the other end of the scale, knowledge areas could be identified in which the questions that could be asked at any given time, with some reasonable expectation that they might be answered, were virtually unlimited, while the number of those engaged in answering them was negligible in comparison. In order to elucidate the idea of the people-to-problem ratio, it will be tactically useful to focus on the extremes of the spectrum, while acknowledging the existence of many intermediate instances where the ratio is neither spectacularly high nor strikingly low.

There are certain areas in almost any knowledge domain, whether it be pure or applied, hard or soft, which from time to time enjoy a high level of active interest. Sometimes, the attraction may stem from what appears to be a strikingly novel perspective with powerful implications – in Kuhn's (1962) terms, a revolution based around a newly emergent paradigm. But in the case of a thoroughgoing conceptual reassessment, though the initial problem base may be small, it must soon widen out to encompass all or most of the intellectual territory whose existing paradigm is in dispute (an attempted coup which is eventually confined only to part of the hinterland is accorded no more than the status of a minor insurrection). In such a case, the people-to-problem ratio remains abnormally high only for a short while, until the process of 'normal science' is set on its realigned course. The same is true of other, more transient population movements, focused on the fashionable topics referred to in Chapter 5, to which academics who are not committed to substantial investments in rival concerns may be attracted for one of a variety of reasons, whether personal or professional or both. Where the occasion is recognizable in hindsight as no more than a passing fad, the residual population – regardless of how large or small the problem scope might be – is likely to dwindle to a point at which the people-to-problem ratio is not much changed from its original level (yesterday's fashion is as marginal as tomorrow's, lacking even its anticipated glamour).

There remains, however, a significant group of specialisms that continue to attract a level of interest high enough to exonerate them from the charge of mere faddishness, while they remain concentrated within a sufficiently narrow cognitive framework and stable enough in terms of their associated social structure to be disqualified from revolutionary status. A further distinction, subtle but important, needs to be made here between a school or sect (terms that imply a relatively rigid and static set of intellectual beliefs)[1] and a close specialist community which is at a constantly high pitch of intellectual activity.

A sectarian approach, in the academic as much as in the religious context, combines a narrowness of outlook with a breadth of application. It is a matter of seeing the world which one inhabits only from one particular angle: but it is the whole of that world, and not simply a limited part of it, which falls within the scope of the sect's defining dogma. Along another dimension, one might say that a sect is a revolution which has become established without achieving orthodoxy, permeating the whole of its relevant domain but winning the hearts and minds of only a minority of the population. In any event, however many adherents a particular school of thought may have, since the interests of those adherents are cast across a broad field, the people-to-problem ratio is liable to remain small. It is only in the second category – the tightly knit but dynamic specialist group in a closely defined knowledge field – that the population can become for more than a short time (the passing of a fashion or the establishment of a successful revolution) heavily concentrated on a limited number of problems.

Framing an analogy between urban and rural ways of life, we may liken specialisms which have a high people-to-problem ratio to urban areas, and those with a low one to rural areas. In the first, there is alongside a densely concentrated population a generally busy – occasionally frenetic – pace of life, a high level of collective activity, close competition for space and resources, and a rapid and heavily used information network. By and large, the rural scene, though it may offer frenetic and competitive moments, occasions for communal involvement and a potential for spreading rumour and gossip like wildfire, displays the opposite characteristics.

Urban and rural scenarios

Urban and rural specialisms differ in a number of ways, not only in their communication patterns, but in the nature and scale of the problems on which their inhabitants are engaged, in the relationships between those inhabitants, and in the opportunities they have for attracting resources. Urban researchers characteristically select a narrow area of study, containing discrete and separable problems, where their rural counterparts typically cover a broader stretch of intellectual territory in which the problems are not sharply demarcated or delineated. The urban population is clustered around comparatively few salient topics, as against being spread out thinly across a wide range of themes. The urban mode is to tackle questions with relatively quick, short-range solutions, whereas rural researchers are liable to become engaged on long-range issues, which may take years to puzzle out.[2] However, the HE policy environment and other aspects of a dynamic context can influence the extent of these patterns. The almost-global phenomenon of research audits by state or quasi-state bodies and the associated bibliometric techniques can have important effects in this regard. McNay's report (1997) identified a trend towards more rapid research dissemination practice as a result of the English Research Assessment Exercise: researchers were quicker to publish than before audits were instituted. Though this effect was seen to relate to dissemination rather than to research itself, McNay argues that the cumulative effects of successive exercises are likely to sustain this trend, pushing more disciplines towards an urban rather than rural form and creating a Procrustean bed for some. The more recent study by Kogan and colleagues, reported in Henkel (2000) and Kogan and Hanney (2000), suggests that research practices themselves have been affected by bibliometric exercises such as the RAE, emphasizing production as distinct from reflection.

Competition in urban life can become intense, even cut-throat, taking the form of a classic *double helix* pattern:[3] an all-out race to find the solution to what is seen as a seminal problem. In rural life, it makes better sense to adopt the principle of a division of labour – there are plenty of topics, so there is no point in tackling one on which someone else is already engaged. Teamwork is another feature more common in urban than in rural settings. Where several people are engaged on the same issue, it may pay to work collaboratively with a group of colleagues: joint activity has less occasion, and a less obvious justification, when there is ample opportunity to avoid close overlap with others. A competitive urban environment carries other implications – fears of plagiarism, a temptation to be secretive, and a concern with rapid publication to ensure priority – which we consider below in more detail.

There were frequent illustrations of these contrasts in the original research data. Independent corroboration of them may be found in a number of places in the literature. To take one example, the investigation by Gilbert (1977a) of radar meteor research in the 1940s and 1950s (a rural branch of radio astronomy) offers a striking juxtaposition with the study by Gaston (1973) of high-energy physics in the 1960s. Gilbert's analysis shows that 'the ratio of the number of authors to the number of topics' in the group of researchers he studied was typically as low as 1.5, i.e. 'there were about three participants for every two topics under investigation'. Taking into account the fact that 'over the years 1945–1960 the average number of authors per paper varied about a mean of 1.6', this implies that 'there were on average approximately the same number of collaborating groups of researchers as there were topics. It is therefore unlikely that competition on a significant scale would have occurred.' Gilbert contrasts this situation with the one described by Gaston, remarking that 'competition will be prevalent when there is general agreement among the participants of a research area on the overriding importance of finding solutions to one or a small number of clearly defined problems'. Gaston (1971) himself argues that 'in fields of science in which there is not such a concentration on so few problems . . . there is less risk of anticipation and competition is less likely. In another clear instance of a rural pattern of activity, Griffith and Miller (1970) observe of one specialism in psychology that:

there are so few active researchers in this area that there is little perceived danger of overlap among research efforts. This may . . . reduce the need for rapid informal communication, since there appears to be little need to determine whether anyone else is doing research on similar problems.

The urban and rural research environments are as noticeably different as the activities that take place within them. The urban world has touches of modishness and occasional moments of intense excitement, which are lacking in the measured pace of rural life. It can, where necessary, command sizeable resources and a high level of technology, where rural research is more modestly equipped and provided for. Research Councils and Foundations tend to concentrate their energies and funds on urban groups, both because they have a higher profile than rural ones and because they more commonly make large claims for supporting grants. For the most part, the urban context favours 'big science'. The rural setting embraces a number of 'little science' specialisms, but also takes in most soft pure, hard applied and soft applied areas as well.

Informal communication channels

Some of the most striking urban/rural differences emerge in the characteristic forms of communication within and between the various kinds of specialisms and networks discussed in Chapters 4 and 5. In the exploration of this theme a distinction needs to be made between the procedures involved in published work of a conventional kind (books, monographs, journal articles, reviews and the like) and the less formal mechanisms which do not fall so evidently and unrestrictedly within the public domain. To begin with the latter, a good deal of interchange takes place by word of mouth or in private or semi-private writings, email exchanges or electronic discussions. Besides the everyday mechanisms of shop talk, gossip, and other familiar modes of personal contact, there is a clear incidence in certain fields of what are commonly termed 'preprints'. The phenomenon is one that has arisen mainly in urban research specialisms. It involves a fairly large-scale, semi-private circulation of photocopies of papers in typescript before they appear in orthodox journal form (as a sizeable number subsequently do). This practice has the advantage of helping to establish the priority of the authors' findings without the delay often attendant on formal publication: its disadvantage is that it serves to create a privileged network of those who are on the mailing list, at the expense of equal access by those who do not enjoy insider status. More public versions have however come into existence in a number of disciplines in the form of facilities for the electronic pre-publication of drafts of conference papers or early versions of journal papers. Listerservers, and other on-line discussion groups have opened up previously private and closed discussion, though only where list owners or discussion moderators allow open access (Burbules 1998). Increasingly, academic conference organizers require paper presentations to be available on-line soon after or even before the conference, hence shifting the informal and semi-private into the more formal and public domain.

The contrast between insiders and outsiders is, though, sustained by the tendency in urban circles to hold invited lectures by leaders in the field, engage in small, invitational conferences and symposia, undertake fairly frequent visits to laboratories in other centres, and exchange letters, emails and telephone calls on a regular basis. The move towards closure of this kind, with its attendant risk of exclusiveness and inbreeding, can in some contexts become very pronounced: one respondent drew the comparison with an unstable economic system in which there is more traffic in black market currency than in legitimate coinage. The growing use of information and communication technologies has not lessened this tendency but has merely augmented the number of options.

Word-of-mouth communication is a common feature of urban and rural settings alike, though it takes a different form in each. Generally speaking, the more hectic the pace of urban research, the more the reliance on informal sources. Gaston (1972) notes that, within the intensely competitive British high-energy physics community, experimentalists go in more for verbal information and theorists more for written information; Traweek (1982) singles out a common preference of American and Japanese practitioners in the same field for 'informed gossip', with little attention given to reading the relevant journals; and Crane (1972) finds a similar distinction across the broader groupings of physicists and chemists: 'Physicists placed a higher ranking than did chemists upon informal sources of locating information such as conversation and correspondence.'

Gossip is rife, too, in the small rural communities characteristic of anthropology (Cohn 1962), sociology (Kleinman 1983) and, as became clear from the interview data, in British academic law. Here, however, it takes the form of rumour and the dissection of personalities rather than the more sternly professional shop talk indulged in by serious-minded scientists – though it may also leave room for folklore of the sort common among less enclosed semi-rural groupings such as those in history. Historians, for example, 'tend to gossip about their sources, about their merits and whereabouts – they talk more about the tools of the trade than the trade itself.' They 'don't talk much shop', perhaps because the nature of the subject lies in details, so that a problem cannot often be adequately defined in conversation.

It is understandable that urban academic groups with a closely shared set of problems should be more occupationally gregarious than rural groups whose work shows little overlap even with that of their few near neighbours. Besides the more private social activities attributed to them above, urban researchers typically attend more national and international conferences than their rural opposite numbers. In the sample of academics interviewed, the variation both between and within disciplines in this respect was noticeable. One senior and cosmopolitan biologist in a hot area claimed to be involved in a dozen gatherings a year, a couple of them overseas (as against most proponents of the same discipline, who regarded conferences, in the words of one respondent, as 'pleasant but inessential', and who normally reckoned to attend only two or three annually). Modern linguists, whose research predominantly follows a rural pattern, might typically go to one national conference in a 12-month period and one international conference once every 3 years.

Formal modes of interchange

The published literature of any field is its most accessible and durable manifestation of the research activity it embraces. The types of informal contact which have so far been considered, while they may assume a particular importance in accelerating the flow of ideas within an active urban community, are both less visible and more ephemeral than the commonly accepted means of recording and transmitting new findings through the medium of the printed word.[4]

The importance accorded to written communication is evident in urban and rural specialisms alike. But the resemblance hardly goes beyond that point, since even the most superficial observation reveals a host of consequent differences between the two. It may be argued, for example, that urban research activity favours the writing of journal articles at the expense of books, whereas in rural research the priorities are reversed. Whitley (1984) puts this contrast in practice down to the greater 'technical task uncertainty' of some specialisms, which means that they:

> have to be able to convey how research is undertaken, its purpose and implications in greater detail than where tasks and outcomes are more standardized. The high degree of ambiguity of results means that their presentation has to be more elaborate and has to justify the particular interpretation being put forward. Thus typical articles are quite long and often work is communicated through books, whereas a lower degree of task uncertainty enables research to be effectively communicated in a short space through esoteric and standardized symbol systems.

Griffith and Small (1983) make a similar point, more succinctly, in relation to 'the social and behavioural sciences literature': 'The journal article is, for many parts of social science, a poor vehicle of communication, ill-suited to discuss extremely complex issues. Books are, in fact, the medium through which change is really effected.'

Steig (1986), in her turn, explains the contrast between history, with its multiplicity of monographs, and physics, with its relative paucity, in terms of the 'loosely organised character of Western historical scholarship', adding that:

> monographs and therefore book reviews are a major method of disseminating and evaluating historical research[5] . . . since history first emerged

as a scholarly discipline, the monograph has been the dominant form of publication, and the article has never successfully challenged its preeminence . . . Articles have been perceived as a way of getting started.

Book reviews, as Steig indicates, are a significant element in historical scholarship, accounting for over half the text in the leading academic journals (Becher 1987b). They are also prevalent in other disciplines in the humanities and social sciences, though virtually non-existent in hard pure and hard applied subject areas, where they are commonly replaced by thematic surveys of particular topics. *Reviews of Modern Physics* provides a typical example of the genre. Here, each contribution offers a conspectus and synthesis of the main recent contributions to its chosen theme, with a list of references that will normally run to two or three double column pages. Almost invariably, the cited papers are discussed in factual rather than evaluative terms, the only obvious form of criticism being omission.

At the level of individual disciplines, a clear set of distinctions emerged in the sample between history and modern languages, where books were clearly held to earn more prestige for their authors than articles, and the hard pure and hard applied subjects (physics, chemistry, engineering and pharmacy), where book publication (apart from student texts) accounted for only a small minority of the written output. Mathematics and biology allowed for some longer publications in monograph form. In the pure and applied social sciences (economics, sociology, geography and law), respondents indicated no strong preference between book-length and article-length treatment. In economics, articles seem to be the norm for developing the more quantitative topics, and books for the more qualitative ones (such as the history of economic ideas); similarly, in sociology, books are more important in the social thought tradition than they are in the more technical specialisms. Stoddart (1967) suggests that books have tended to become less significant than articles in geography, particularly in quantitatively oriented subject areas. In law, books commonly take the form of student texts on particular topics rather than scholarly analyses of a major field or central theme. Translating this in terms of the spectrum from urban to rural specialisms, it may be held to support the earlier contention that books are a predominantly rural phenomenon and articles a predominantly urban one, a finding which in its turn would seem to reinforce the claim that urban researchers tend to focus on limited and short-term problems whereas their opposite numbers in rural settings show some preference for global issues whose resolution calls for more sustained and longer-term enquiry.

The rise of digital texts has important implications for scholarship and the criteria for academic evaluation of research. Burbules (1997, 1998) points out that as more and more academics read and seek publication through on-line journals, web pages and other manifestations of information and communication technology the boundary between what is and what is not a 'publication' becomes increasingly fuzzy. The importance of prior refereeing, as a measure of quality assurance, is also diminished.

Speed, frequency and length of publication

The publication process is subject to the influence of many variables, including the scope and nature of the message to be conveyed, the form chosen to convey it (article, book or whatever), the number of people involved in generating it, and their age and reputation. It would therefore be surprising if any very clear statistical pattern were to emerge from the attempt to analyse the products of the research enterprise in quantitative terms.[6] None the less, there was a rough-and-ready consistency in the testimony given by respondents which it may be worth touching on, even though the material is too flimsy to bear much weight of inference.

Three main sets of considerations were covered in the interviews: a rough estimate of the length of time it would take for a journal article to appear after its initial submission; the approximate length of a typical contribution; and the number of papers an individual author might expect to publish in a reasonably good year. It must again be emphasized that the original study was focused on elite academic groups, so the results are confined to the upper end of the scale of prestige and productivity: active researchers concerned with acquiring or maintaining a professional reputation, and accordingly tending to submit their papers to the more prestigious journals in their field.

In terms of publication delays in refereed journals of a traditional kind, it may be best to begin by drawing attention to a special feature of the very fast-moving hard pure specialisms, especially those within physics, chemistry and biochemistry. Here, the need for the rapid public announcement of findings has resulted in specialist publications that minimize delay by restricting length. A typical example is *Physical Review Letters*, in which highly topical results may be published within 3 months or so of their submission, provided that they are kept within the compass of three or four pages.[7] That such public mechanisms exist alongside a flourishing private preprint network gives a clear indication of the anxiety of authors to win first place in a sprint to the finishing-post.

The waiting period, as one might expect, tends to be longer in specialisms where the population density is lower (so that there is less overlap of topics and little consequent concern with priority). Delay times may vary considerably from specialism to specialism, especially in heterogeneous subjects such as biology, and between the more rural areas of chemistry, such as analytical chemistry, and the dense urban groupings at the biochemical end of the discipline. But the rough averages are indicative. Full-scale journal articles in physics may be held up for 9–12 months, and those in economics for 9–18 months. The comparable figures in engineering would appear to be between 1 and 2 years; in mathematics and in mainstream biology the lower limit is similar but the upper one rather higher. At the other end of the spectrum, modern linguists may have to try their patience for as much as 2 or 3 years before their papers appear in the established journals (though there are less prestigious outlets where the time lag may be as low as 6 months). History and sociology fall somewhere in between, with typical waiting times of around 18 months or a couple of years.

Where time-lags give an appropriate indication of competitive pressures, the length and frequency of an individual author's output say something about the nature and scale of research topics. Again, there is considerable variation in those disciplines with a diversity of types of specialism. A reasonably productive biologist in a setting that might be described as suburban would perhaps reckon to publish one or two journal articles a year of moderate length (say 4000–6000 words), though there is also some pressure to produce the occasional monograph of 20 000 words or more (the figures for mechanical engineers are similar – 'between, say, 30 and 60 papers in a lifetime' – though in their case alternative modes of output commonly take the form of consultancy reports and conference papers). However, in the more descriptive areas of biology (e.g. taxonomy), the annual production rate might be as high as 10–15 short papers. An output of ten or more, often of less than 2000 words and with multiple authorship, would also be characteristic of the hotter specialisms such as biochemistry.

Chemistry is a discipline in which many of the topics are relatively easily broken down into small components: this is manifest in the relative brevity of chemists' writings (4000 words tends to be on the high side), in their tendency to put such components together into papers with several authors (see also the section later in this chapter on collaborative research), and in the volume of their output. Ten or a dozen contributions a year is not uncommon, though the rate may decline somewhat with increasing age: the most prolific researchers can notch up totals of four or five hundred titles over a successful working life. In mathematics, there are fewer co-authors. The average length of article is about double (some 6000–8000 words) and the average output about half that in chemistry. Active economists can be counted on to produce two to four articles a year (at least, those who are not simultaneously engaged in writing books), though in their case the upper word limit of about 8000 may be imposed by leading journals in the interests of accepting more articles and reducing publication delays. Where research topics are free-standing rather than cumulative (so that there is not an already established starting point for the work) the rate of output is understandably lower and the length of contribution greater. Reputable historians and modern linguists in particular may thus do well to produce an annual average of one 8000–12,000 word article a year, particularly as they may also be working on a book at the same time.

The audit of research output, the intensification of academic work, the accelerating growth in knowledge and the competitive pressure to achieve research status among institutions, departments and individuals in many countries have collectively built up the pressure to accelerate research 'output' and have imposed demands on academics' time. Despite this pressure, research productivity, as measured by the number of presentations and publications, remained constant in the USA between 1987 and 1992 (NCES 1999), only increasing in the 1990s, particularly among women academics (Sax *et al.* 1999).

These pressures may lead to further divisions between researchers who produce significant numbers of publications and academics who devote their attention to other tasks. In Australia (Ramsden 1994), the USA (Boice 1992) and elsewhere, highly productive academics now represent only a small proportion of the total.

It is not only external environmental factors that condition academic productivity, however. Ramsden's (1994) research indicates that the characteristics of the department in which an academic operates may be significant. He concludes that productivity is raised where the management style, governance and leadership are cooperative, participative and collaborative, though. Kekäle's (1999) research indicates that this may be more true for soft, pure, divergent and rural disciplines than for other categories.

Citation practices and their implications

Citation – the inclusion in academic writing of formal and explicit references to the work of other authors – is a feature of every discipline. The study of it as a phenomenon can be revealing in a number of different ways.[8] Those with an interest in information science often adopt a quantitative approach, using citation counts and patterns of citations to underline the disparities between more and less prestigious authors or to characterize the rate at which knowledge becomes obsolete in different fields. Those who are interested in research practices tend to favour a more qualitative approach, concerning themselves with questions about purpose and function.

The evidence from the original interview data, used here as a starting point for a brief discussion of the topic, was of the latter kind. There was some indication, as one might expect, of disciplinary differences in the incidence of citation. Perhaps, as one informant, a biologist, speculated, 'the softer your subject-matter, the more citations you need to give'. Certainly, a number of mathematicians confessed themselves to be somewhat slapdash in referring to previous work, partly at least because of a preference for approaching certain problems with a freshness or vision unclouded by the knowledge of how others had tried to tackle them before. People in less hard disciplines thought it important to be punctilious in their referencing, for a variety of reasons.

In biology, you are expected in social terms to 'prove that you have read everything relevant' and in cognitive terms to 'acknowledge the foundations on which you build'. In sociology, there are temptations not only 'to use other people's writing to reinforce the statements you put forward – citing other people suggests a greater measure of support for your case', but also 'to cite famous people so as to suggest that you are keeping good intellectual company'.[9] Citation, one historian suggested 'serves a social and institutional as much as an epistemological function'. It enables you to engage in debate with other writers; it protects you from reviewers' criticisms of your failure to acknowledge X's arguments or Y's findings; and more generally it serves as a mechanism for preserving solidarity among historians. After all, 'if we don't read them, perhaps they won't read us'. But more fundamentally, footnote references to primary and secondary sources 'give the reader a sense of interplay between data and argument – an almost literal sense of tension as the reader's eye moves constantly between the one and the other'. Admittedly, the citation of secondary sources can 'get out of hand, and become over-elaborate'. A number of US respondents considered themselves less extravagant in this regard than their British counterparts.

Hyland's study (1999), using close linguistic analysis of citation practices in 80 research articles across eight disciplines, confirms the conclusions from the interview data. Hard pure disciplines tend in general to use fewer citations per paper and per 1000 words than soft disciplines. So, while sociology, marketing and philosophy average around 100 citations per paper, physics and mechanical engineering have around a quarter of that, and some half the number of citations per 1000 words. Perhaps contentiously Hyland attributes this variation to differences in the authority accorded the individual as against the validity of the research procedure or the significance of the findings. That molecular biology is something of an exception is attributed to the fact that 'it is neither fully established nor prototypically "scientific"' (Hyland 1999: 356–7), though some would take issue with this.

In the less highly structured and strongly specialized disciplines among the initial sample there was a general expectation that people will read widely outside their own current areas of concern. In history and modern languages, for example, interesting and potentially relevant ideas may be gleaned from a variety of sources, as both the widely dispersed citation patterns and the comments from informants on the virtues of a broad knowledge of the field made plain. As we noted earlier, some have interpreted this as poaching across tribal boundaries. This is likely to be related to the issue of mutual intelligibility between specialisms. For example, in some fast moving areas of biology it was held to be very difficult to keep up with developments outside one's specialism, not only because of time pressures but also because of the incomprehensibility of language and logical structure, even in neighbouring territories: 'Built upon a widening array of disciplines and specialities, [the academic profession hosts tribal] subcultures that speak in strange tongues of econometrics, biochemistry, ethnomethodology, and deconstructionism' (Clark 1997: 21).

A characteristic view in slower-moving areas within the discipline, however, held that it was 'important to keep in touch with developments in other fields . . . what you learn about other specialisms helps you to change your attitude towards your own – and you can sometimes pick up useful concepts and techniques which other groups have developed'. However, for some disciplines this ideal has been more often observed in the breach than the observance, as Nehamas notes of philosophy:

What philosophers read is by and large specific to their immediate interests, which are reflected in the proliferation of specialized
societies, conferences and journals. We seem to be lacking the most
elementary lingua franca to discuss our field in general [and] the most
rudimentary notion of a set of problems that are common to the
discipline . . .

(Nehamas 1997: 222)

How easy or difficult it is to understand colleagues in different parts of
one's discipline is an important aspect of the style and accessibility of scholarly writing, which is the topic to which we now turn.

Questions of style and accessibility

A distinction may be drawn between hard and soft knowledge areas in
terms of the extent to which they use mathematical symbols as against
common parlance. On the one hand, most writings in mathematics and
physics and many in academic engineering are unintelligible to the lay
reader, not merely because their content is unfamiliar but because they
convey meaning in a special, highly compressed, quantitative code. On the
other hand, articles and books in most humanities subjects, though they
may use the occasional technical term, are couched in familiar, everyday
language and are – on the surface at least – readily accessible to those
outside the field. Between the two extremes, disciplines such as chemistry
and pharmacy employ a symbolism of their own; researchers in biology,
geography, sociology and academic law make varying use of specialist words
carrying particular meanings with which outsiders are likely to be unfamiliar or may misconstrue.

There seem to be two main factors at work behind such evident and
widely recognized distinctions. The first is cognitively derived, concerning
the extent to which research is subject to a contextual imperative, as against
a weaker contextual association; the second is social, and is related to the
degree of legitimacy allowed within the discipline to public communication
with external audiences.

To decompress these statements, it has been remarked on a number of
previous occasions that hard pure knowledge in particular develops in a
restricted and relatively clearly defined sequence. Its cumulative character
depends on the degree to which the central topics of current concern are
determined by those in the recent past, and the extent to which they serve
in their turn to identify those needing to be tackled in the near future.
Most hard pure problems are thus formulated in an established knowledge
context. In contrast, the topics in soft areas, though they may in some cases
be subject to fashion, and hence grouped together in a more or less close
association, do not convey the same sense of obeying an imperative
demand. The consequence is that in many hard areas research takes place,

and can be reported, within a known framework of assumptions; in soft areas, the context has often to be separately elaborated.[10]

This affects both the length of typical contributions, as has already been noted, and their general style. Both Bazerman (1981) and Whitley (1984) remind us that where relevance to current developments in research is an important criterion, the succinctness and precision of communication is prized above its stylistic qualities. In specialized scientific fields, there is 'an elaborate communication system which uses a highly formalized symbol structure to co-ordinate research across geographical and social boundaries. Ambiguity is reduced by standardizing and formalizing reporting procedures.' In contrast, because of the 'limited degree of standardization of cognitive objects and work processes', and because 'the meaning and significance of results are ambiguous', writers in the human sciences have to tailor their style 'to the particular message being communicated' (Whitley 1984). Developing the point:

> The sociological literature . . . is . . . diverse, unsettled and open to interpretation: therefore, the essay must reconstruct the literature to establish a framework for discussion; in the humanities, the literatures . . . tend to be particularistic and used in particularistic ways . . . Codification, if it can be called that, is entirely personal.
>
> (Bazerman 1981)

Here, as Whitley adds, 'an individual's style of writing is an important component of his or her reputation'.

Such considerations do not fully explain why, for example, biologists, and to a lesser extent geographers, place such a high premium on literary and stylistic qualities. From the pointers given by informants in a number of disciplines, we are inclined to ascribe this to the existence of a tradition of lay participation, or at least of lay interest. History offers a good case in point. Historians, along with most other academics, are scornful of 'professional popularizers', people who are seen as making money out of other people's ideas; though many of them would like their own ideas 'to reach a wide – though preferably a discerning – public'. Amateur practitioners in history are not subject to the same degree of obloquy, and may even, in areas such as archivy and local history, be acknowledged to serve a useful purpose. The amateur tradition is strong in biology as well: active amateurs can play a significant supporting role in ecological research and in studies of animal and plant populations; passive amateurs help to create a ready market for books in the style of *The Blind Watchmaker* and *The Selfish Gene*. Geography has its tales of polar exploration, not to mention the *National Geographic*; astronomy its active gazers at the stars through the telescope and its passive watchers of their interpreters – stars from a different mould – on their television screens. Because of their openness to public view, such disciplines would seem more conscious of the need for, and benefits of, skills in lucid communication.

The more strongly specialized, professionally closed and linguistically impenetrable disciplines leave no such scope for outside involvement. Nor are they tolerant of attempts to go over the heads of the research community to enlist a wide public interest in new developments. It is firmly understood that even the more newsworthy discoveries must be announced within the family before they are made known outside it. In physics in particular, as Reif (1961) and Geertz (1976) imply, and Traweek (1982) makes plain, there is a strong resistance to premature communication in the popular media, which is seen as a transgression of community boundaries.

The closed nature of academic research, partly achieved by the development of inaccessible modes of communication, has been the object of critics' attention for some years. Some argue that obscure language is no better than a form of sorcery to mask an insubstantial message: Andreski made this point about the social sciences in 1972 and Sokal and Bricmont (1998) echoed it more recently in relation to postmodernist writers. Tooley and Darby's critique of educational research standards similarly concluded that 'the majority of the research was either reported in language which would alienate many practitioners, or concerned topics which would not capture their interest' (1998: 65). Happily Scott (1999) suggests that this is not true of the bulk of higher education research.

This discussion has already taken us some way from the central business of communication – the kinds of messages that are conveyed, the means of conveying them, the time pressures to which they are subject – and into a consideration of its social milieu. The rest of the chapter concentrates on the latter aspect, picking out three main features of the environment in which the interchange of ideas takes place. We begin by considering the various forms of competitiveness in the exploration and transmission of new insights, and some of their side-effects. This will lead on to a brief review of collaboration and teamwork and its manifestation in joint or multiple authorship. In a subsequent section, we look at the situations in which the exchange of ideas degenerates into the exchange of hostilities as communication breaks down into controversy.

Competition

The competitive nature of academic life is a function of the emphasis placed on gaining a professional reputation, though more commercial competitive pressures are becoming increasingly important in scientific disciplines. In rural areas, such competition takes a more subtle form than that of a contest to publish one's findings before they are 'scooped' by somebody else. It may rather be manifested, in the words of a biology respondent, by 'an emphasis on publication, aggressiveness at meetings and a high degree of single-mindedness'. Rivals seek to surpass each other in the quality and significance of their work, in the esteem in which they are held by professional colleagues, and in the honours that are bestowed on them; they may vie for the same jobs, but they seldom engage in battle over the very same area of intellectual territory. It is in the most heavily populated urban pockets that the fiercest tussles take place over the division of the spoils of research. As Gaston (1971) writes:

> In their attempts to gain recognition for their accomplishments scientists work in a competitive situation which is quite different from that of other professions . . . Competition in science is more like a race between runners in the same track and over the same distance at the same time.

However, not all hard knowledge is associated with a highly competitive urban research community. Hagstrom (1965) instances mathematics as a discipline in which 'competition tends to be less prevalent because of the absence of agreement on the relative importance of mathematical problems'. Griffith and Miller (1970) suggest that 'positions, resources and facilities for which there [is] much competition' are likely to be a special feature of highly coherent groups. Among the chemists interviewed, one developed the point in an unexpected direction:

> Some people are quite competitive and secretive, but there are others who don't feel that they are in a rat race. They see themselves as being in competition with nature, not with other scientists. The race is only of secondary importance, because the job needs to be done. On the whole, if there is a race for the solution, that solution is probably rather obvious, and not really on the frontier of the subject. The more important parts of science don't necessarily end up as a fight for the finish.

Where strong competition does exist, it has its positive aspects in generating intellectual excitement, personal involvement and a heightening of research productivity; but it does also tend to give rise to a number of problems and pathologies. One is a tendency to produce hasty, essentially unfinished, work in the interests of rapid publication: something which the research assessment exercise in the UK (and doubtless equivalent bibliometric audit exercises elsewhere) appears to have exacerbated, as we have previously noted. Both Gaston (1971) and Reif (1961) single out this feature for discussion. The latter quotes a revealing editorial in *Physical Review Letters* in which it is noted that:

> when a 'hot' subject breaks and many groups initiate related work . . . [b]ecause of the rapid development and the intense competition we have found it necessary to relax our standards and accept some papers that present new ideas without full analysis, relatively crude experiments that indicate how one can obtain valuable results by more careful and complete work . . . Such incomplete papers have been accepted reluctantly since we realize that thereby we penalise some physicists who, working along the same lines, want to do a more complete job before publishing.

Another consequence of working in a hot climate is the fact that one's ideas may be stolen – if not directly in the form of plagiarism (which, if proven, carries a heavy sanction), then in the more cunning guise of picking up someone else's idea and running with it fast enough to win the race:

> What is stolen in such cases are ideas, general information about the goal sought and the means to be used. Usually the thief must do considerable research himself . . . A chemist will learn about an experiment which is planned, but he is obliged to do the experiment himself if he is to publish first.

> (Hagstrom 1965)

And there are of course cases where the borrowing is unconscious, where someone remembers an idea as his or her own, even though it may in fact have been suggested by someone else.

The fear of theft, if not the first-hand experience of it, is one of the motivating sources of secrecy. Another is the direct obverse of the concern for over-hasty publication – the urge fully to exploit the consequences of a promising idea before bringing it out into the open and allowing others to do so. One interviewee, a physicist in an urban network, spoke of a tendency to 'play your cards close to your chest . . . to be open about publishing last year's findings, but not this year's'. It is not unknown for 'laboratories to be kept locked, and progress reports to be given in a very guarded way'. The dilemma, as Hagstrom (1965) points out, is between withholding publication with the 'danger of being anticipated in presenting the central idea' and being 'forced to share recognition for its elaboration with others'.

As an aside at this point, it is interesting to note how many writers see the incidence of secrecy as an important distinguishing mark between pure science and technology. Price (1970) contrasts the technologist's opportunity to make capital from discovery with 'the open publication that determines intellectual private property for the sciences'. Dasgupta and David (1985) make a similar point, arguing that scientists regard knowledge as a public consumption good, whereas technologists treat it as a private capital good, with related strategies of disclosure and secrecy. Baruch (1984) sees the cultures of scientists and technologists as 'almost opposites', in that the former 'leave as their legacy public scientific knowledge', whereas among the latter knowledge 'is developed in secret. Publication is anathema, and the final test of validity is public use.'

It must be said that there was very little evidence of this distinction in the interviews with physicists, chemists and biologists on the one hand, and mechanical engineers and pharmacists on the other. The reason may possibly have lain in the nature of the sample: the technologists interviewed were in relatively prestigious departments, where there was clearly a stronger emphasis on contributing to theoretical development than on generating patentable products. It may be that departments with a strongly applied emphasis would have shown a closer concern with keeping promising inventions under wraps, with a view to circumventing the academic equivalent of industrial espionage. Or it might have been that people preferred not to talk about such issues, because they were not thought to be entirely respectable.

The NewU study (Trowler 1998a) revealed another motivation in lower status institutions, explicitly stated by respondents, for keeping applied work under wraps. Here the lack of a strong research base within the university and the close links with industry in domains of study such as those related to design (for example fashion design) and to the media professions combined to result in a pattern of independent consultancy work among staff in particular disciplines. Some of them explained their desire to keep this work and the developments stemming from it covert in terms of the institution's proclivity for taking a substantial cut of income earned.

Another possible motivation, which applies in both elite and non-elite contexts, derives from the fact that many technological specialisms lie towards the rural end of the spectrum, where the number of people working on the same or closely similar topics is relatively small, the competitive pressures are less evident and the consequent urge to establish priority less pronounced than in the densely urban areas within pure science. In this spirit, one mechanical engineer claimed, 'It's often wise to wait for your work to mature – to be sure you've got it right before you send the final typescript off'; another listed the priorities as 'wanting first to be right, second to be useful and only third to be ahead of the field'; and a third claimed that 'priority in reaching a result isn't all that important, particularly if someone comes along shortly afterwards with a better technique and more accurate measurements . . . progress is a matter of making incremental changes, refining measurements and looking at new variations on existing techniques'.

The work of Slaugher, Leslie and Rhoades (Slaughter and Rhoades 1993; Rhoades 1997; Slaughter and Leslie 1997) on intellectual property, technology transfer and academic labour has thrown into sharp relief the commercialization of scientific research in recent times. Changing statutes and policies on the issue both in state legislatures and within universities have reinforced competitive pressure on scientific academic research and generated incentives to protect rather than share intellectual property. Saleable knowledge accordingly comes to be seen as a goal rather than a product of academic research. Distinctions between the haves and the have-nots in the academic world are likely to sharpen as links to the market and technology transfers between universities and industry increase. Commercial pressures of this kind give rise to effects on professional and organizational cultures and have important consequences for how HE researchers perceive them:

> we must move beyond dualistic theory that divides all organizations into public or private and all personnel in the academy into administrators or professionals. Such categories carry unnecessary connotations and cloud our perception of new organizational forms and new patterns of professional stratification. Instead, we need to theorize relations between public and private sector, and between managers and professionals as fluid, permeable, changeable, and in some respects

even undifferentiated. States, universities, professions, and private sectors, are more dynamic and multifaceted than our concepts and theories. Our data point to such complexity, and to the need for post-structural theorizing that will help us to better understand the relatively unmapped borderlands of so-called public and private sectors, the opportunity structures being created by state bodies that use public monies as venture capital for university start-up companies, and by state subsidized academic and administrative entrepreneurs.

(Slaughter and Rhoades 1993: 309–310)

Some academics, whether or not concerned with such issues, clearly enjoy the challenge of direct competition, while others prefer to avoid it. In most rural areas, there is little choice in the matter, since there is no one else hell-bent on getting there first. But in those disciplines where there is some option, quite a few people – according to Whitley (1984) – prefer 'differentiation and security to coordination and challenge'. Gilbert (1977a) is at pains to emphasize that 'recognition and career success for scientists working in most research areas depend on their being in a position to find and follow up research problems which differ substantially from those being pursued by other participants'. In their study of radio astronomy in Britain and the USA, Mulkay and Edge (1973) note that

> Research groups tend to avoid competition by concentrating, wherever possible, on techniques and problems which are not the main focus of interest elsewhere. Once one group has achieved a clear lead in a particular field, other groups will tend to choose different areas rather than face duplication and open competition.

As one of the respondents, a botanist, put it: 'There are some competitive areas, but you need to be careful with them – you may want to be near enough to share the warmth, but not so close that you get roasted alive.'

Another means of avoiding a direct conflict of interest is through collaboration (whose implications we explore in the next section). 'Outside the more competitive areas', observed one of the zoologists interviewed, 'there aren't so many people working on the same problem, and those that are usually know each other and keep in touch with progress'. A chemist made the similar comment that 'where different groups turn out to be working on the same problem, some people are bastards and start to clam up, but very often you don't have to make a fight of it – you either divide up the field or agree on a joint publication'.

Collaboration

There is considerable variation in collaborative practice between the hard and soft ends of the continuum. Henkel (2000) and Knorr Cetina (1999) report that in astrophysics and particle physics huge collaborative teams are the norm. The complexities of such collaboration can be enormous, requiring careful planning, negotiation and communalism rather than competition. Publications resulting from research in these fields can involve up to a hundred people. By contrast 'the ideal in the humanities and the social sciences remained that of the individual scholar pursuing his or her interests according to his or her own rhythms' (Henkel 2000: 195). However, recent changes in funding regimes and in higher education more broadly have meant a push towards collaborative activity even here. Within the broad categories of hard and soft disciplines, however, there is considerable diversity of practice. Let us examine, then, the motivations underlying collaborative activity and the form it commonly takes.

On the face of it, an individual academic's reputation is likely to be most decisively established if the person concerned takes full, unambiguous responsibility for his or her work. As several of the respondents in such fields as geography and economics contended, once you start publishing with other people it becomes difficult to know who has done what. It might therefore be supposed that, other things being equal, the preference would be for publishing solely under one's own name.[11]

Other things are not always equal, of course. There are various good reasons for wanting to work with other people (the avoidance of competitive duplication has already been mentioned as one of them). Research funding from the European Community is usually conditional on collaborative research across the Union, the aim being to further integrate the research effort of different countries and to assist in the development of the research cultures of institutions and countries which are less advanced: the *Socrates* programme offers an example.

In some areas of 'big science', there is little choice in the matter. Knorr Cetina (1999) points out that only collaboration by legally and financially independent physics institutes and European member states could fund the CERN accelerator, computing facilities and services. As a result experiments at CERN are large-scale collaborative enterprises. In some comparatively modest 'little science' areas such as organic chemistry, as was remarked earlier in this chapter, it is easy to divide substantial problems into smaller related components; the resulting possibility of a division of labour may enhance the attraction of collaborative work. In other cases, the resolution of difficult issues may demand an unusual combination of skills: here, there may be a premium placed on working with colleagues who have complementary contributions to make. Productivity may be enhanced by working collaboratively: an important consideration in a highly audited academic environment. Traore, Godin and Landry's study (1996) based on a survey of 1500 scientific researchers in Quebec, backed up by a literature review, concluded that both researcher-researcher and researcher-industry collaboration in scientific disciplines increased productivity in comparison with individual research.

These observations are consistent with the findings of a small-scale study of four social science disciplines (sociology, psychology, economics and political science) by Fox and Faver (1982), concerned with the strategies adopted by research partnerships. One approach they identified was to 'share the parts' with collaborators working together on the same task at the same time; another was to 'separate the parts', where each collaborator again tackles the same tasks, but this time working individually before the results are 'exchanged, mutually reviewed and combined towards a final draft'; a third was to 'divide the parts', so that each collaborator works separately and on different tasks. Fox and Faver suggest that division of labour is the most common strategy for routine research activities, for those under time pressure, and for those demanding complementary competences, but that 'more complex tasks ... may benefit from some combination of sharing and separating the parts'.

The interviews with chemists and physicists confirmed that the processes which underlie apparently similar examples of teamwork are not necessarily homogeneous, a point also forcefully made by John-Steiner *et al.* (1998) in their critique of the work on research collaboration by Clark *et al.* (1996). The areas of physics that favour large-scale research collaboration and result in papers with as many as one or two score authors are nearly always examples of 'big science', in which the teams may be likened to those in, say, American football, demanding a high degree of mutuality and involving both shared and divided tasks. The membership is typically composed of groups from two or more institutions with a number of senior academics working alongside more junior tenured and untenured staff, postdoctoral fellows, doctoral students and technicians. The teams in certain of the more populous specialisms in chemistry, though sometimes comparable in size, share few other common features. The demands of instrumentation are far less dominant, so the pressures for inter-institutional collaboration are not so severe. There is seldom more than one senior academic – the unquestioned leader – in the team, the other members being untenured academics and other ranks (technicians, research fellows and students). Tasks are systematically divided out between participants, though there may be some sharing on a small scale, with perhaps three or four people working on the more demanding components of the overall project. The pattern is thus quite unlike that of a team sport and more reminiscent of that of an orchestra, with the conductor taking sole responsibility for bringing together into a harmonious whole the disparate contributions of the various sections of the orchestra – strings, brass, woodwind and percussion.

The distinctions between these two cases help to underline the importance of attending to cognitive as well as social factors in any attempt to make sense of academic interaction. Large-scale, collaborative research reporting in physics is commonly a product of substantial and not always readily divisible problems demanding complex instrumentation; but superficially comparable cases of multiple authorship in chemistry would seem to derive instead from the atomistic, easily fragmented and easily combined nature of the problems in its knowledge field. To quote one informant:

In particle physics theory drives the whole thing – the different parts are inseparable, and the teams tackle a large, unified operational task. In chemistry, the problems can be broken up, and each part solved separately, before they are put together again.

Knorr Cetina reports that over a decade teams in the field of high energy physics increased in size from around 100 scientists to more than 1500, representing over 150 collaborating institutions (Knorr Cetina 1999: 20). Mathematics offers another interesting example of the complex reality behind an apparently simple facade. There is only a modest amount of joint publication in mathematical research: the statistics quoted earlier, together with observations from the initial study, suggest that it is roughly comparable with sociology in this regard. Yet it was quite evident from the interview data that the sociologists who worked alone seldom went out of their way to discuss their work with colleagues, whereas many of the solitary-seeming mathematicians placed considerable stress on the need to talk over their problems with other people.[12] One way of accounting for this anomaly is to observe that research in many areas of mathematics, though not as tightly structured as that in some of the more urban parts of physics and biochemistry, is nonetheless subject to quite strong contextual influences. Ideas and techniques from neighbouring, or even sometimes apparently distant, specialisms may turn out to help in the resolution of an initially intractable problem: so if you find yourself getting stuck at a certain point, it helps to bounce suggestions off other people and get them to bounce suggestions off you. On the other hand, many mathematical arguments are organic rather than atomistic in character: they cannot be carved up into discrete pieces, but demand to be understood as complex wholes – an endeavour that can call for an intense, essentially individual effort of concentration. Such formal collaboration as exists is often between no more than two people, based on the sharing and separation rather than the division of tasks ('brainstorming' an idea together, or each – as one informant put it – 'going home trying desperately to sort out an idea before your collaborator does, spurring one another on towards the solution').

The preference of many sociologists for solitary over collective research reflects a different set of social and cognitive norms from those of mathematicians. In this discipline, Kleinman (1983) argues, there is an in-built bias against collaboration and in favour of the 'lonely scholar' image. Doctoral students 'learn that the "real work" of sociology – research and writing – involves distinguishing oneself from one's peers . . . Professional development . . . is synonymous with increasing individuation.' More than one of the sociologists interviewed pointed out that collaboration tends to occur more often between empiricists, who may be able to share out fieldwork, than between theorists. To the extent that certain biological and sociological specialisms exemplify the predominantly interpretive character of historical or literary research, another factor comes into play. Interpretation is a characteristically individualistic process, as the respondents made plain: 'In taxonomy it's virtually impossible to work with other people – like judges, taxonomists can give opinions, but they don't give joint opinions.' As for theoretical sociology, 'how can three people write with one pen and speak with one mind?' In modern languages, 'one's research and one's writings are not really separable – and both are very personal'. In history, it needs 'a single intellect to turn over the material'; 'ideas have to be shaped in the mind of the individual scholar'. When one adds the consideration that, in the soft pure areas of knowledge, there is a great range of choice in style, taste, and subject matter, and sometimes in theoretical orientation as well, it is perhaps scarcely surprising that joint research enterprises are the exception rather than the rule, and that disagreements are at least as common as the taking of a shared stand.

Controversy

In academic disciplines, as in political parties, a good, blazing row is as capable of arousing vicarious enjoyment as it is of damaging credibility and reputation. Both features were evident, for example, in the much-publicized squabbles of the English Faculty at the University of Cambridge (particularly in the early 1980s, when a young, vocal proponent of structuralism was refused tenure but subsequently obtained a professorship elsewhere; see Bergonzi 1990). When people's identities are at stake, passions run deep. This may be one reason behind the tendency in areas in which values are highly charged – sociology is an obvious case in point – towards a disproportionate incidence of rifts and schisms.[13] A dispute between postmodernists ('pomos') and the rest has been running for some years in that discipline, spilling over into others.

Yet even in the overtly more dispassionate domain of empirical science, as Kuhn and others have shown, controversies may become too bitter to remain concealed beneath the public veneer of amity and consensus. Apart from the tactically dubious recourse for adjudication from parties quite outside such disputes, other expedients include the attempt to call in aid the history and traditions of the discipline, often with a generous degree of retrospective reinterpretation (see, for example, Taylor 1976 and Graham 1983). There is a contrast to be drawn here between specific, relatively localized arguments and broad dissensions over basic theoretical stances. A mildly entertaining, if somewhat voyeuristic, example of the former is given by Kemp (1977) in his case study of an increasingly acrimonious wrangle between two eminent biochemists (scientists exposed as nothing other than ordinary human beings). Another example offered is the 'cold fusion' controversy in physics, which concerned experimental data apparently indicating that a nuclear fusion reaction involving hydrogen isotopes could generate heat by an electrochemical process operating at room temperature. As a result of an unseemly rush in 1989 to publish their highly controversial results, the two scientists at the centre of the dispute, Fleischmann and

Pons, quickly found themselves at the heart of an acrimonious dispute. Such conflicts, however, usually make little or no difference to the evolution of the discipline in whose name they are conducted, and have none of the grand, titanic flavour of the battles between the proponents of fundamentally opposing paradigms.

But in cases of major controversy, as in more parochial disputes, there is a discernible tendency to steer clear of arguments. The respondent who commented that his discipline 'is organized in a way that minimizes quarrels – it gets people engaged in fiddly problems rather than major issues' was speaking, on the evidence of the interview data, for more than a few other subjects as well. Documenting the ways of political scientists, Ruscio (1985) exemplifies how the absence of communication on major issues between rival groups may come about:

> Journals in the subfield [of political philosophy] have become extremely focused. Straussian journals circulate submissions among Straussians, for example, while Marxist journals send their submissions to Marxists, so that Marxists and Straussians seldom review each other's work. When the articles are submitted to the mainstream journals which cover a broader range of articles, the Straussians and Marxists frequently 'kill each other off' by critically reviewing submissions from the opposite perspective. The result is 'well-established little cadres of people who don't argue any more about how political theory should be done'.

This phenomenon of the systematic avoidance of overt controversy, both on a localized and on a more global scale, was captured in summary form by one of the economists in the interview sample:

> Disagreements sometimes become public, but it's more common simply not to communicate with people who hold a radically different viewpoint. Those who are in opposing camps just talk past each other. In the last few years, a polemical argument has been raging over a very abstract technical question, but it's been a pointless argument because it hasn't changed anyone's views. On the whole, orthodox and non-orthodox economists have their own journals and keep to their own circle. Inside any particular camp economists don't criticize each other much. When they do, their comments are usually technical ones.

The inclination to play safe – to minimize the risk of making professional enemies by not opposing or being critical of colleagues' views – is also reflected in the preference, noted earlier, of many academics to steer clear of direct competition with others. It is often the consequence of a deliberate career decision of the kind discussed in the next chapter. But as far as the present topic is concerned, one might reflect that the reluctance to say what one thinks, the refusal to join in contest or debate, is the direct antithesis of the view with which this discussion began: that free communication is of the essence of intellectual progress.

Some significant distinctions

Detailed attention has been accorded in this chapter to the varying forms in which ideas are transmitted across disciplines and across specialisms within disciplines. The study of communication patterns has served to bring out certain identifiable features of knowledge communities and to underline various aspects of the knowledge forms to which they relate. We can now begin more systematically to enumerate a number of key sociological and epistemological contrasts, and to discern some apparent connections between them.

The urban-rural dimension, which formed the main initial theme, has proved a significant one. Although it is itself based on social considerations, it has helped to mark the way in which hard knowledge, subject to contextual imperatives, gives rise to characteristic modes of communication that differ fairly consistently from those which typify soft knowledge, subject merely to contextual associations.

Where knowledge is, or is treated as, both cumulative and amenable to fragmentation, research labour can be parcelled out and progress thus often accelerated. The ready identification of currently significant problems can give rise to a competitive race to solve them, and to a corresponding tendency towards secretiveness. That in its turn encourages a rapid and intense style of interaction which relies as much on the spoken as on the written, on the unpublished as on the published, word. In this context, citation is relatively frugal and time-constrained. At the other end of the hard-soft spectrum, where knowledge is reiterative and where problems are not easily divisible, there is no clear notion of progress and no strong incentive for the sharing of labour. There is rarely any competition in reaching a conclusion, and hence a general inclination towards openness, but little sense of urgency, in communication. Information is conveyed mainly through the printed text; citation tends to be copious and to cover a wide time-span.

Cognitive features reinforce and ramify the distinctions in working practice. They can, for example, be discerned through the varying length of typical publication forms: a preference for book-length exposition signifies a contextual association, where assumptions have to be developed *ab initio*, whereas that for article-length pieces signals a contextual imperative, where much of the background argumentation can be taken for granted. Variations in the scale and complexity of problems are also the occasion for differences in the frequency with which active researchers publish their findings. Again, soft knowledge areas, which depend on the exercise of individual interpretation, are generally less amenable to collaborative publication than hard areas, which rest on commonly defined criteria of validity. The scatter of problems characteristic of a loosely structured knowledge domain is reflected in the dispersion of literature across a wide range and variety of sources, whereas tightly structured knowledge tends towards concentration in relatively few journals.

Other contrasts that have been touched on include the gregarious as against solitary social patterns associated respectively with hard pure and soft pure knowledge areas, along with the differential tendencies towards plain as against specialized language and the related degrees of accessibility to non-specialist audiences. We return to a number of these issues in Chapter 9, where a further attempt is made to clarify the relationships between the various social and cognitive categories to which the analysis has given rise.

Notes

1. Crane (1972) observes that:

   A school is characterized by the uncritical acceptance on the part of disciples of a leader's idea system . . . it rejects external influence and validation of its work. By creating a journal of its own, such a group can bypass the criticism of referees from other areas . . . In extreme cases . . . such groups forego the attempt to obtain empirical verification of their ideas altogether.

2. Whitley (1982) notes that 'if . . . the number of practitioners seeking reputations in a particular field, which already has a fairly formalized communication system, increases, the scope of problems tackled is likely to decrease as specialization of tasks and skill becomes higher'.
3. As documented by Watson (1970).
4. Writings in the public domain, because of their ready availability for scrutiny, are the predominant sources not only for practitioners but for those who study them: the historians, philosophers and sociologists who choose as their topic the nature of academic knowledge and academic communities. Among the latter, the use of oral testimony is relatively rare.
5. In quantitative terms, 'In 1970 in the United States, 1,995 books on history were published; in all the pure sciences . . . eight or nine disciplines . . . accounted for 2,358' (Steig 1986).
6. This contention is borne out by the highly technical and complex discussion in Allison (1980).
7. Announcements of this kind, because they are refereed, enjoy more kudos than preprints, over which little quality control is exercised: announcements of results are not invariably followed up by full publication of the details in standard article form.
8. Cronin (1984) provides a thoughtful and reasonably comprehensive review of the relevant literature on the natural and social sciences, but has relatively little to offer on the humanities or the technical or social professions.
9. Even in the apparently dispassionate and value-free area of physics, Gilbert (1977b) suggests, the same tendency may be identified: 'many references are selected because the author hopes they will be regarded as authoritative by the intended audience'.
10. It seems reasonable further to suggest that the degree to which the background to a problem can be taken for granted, as well as the relative incidence of technical and non-technical language, is connected with the universalistic character of hard pure, as against the particularistic nature of soft pure, knowledge (see Chapter 2).

11. It nevertheless came as something of a surprise that there were so few examples of large-scale teamwork among the natural scientists and technologists in the interview sample. The 'teams' often consisted of no more than the occasional postdoctoral researcher, a couple of postgraduates and perhaps a part-time technician, engaged on a 3-year funded project under a single faculty member. In the physical sciences, and even more in biology, mechanical engineering and pharmacy, a sizeable number of respondents were working in isolation among their departmental colleagues.

12. Crane (1972) reports that in her particular sample of mathematicians, 'isolates were even more likely than members of large groups to report that informal communication was very important to their research', and that 'isolates and members of two-person groups attended . . . conferences as frequently as members of large groups'.

13. 'Social scientists operate in a much less predictable and therefore more anxious environment than physical scientists . . . This continuous struggle to reach consensus in a relatively unpredictable and uncertain environment is likely to generate high levels of conflict' (Lodahl and Gordon 1972). It is also relevant to note the references in Chapter 3 to the testimony of respondents on the divisiveness and factionalism of the sociological community.

7

Academic Careers

Personality and environment

In the preceding chapters, we have explored academic activity mainly in aggregative terms, tracing the common cultures, internal structures and modes of interaction of disciplinary tribes and their constituent networks. But just as there are new insights to be gained by moving from a broad to a narrow epistemological framework, so too there are benefits to be won in the social dimension from supplementing a conspectus of the large picture with a scrutiny of the small detail – the individual academics who might be labelled as the elementary particles of the intellectual world.

As one begins to speculate on the match between academic fields and the people in them, the familiar rivalry of nature against nurture manifests itself. Is it that particular kinds of people choose certain sorts of disciplines and bring particular things with them (the 'presage' argument), or is it rather that disciplines shape and condition their adherents into becoming particular kinds of people (the disciplinary socialization argument)? The older literature on HE (e.g. Crane 1972; Clark 1987a, esp. page 107) tends to take the latter position, arguing for the strength and distinctiveness of academic culture. Later literature (e.g. Huber 1990; Thomas 1990; Greed 1991; Tierney 1997; Välimaa 1998 and most feminist writing) stresses the former, pointing to the power of social structural factors, including socialization in the gender role, in shaping personal, professional and disciplinary identity and in delimiting potential career choices as well as more general notions of what is normal and appropriate. However in some of the most recent literature (Prichard 1999, 2000; Parker 2000) notions of professional and personal subjectivities as dynamically constructed in specific social contexts have brought the theoretical wheel full circle. Grbich's interesting study of the socialization of academic researchers in two different Australian universities uses, alternately, modernist and postmodernist perspectives to interpret her results, enabling the reader to make a comparative analysis of alternative theoretical lenses in viewing the same data (Grbich 1998).

The classical escape route from most dilemmas is to repudiate them, arguing that the choices they pose are as false as they are stark. Careful empirical studies such as that by Perry *et al.* (1996) that show that a combination of factors (including, in that case, the individual academic's locus of control and the type of institution they enter) are likely to be nearest the mark. Grbich would describe this as a modernist position, the postmodernist one would stress the diversity and dynamism of situations that renders inappropriate the weighing of alternative variables and strong claims for comparability across settings.

The claim in the present context is that academic careers are subject to a range of causal factors, none of which can be shown as predominant in every case. The activities involved in the transmission and creation of knowledge, Ruscio (1987) writes, 'reflect individual preferences, disciplinary backgrounds and institutional imperatives' in a varied mix of ingredients. It is in the nature of the present study that the second of these should enjoy pride of place, since it is around the notion of disciplines that most of the evidence has been collected; something nonetheless needs briefly to be said about the first and third.

The relationship between personality and learning style is a longstanding topic of psychological enquiry. Research in the 1970s and 1980s acknowledged more clearly than earlier work in the field that apparently homogeneous disciplinary categories may themselves embrace a fair amount of diversity. Wolfe and Kolb's review in 1979 (drawing on a number of investigations of student learning styles, including Kolb's study of '800 practising managers and graduate students in management') remained cautious about the tendency, discerned by Bereiter and Freedman (1962), 'of fields to attract people similar to those already in them':

> What these studies show is that undergraduate education is a major factor in the development of learning style. Whether this is because individuals are shaped by the fields they enter or because of selection/evaluation processes that put people into and out of disciplines is an open question at this point. Most probably both factors are operating – people choose fields that are consistent with their learning styles and are further shaped to fit the learning norms of their field once they are in it. When there is a mismatch between the field's learning norms and the individual's learning style, people will either change or leave the field.

This conclusion matches that of Huber (1990), Joseph (1978, 1980) and Greed (1991) who each argue that the origins and individual characteristics of academics play an important part in influencing their early choice of discipline. This brings these authors into a degree of conflict with Clark (1987a: 107) who claims that 'characteristics imported into the academic profession by individual members from their personal background and prior experiences are relatively unimportant in conditioning their subsequent attitudes and behaviour'. However, recent thinking and research about both learning styles and personal identity lend weight to Clark's position that current context is more important than any relatively fixed consequences of presage. Research on approaches to study nowadays sees them as conditioned by curricular and assessment arrangements and by teaching styles rather than being more or less permanent individual characteristics (Reynolds 1997). Similarly identity is seen 'not as an essence but as a project' (Henkel 2000: 14), a shift towards agency marked by the use of the word subjectivity rather than identity by some authors (Prichard 1999). Thus, micro-social context both shapes and is shaped by the subjectivities of the participants involved (Trowler and Knight 2000).

Such claims are not inconsistent with, though they go a fair theoretical distance beyond, the observations about matches between personality types and subjects of study gleaned from the interviews. The biologists, along with the historians, tended to the view that theirs was 'a discipline for loners'. Much as Evans-Pritchard (1951) had referred to anthropological fieldwork as requiring 'in addition to theoretical knowledge and technical training a certain kind of character and temperament', one of the physicists in the sample spoke of choosing a research area to match one's temperament, and another of picking a problem to suit one's personality; and a geographer observed that graduate students will usually have a good look at the mode of working as well as the content of subdisciplines, and make a selection on the basis of what they see as their own talents.

For undergraduates, the influence of the institution may be as strong as, if not stronger than, that of the discipline (Parlett 1977). Beyond the point of graduation, institutional influences remain – as has already been remarked in Chapter 5 – a significant force in determining academic career chances. On the basis of nearly 150 interviews in a wide range of institutions with academics in physics, biology, political science, English, business studies and medicine, Ruscio (1987) concludes that 'the nature of research is determined in part by the organizational setting . . . other major influences . . . are its rationale or purpose and the institutional attitudes towards it'. He shows convincingly how the interpretations of what research is, and the emphasis which is accorded to it, differ from one type of institution to another:

> Each sector seems to worship the god of research, but organized religion reflects the local culture . . . At a leading research university, the demands for excellence in scholarship are apt to be precise and well understood. On the other hand, scholarship at a liberal arts college may be more broadly defined.

The original study informing this book, concentrating as it did on elite institutions, fully supported his contention about the strength of their research norms: virtually none of the people interviewed for it – even the most junior postgraduate students – seemed in any doubt about the expectations placed on them. Clearly though there are important differences in this regard when we shift the focus to non-elite institutions. Clark's 1987a study showed very clearly that role ambiguity increases as one moves down the institutional status hierarchy in the USA. While faculty in high status institutions were very clear about institutional expectations and criteria for professional success, those lower down the ladder operated in a more ambiguous environment. Here staff were often expected to engage in teaching, research and substantial administrative duties in a situation of vague institutional priorities. This meant a greater degree of uncertainty about where best to direct energies and time. This led to lower levels of satisfaction with the academic role in these contexts generally. Henkel's more recent (2000) British study reached similar conclusions, though focusing more on issues of ambiguities in the construction of professional identities.

Recruitment and the choice of specialisms

Disciplinary differences are evident at the very beginning of an academic career. In most well-established 'pure' subject areas it is now more or less obligatory to begin by acquiring a doctorate, but this is by no means the case in those applied, vocationally oriented disciplines in which the professional component is significant within academia as well as outside it. In pharmacy, as in the law, a professional qualification can only be acquired after at least a minimal period of practical experience in the field, and a majority of aspiring academics will choose the safety net of becoming employable as working professionals before beginning to apply for posts within HE. In engineering, the main motivation is different, though the outcome is the same: starting salaries in industry are so much more attractive than the financial prospects for a doctoral student that very few graduates are tempted to stay on at university. Recruitment to posts in engineering departments is therefore largely confined to those practising engineers who subsequently come to recognize the attractions of an academic life. It is understandable that in all such fields admittance to the relevant profession serves as at least an initial substitute for a doctoral degree – though the more ambitious academics, once appointed, make it their business to acquire a doctorate as well. The consequence is that in applied subjects, those entering the academic community tend to do so later in life than those in other disciplines (sometimes, in the case of mechanical engineering, at quite a senior level, in mid- to late career); that they may, atypically of academics at large, acquire tenured posts in elite institutions without a higher degree (in one leading law faculty in 2000, there were 16 members out of 37 with doctorates); and that, with some practical experience and professional contacts behind them, they may stand a good chance of augmenting their academic salaries with a reasonable amount of consultancy work.

For the rest, however, as the academic world has itself become more professionalized (Clark 1987a, 1987b), a doctorate has become a standard requirement, at least in the more elite institutions (only a negligible proportion of those interviewed in hard pure and soft pure disciplines lacked such a handle to their names). It is therefore on this rite of passage to the scholarly life that we shall for the moment concentrate attention.

In pure, as against applied, disciplines, a further series of broad distinctions emerges between the hard and the soft. In both alike, as has already been indicated in Chapter 5, it is prudent for the novitiate to seek out the most prestigious available department in his or her field (since this will serve to enhance initial research visibility), and to attach himself or herself to the most prestigious available research supervisor (since the benefits of patronage, at least in acquiring one's first paid job, are generally agreed to be more than negligible). There are certain trade-offs even here, since departmental prestige will no more guarantee a good match for a given individual's needs than will an eminent mentor necessarily have time to spare for providing the ideal amount of guidance and support. However, when the initial engagement is being negotiated between a successful applicant (the quality of whose first degree is, at this stage, though not so much later, an important consideration) and a potential supervisor, the extent of available choice of research topic is significantly different from one knowledge area to another (Becher *et al.* 1994; Parry 1997).

Generally speaking, the stronger the contextual imperative, the less scope there is for negotiation over the subject matter of the doctoral thesis; the weaker the contextual association, the greater the latitude of decision allowed to the candidate. There are two related reasons for the constraints in hard pure settings. First, it is quite common for a graduate student to be taken on as as junior member of the supervisor's research team, and to be expected to carry out the task or tasks allocated by the team leader; second, the student, being relatively unfamiliar with the field, will not usually be in a good position to judge which problems or parts of problems are both relevant to current developments and at least in principle amenable to solution within the timespan of a doctoral programme. One of the requirements of a good supervisor, in subject areas of this kind, is to be able readily to supply newcomers with topics that are neither too easy nor too hard to meet the requirements, while at the same time ensuring a useful contribution to the work of the group as a whole.[1] Few such restrictions obtain in knowledge domains where the choice of theme is virtually unlimited, where a theme, once chosen, may be addressed in a diversity of ways and at a variety of levels of sophistication, and where the norm (at least at the doctoral stage) is for individual rather than group research.

Research groups in laboratory-based and field-based sciences are for the most part closely knit, so that group leaders will tend to have regular weekly (and occasionally even daily) contact with their doctoral students, and will thus be quite strongly involved in guiding and overseeing their work. At the other extreme, a lone doctoral candidate working on, say, a relatively narrow topic in eighteenth-century history or the interpretation of a hitherto-neglected text in Renaissance Italian literature can usually expect less collective, corporate activity or close supervisory attention. Levels of contact between student and supervisor may vary over time, being generally more intense early and late in the evolution of the thesis. Monthly or less frequent sessions, interspersed with lengthy bouts of solitary reading and writing, were the common pattern, at least until the advent, in the UK, of the wide-spread adoption of research training courses (Deem and Brehony 2000). The experiences of full-time as against part-time, home as against international students and male as against female students also differ significantly, as Deem and Brehony and others (e.g. Acker *et al.* 1994) show.

The disciplinary contrasts throw up another, more complex and subtle distinction. There are some fields in which it is not unusual for a doctoral student to produce a paper of publishable standard. When it appears in print, there are certain disciplines or specialisms within disciplines in which it will be routinely expected to bear the name of the research supervisor as joint author. Various grounds for this practice were put forward by respondents, both in those disciplines where the practice is widespread (chemistry notable among them) and in those in which it is more patchy. One justification is that since the supervisor chose the topic and had a close hand in its resolution, he or she is rightly entitled to a share of the credit. One respondent compared it with the levying of a tithe by a landlord from his tenants; others saw it as a kindly way of giving the student a leg up by association with a more prestigious author, or as a way of underwriting the quality of a piece of work whose value it would otherwise be difficult to assess, in contrast, those who chose not to adopt the practice – or who were at its receiving end – confessed themselves embarrassed by its exploitative overtones and its implication that research students were 'slave labour' or 'cannon fodder'.

Much as standard lengths of articles differ between one knowledge domain and another, what is required in the way of a PhD thesis will vary from an occasionally highly concise proof of a significant theorem in mathematics to a treatise running to 300 or more typewritten pages on a topic in the humanities, though some universities currently impose an upper word limit to discourage this. Somewhere in the middle, even the more prestigious departments of economics will allow a doctoral award for three scholarly papers published in a refereed journal or judged to be of comparable standard, one of which may be jointly authored with the research supervisor. This, it is argued, is more in keeping with the current professional research norms in the discipline than is the conventional lengthy and monolithic doctoral dissertation.

These considerations make it plain that even in their initial stages, the lines of academic development may vary substantially from one knowledge area to another; that there is no such thing as a standard career pattern which spans the range of intellectual activity. The claim, as we shall see, is borne out unequivocally in all the subsequent phases of the life-cycle.

The achievement of independence

Because the job market and the disciplinary traditions bear differently on different subject areas, it will take longer in some than in others to become launched on an autonomous career as a scholar or researcher in an elite institution. Across all disciplines, however, the reduction in the proportion of tenured, 'core' academics as compared with those on temporary contracts in many countries, discussed in Chapter 1, has led to an increase in the average length of time it takes to gain a permanent post, with many more aspirants than in the past never doing so. In those disciplines in which there is a strong pattern of team activity, along with the availability of substantial grant funding – largely, that is, in the pure sciences, together with some hard applied areas (notably medical and paramedical research) – the intending academic may be expected to occupy 3 years or more in the limbo of a postdoctoral research post before being offered a job leading to tenure. While this is regarded in some fields as useful further experience, it is essentially a period of marking time in career terms. Except in periods of expansion, it does not in any way guarantee a tenure-track post in a prestigious department. Even among those who survive the postdoctoral stage, many will end up in teaching jobs with few if any research opportunities, or in posts outside academia. Postdocs enjoy more independence and more responsibility than doctoral students, but they are still essentially what one non-scientist, critical of the system, regarded as an army of 'hired hands and dogsbodies',[2] dependent largely on the goodwill of their seniors. Lacking the necessary institutional standing, they cannot in many universities supervise research students or apply for grants in their own names: they are not fully-fledged freemen in the scholarly community.

The academic career proper begins – in disciplines having a postdoctoral tradition, as in those that lack one – with a salaried but usually untenured and probationary appointment on the lower rungs of the promotion ladder (an already mentioned exception being through recruitment to more senior ranks on the basis of outside professional experience). The provenance of the first regular post is important, since it is less usual to move up the scale from a lower-ranking institution than it is to move down it from a higher-ranking one. Let us, however, at this point, focus on the early research career of a successful survivor of the various initial hurdles, typically someone with a good first degree and a doctorate – both preferably (as far as their possession is concerned) acquired from well-regarded departments in leading institutions – together with, where appropriate, a spell of postdoctoral work in a group run by a well-known researcher.

Since our central concern is with the creation and development of knowledge rather than with its transmission, we will do no more than mention here the paradox that the standard route to a research career is through what is formally a teaching appointment, while a research post as such, except at the highest level, carries little status and no long-term prospects of advancement. It is nonetheless important to recognize that the common pattern in the UK and the US – though it is not so pronounced in other national HE systems – is for elite researchers to have teaching obligations as well. These will often be quite substantial in the period before tenure is granted, so rendering it harder than it might otherwise be to make a major research contribution in early academic life. The situation is, of course, different in universities where teaching is the main function. Here the criteria for getting on will lie in a successful record as an academic manager, either of students, of colleagues or both (Boice 1992).

The requirement to teach places a high premium on the choice of both an initial research specialism and a particular topic within it. To gain the early visibility commonly associated with a strong professional reputation, a budding researcher needs to concentrate the available research time – that is, the time which remains after the necessary teaching commitments have been met – on an area of activity that is capable of yielding significant results in a reasonably short period. The selection of this activity is arguably the most strategic decision that faces academics in the initial stages of their careers.[3]

We shall need to distinguish more sharply at this point between a specialism and a specific research topic. Although the beginnings of a specialized interest may sometimes be traced back to the late undergraduate phase, intellectual identities necessarily become more pronounced in the course of choosing and pursuing a doctoral topic. Some individuals may stay with, or close to, their initial choice of specialism for the rest of their lives, selecting a series of research problems which continue to fall within it. On the whole, however, as we see in the next section, a strong academic reputation may depend on a reasonable degree of mobility between different specialist areas.

One of the most prized assets of an appointment to a tenure track academic post – identified as such by respondents in each of the 12 disciplines covered by the initial inquiry – is the perceived freedom to choose the subject matter of one's research. In reality, that freedom is hedged about by constraints – including the lack of necessary resources, the scarcity of time, and in some contexts the absence of incentives. These constraints are becoming tighter and more defined by external forces (Henkel 2000). Nonetheless, the degree of autonomy, and in particular the liberty to determine the intellectual issues with which one wishes to engage, is held to be significantly greater than it would be in other walks of life. Indeed, research consistently finds that this is the main reason why academics choose, and remain in, their profession (Halsey 1992; Adams 1998; Trowler 1998a).

The scope for matching activities to temperaments has already been noted. That scope is enhanced by the considerable variety of types of research on offer within virtually every discipline. The individual specialisms an apparently homogeneous subject area embraces will often span the continuum from hard to soft modes of investigation. To give only a few examples, the quantitatively inclined historian may be free to register a commitment to economic or demographic history; the modern linguist may choose between the well-hedged confines of philology and the open pastureland of interpretive criticism; the economist may espouse the mathematical rigour of pure theory or the less easily tamed complexity of the labour market; the mechanical engineer may select from a menu that includes the creative uncertainties of design as well as the numerical precision of studies in fluid mechanics; the biologist may opt between the narrow and relatively certain worlds of taxonomy or microbiology and the broad and unpredictable studies of particular species or habitats; the physicist may escape the urban demands of research into particles or solid state by choosing to investigate such comparatively rural areas as meteorology, relativity or gravitation. The option may not of course be an entirely open one. Echoing a point made earlier in this chapter, one informant remarked that 'literature and linguistics demand different mind sets – one could view the choice between them as being temperamentally determined'.

Although a commitment to a given discipline does not dedicate one irrevocably to a specific pattern of thought or mode of enquiry, this is not to contradict the claim (argued in Chapters 2 and 3) that, when viewed from a distance, particular disciplines and groups of disciplines display certain aggregated characteristics which distinguish them from others: it is merely to emphasize the variety within the uniformity. The resulting catholicity within disciplines may be seen as a fortunate epistemological characteristic, in that it allows in the social dimension for a wide range of intellectual opportunity.

Even when the important choice of an initial research specialism has been settled – usually deriving, as we have seen, from the decisions entered into at the doctoral stage – there are still two well-marked escape routes from what may have transpired as a less than entirely successful match between theme and temperament. The first, to which we shall return shortly, lies in the sometimes far-reaching decision to change from one specialism to another; the second, which we shall now consider, rests on the choice of a particular research topic within a specialism to which a firm commitment has already been made.

Inside their necessarily narrower limits, specialisms themselves may offer something akin to the options that most disciplines can be seen to provide. That is to say, certain topics will be seen as central, and others as more peripheral; some as demanding, and others as comparatively tame. The decision that this calls for, whether to gamble with large stakes for high dividends or to play safe for lesser rewards, is a quite serious one in career terms. As one respondent, a chemist, put it:

> In underpopulated areas within the discipline, there are fewer grants and fewer fringe benefits – less communication, less meetings, less opportunities to share interests, less of the things that motivate people. Because such areas aren't competitive, they promise better results – but the credit is not so great. People drift into such an area if they are loners and isolated individuals who don't like the limelight. Highly competitive people wouldn't be attracted by fields of this kind.

The strategic issues were elaborated in another of the interviews with chemists:

> Problems take different lengths of time to solve. It isn't necessarily a good strategy to go for the quick solutions. Although these result in a

greater number of publications, they don't necessarily count for much. The result may just be 'shotgun science', with very little coherence or quality. In fact, you need to find a good balance between short and long problems as a matter of expediency. You have to do things with rapid results as well as tackling long-term issues. A large problem can be a large gamble too. It can bring a lot of credit – but you may not be able to complete its solution.

The successful selection of research themes in pure mathematics, incidentally, is celebrated by the epithet 'good taste'. Much like the same phrase used by a connoisseur of the arts, it denotes the independent identification of what is consequently recognized as valuable. It is 'a matter of finding significant and soluble problems not amenable to traditional approaches', problems that are 'difficult, deep as opposed to shallow, and worthwhile in terms of the new possibilities they give rise to'.

If the choice is less firmly underscored in soft pure, hard applied and soft applied domains, it is nevertheless there to be made. There are topics which, on most people's reckoning, are minor and perhaps rather trivial, but may nonetheless lead to a publication of sorts; and there are those on grander themes which promise to become the subject of widespread critical attention. Not everyone is prepared to make the large commitment which may, or may not, even after years of endeavour, be judged to result in a significant intellectual coup; as in the hard sciences, there is the countervailing temptation to stick to a series of minor, more manageable contributions.

Whatever the area of knowledge, however, the dividends are not necessarily confined to hot (mainstream or currently fashionable) topics. Indeed, the potentially greatest pay-offs may come from apparently marginal areas. It is there that many of the successful revolutions are bred: consider, for example, the lonely wilderness years of a Ladurie in history or an Einstein in physics. But to follow in their path is a high-risk strategy indeed, since the chances are that at the end of the day one's efforts will prove inglorious and one's endeavours remain unsung.

The mid-life crisis

We need to make a leap in imagination, here, from the aspiring to the established. That is, we need to assume that the individuals with whose fates we have been concerned have duly achieved both the goal of a professional reputation and the status of a tenured appointment. The mid-career stage does not mark an end to the demands and dilemmas of an academic life; indeed it often signals the onset of a new set of challenges.

The main question that is posed at this point concerns whether or not to continue working within the same specialism, whether to switch to another one, or whether to begin the process of moving away altogether from active research. Consideration of the last of these options is conveniently deferred until later in the chapter, when we review the general phenomenon of ageing and burn-out; so we confine ourselves now to the issue of intellectual mobility.

The most important consideration must be what relative career gains and losses are likely to result from deciding to make a move: but there is of course the prior issue of why, if at all, a change of direction needs to be contemplated. We have already noted, from a collective standpoint, the inertia (though some would prefer the term conservatism) built into the academic enterprise as a result of the often substantial investment needed to attain a special competence in a particular field (see Chapter 5). Anyone who has spent long, arduous years in the achievement of a close understanding of one particular knowledge area or in the acquisition of a particular type of expertise,[4] is unlikely without hesitation to abandon it and repeat the process in favour of a new one. The sense of reluctance, while apparent among respondents in a variety of subject areas, seemed particularly acute where the linguistic and conceptual barriers between specialisms were high, or where one complex but well-established technical skill had to be replaced by another.[5]

Henkel's research, however, notes that despite such difficulties and preferences sometimes it was necessary for academics to shift their specialism in the face of changes in student demand for courses, for example from physics to more domain-based subjects (Henkel 2000: 215–16). However in the face of such disincentives, the motive to change has to be a powerful one. The reasons for making a move tend to be more numerous in cumulative than in reiterative subject areas, being partly dependent on the way in which knowledge has progressed. It was a common theme of the testimony given in interviews by physicists that, in the words of one respondent, 'Ten years is about the maximum life-span of a fashionable topic' and that, in the words of another 'If you're lucky enough to hit on a new technique, you may be able to exploit it for up to a decade.' In the less rapidly moving areas in biology, 'your techniques can carry you through for about fifteen years after graduation, but you tend to run out of steam when you are around 40'.[6] Knowledge of instrumentation also becomes dated: 'my students do things with apparatus which I don't know how to do'.

Those who work in non-cumulative areas may be spared such problems, but they share others that arise from personal considerations. Even when the field itself is not subject to rapid development, it may be affected by the swings of fashion, leaving the researcher to feel that he or she has been left mouldering in an intellectual backwater. Or, more commonly, individuals may conclude that they have done all the work they want to do within a particular specialist area, or that they have become bored with it, or simply that they are stale and in need of a change. Migrating to a specialist area is not a simple or immediate matter, however. As academics in a variety of fields know, even leaving research in one's own discipline for a few years can make it difficult to re-enter later. One of Henkel's respondents, a biochemist, had become embroiled in administrative responsibilities so that he lost focus and continuity in his research. He found it extremely difficult to climb back to a position in which he could publish and obtain research funding (Henkel 2000: 183). Such difficulties are magnified in a move to a different discipline or specialism.

As several respondents in various subject areas pointed out – supporting the contention of Gilbert (1977a) – there is also the crucial difficulty that one is not necessarily able to transfer one's existing reputation to a new specialism; membership of new networks may need to be negotiated, and credibility with funding agencies re-established. Confronted with these challenges, it is perhaps predictable that most people who make a move do not compound their problems by choosing a more intellectually impenetrable area than the one with which they are already familiar. The tendency for migration to take place from areas of high precision to those of lower precision is borne out by the available evidence from the interviews. To take a couple of cases in point: 'it's fairly common for theoretical economists to move into the history of economic ideas or to become economic historians'; 'it's only very rarely that people move from ecology to cell biology, but there are more examples of moves in the other direction'.

The strategy of hedging one's bets by keeping one foot in the old specialism while dipping the toes of the other in the new, is singled out by Gieryn (1978): 'complete substitution of one problem set for a completely different one is . . . a less common occurrence than simultaneous problem change and problem retention'. Data from the interviews suggested that this practice was not confined to the sciences: respondents in other knowledge areas also argued that, to avoid a complete hiatus in one's publications, it was important to continue some writing in the field one was leaving while gearing up to contribute to the literature of the new affiliation.

So far, the discussion has been concerned with the reasons behind migration and the problems that beset it, rather than with its frequency and scope. But something also needs to be said on the latter two issues. Estimates of the incidence of mobility differ to a considerable extent: some commentators write it down as a relatively rare phenomenon, while others claim it to be comparatively common. The divergence may stem from the nature of the population under review. If the whole body of academics is in question, rather than the much smaller group of active researchers, then it could well be the case that 'few scientists change research area during their career' (Thagaard 1987). However the evidence from the initial study of academics from elite departments and institutions was supportive of Mulkay's (1972) claim that 'intellectual migration seems to occur very frequently . . . in most if not all scientific disciplines'; of Hagstrom's (1974) observation that 'scientists typically work in more than one specialty and change specialties often' (more than one-quarter of his sample, he claimed, had changed primary specialties in the preceding 5 years); and of Whitley's (1984) reference to the findings of the US National Academy of Sciences 1972 survey, that 'physicists do indeed "migrate" to a considerable degree between sub-fields with one-third of PhDs changing their major interests in 1968–70'.[7] In the intial interviews the number of respondents who reported some significant change in career direction was much higher in actuality than in expectation, and the extent of the changes was in some cases quite striking.

There were, among the apparently substantial shifts from one discipline to another, a number of physicists who had turned to chemistry and engineering; a chemist who had migrated to biology (as well as a number who had, more predictably, become pharmacists); a biologist about to take up a post in experimental psychology; an anthropologist in a history department (and, again more predictably, an archaeologist in another); a historian who had become a sociologist; and an economist who had changed allegiance to political science. Outside the sample, there are many other well-known cases of intellectual pluralism, including three singled out by those interviewed for this study: Herbert Simon, whose contributions to political science and economics were complemented by those he made to mathematics and psychology; Michael Polanyi, who abandoned a distinguished career in chemistry to become a philosopher of science; and Thomas Kuhn, who started his career as a physicist before establishing himself as a historian.

Movements across specialisms within the same discipline may also at times be quite radical. Examples among the respondents included a physicist who had switched from elementary particles to astrophysics to radioisotope dating to applied energy research; a plant pathologist who had made a new career in studying fish vision; an engineer who had moved on from research on missile structures to a study of machine tool vibration; and a French literature specialist whose interests had evolved from sixteenth-century poetry to modern drama. More limited changes were commonplace in almost every field, and perhaps especially in academic law, where 'there is a traditional notion that everyone should be able to teach every subject', and in those disciplines, such as engineering and history, whose members are similarly encouraged to take the view that they are 'jacks of all trades'.

A substantial section of academics taken as a whole also change direction during their careers, but towards a management role rather than shifting their research specialism. The much-increased incidence of this in the 1980s and 1990s has led Henkel (2000) to talk about the academic manager as a new identity within academia:

> One of the consequences of the deep systemic and institutional changes experienced by universities was the emergence of the academic manager . . . [who was] having to learn 'on the hoof' . . . and sometimes felt that the whole institution or even the whole system was doing the same. 'Higher education is stumbling in a world for which it is not equipped' . . .
>
> (Henkel 2000: 235, 237)

Despite this, however, almost all of the respondents in Henkel's study emphasized their academic identities as of continuing importance to them, indeed some had found new impetus in their research work since taking on a managerial role.

The end-point of active research

For the many academics who manage to survive the challenges and traumas of a mid-career change of life, there are many who do not; and yet others, as we have already seen, who have never faced the necessity or felt the urge to move out of their initial specialisms. They may for our present purposes be grouped together under the category of those whose research careers are at, or nearing, their end; though there are, as often before, significant differences to be discerned among them.

Let us begin by looking at the case of the researchers who, for one reason or another, conclude that they have no more to contribute within their existing fields of expertise, but who lack the incentive to start as virtual novices over again. Among those interviewed, the biologists were particularly informative about the problems that arose and the career possibilities which remained open at this point, so their observations will be taken as illustrative of a wider generality.

There was common agreement that the moment of crisis, at least among botanists and zoologists, occurred somewhere around their late 30s or early 40s. A number of respondents ascribed its incidence to an increasing administrative load, which drained energies away from empirical research, and a mature professionalism, which encouraged an emphasis on the theoretical and synoptic aspects of one's field, where necessary using research associates for data collection. An alternative response was to 'escape into administration' or, for people who were good at teaching, to concentrate on that. Karpiak's research (2000) on mid-life faculty in Canada suggests that in their 50s many academics receive a 'second call': a call to care and to teaching. A new emphasis on relationships with and support for students gave such faculty what was in effect a new, and extremely rewarding, career. There are others again who simply opt to 'rest on their laurels and plod along'. As against this developmental-cum-structural view, however, respondents in the same survey offered an account of the matter more directly linked with the cognitive dimension of the research enterprise. According to the second school of thought, the intellectual menopause had less to do with the obligations of seniority and the growth over time of a reflective approach than it had with the average life expectancy of a research topic or an experimental technique that is, with the problems discussed in the preceding section. The appropriate response, on this interpretation, must be to 'retool your lab and rethink your problems'; to 'pick up the pieces, and update your techniques or change the emphasis of your research'.

Some who favoured the latter view were strongly critical of their older colleagues who had taken up the role of synthesizing elder statesmen: 'It is simply a way of maintaining their self-justification – a cheap and easy way out' said one. 'Such people do damned little work for their syntheses'. Another saw those senior scientists who were content to move out of the laboratory and adopt a supervisory function as 'people who want to "be scientists" rather than to do science in any genuine sense'.

The role of a senior academic as a supervisor of others' work, a synthesizer or a philosopher about his or her discipline, is perhaps more common in hard pure subjects than in other fields – because, as we shall go on to argue, they give rise to a more marked career hiatus. But it is fairly typical for those relinquishing an active research career in any subject to take on a sizeable administrative commitment, either in their own departments or at the institutional level. An added option is to seek office in a learned society or relevant professional association. A few people at this stage decide to leave academic life altogether. But the most common choice of all is to concentrate on undergraduate teaching at the expense of generating new knowledge or supervising the research of doctoral students.

It has already been suggested that the life-expectation of a specialist in a competitive urban field is relatively short. The phenomenon of 'burnout' is most widely recognized in pure mathematics, where the peak of performance is often said to occur in their 20s or early 30s.[8] The older mathematicians in the sample were sceptical about this claim, though some acknowledged that the subject called for lengthy periods of close concentration when working through an argument, and so tended to favour those with high intellectual energy and a capacity for prolonged introspection: 'You have to be able to concentrate intensely enough to see the whole solution to a problem in your head.' Some areas of physics too, particularly the more theoretical aspects closely akin to mathematics, were designated a young person's field by respondents in that area; though in many experimental specialisms experience was said to compensate for age, so that people tended to get better with increasing maturity. The testimony of engineers on this point was ambivalent – again, it may have been related to the level of theoretical content, though the sample was too small to lend confirmation to this suggestion. The majority view, however, was that 'the career profile is a straight gradient – experience counts for a lot'; 'some people remain productive well into their fifties'; 'no-one peters out completely – there are some very active oldsters'.

In soft pure and soft applied disciplines, burning out is not recognized at all as part of a typical career pattern. There is no discernible early peak in research productivity; an increase in age betokens a parallel increase in expertise. A respondent in the field of modern languages maintained that 'modern linguists probably do their best work after the age of 45'; another pointed out that 'late-blooming is partly a matter of the amount of material you have to assimilate and the amount of detail you have to master – but it's also partly a result of the need for emotional maturity, insightfulness and empathy'.

One source of the perceived difference between hard and soft may be traced to the contrast, noted by Hagstrom (1965), between 'powerful and general theories' that can be rapidly assimilated and deployed by energetic newcomers, and 'relatively unsystematic factual material' or 'elaborate and ramified theories' which only long years of study can command. Another, as we have seen, lies in the differential importance of specialized apparatus and techniques, and the tendency for both to become outdated within a comparatively short period in cumulative knowledge areas. Research in the softer domains commonly demands no instrumentation, and such techniques as it calls on are on the whole stable and relatively unchanging.

All that has been remarked so far about the relationship between career stage and research productivity has been based on the subjective impressions of the practitioners themselves. In principle, it should be possible to provide a more systematic, detached and impartial analysis, based on a correlation of published writings with chronological maturity. A number of researchers have in fact attempted such a task, though – with irritating perversity – the objective evidence is as confused and contradictory as the subjective is clear and unequivocal.

The pioneering work is that of Lehman (1953), who set himself the herculean challenge of relating age to achievement – subsequently translated as 'outstanding performances' – not only in academic subjects such as medicine, psychology, philosophy, mathematics and most of the natural sciences, but in music, art, creative literature, politics and 'public leadership positions' as well (though not, interestingly enough, in such fields as history, sociology, anthropology or literary studies). Most of those comprising his sample were deceased, some (e.g. Mozart and Beethoven) long so. He was thus able to compare individuals born in the 1700s with those born since 1850. In his analysis, peaking of productivity appears to occur mostly in the late 30s – the range for chemistry is given as 26–30,[9] for physics and mathematics as 30–4 and for geology and medical sciences as around 35–9. Philosophers, too, are quoted as peaking between 35 and 39, except for metaphysicians, who enjoy a relatively late maturity of 40–4.[10] Lehman stresses, however, that intellectual productivity continues, albeit at a reduced rate, after the peak is passed. Taken as a whole, people beyond the age of 40 make over half the total contributions in any field, but the greatest rate of achievement occurs between 30 and 39.

Critics of Lehman's methods and dissenters from his findings include Dennis (1956, 1958, 1966) and a number of others enumerated in the brief, workmanlike review of the research literature on the subject by Fox (1983). Dennis relies on ageing data in two senses of the phrase, since his sample covers 738 people, born between 1600 and 1820, living to the age of 79 and beyond. He maintains that:

> in many groups [but not among creative artists] the decade of the 20s was the least productive period . . . The highest rate of output, in the case of nearly all groups, was reached in the 40s or soon after. From age 40 onwards the output of scholars suffered little decrement. After age 60 the productivity of scientists decreased appreciably.

His main contention, that 'productivity persists in the later years of life', is echoed in a number of subsequent writings; others discern a twin-peaked pattern, with a second efflorescence of creativity among those in their 50s.

A small group of studies have concentrated on the crème de la crème of academic researchers, in the form of Nobel prize winners. Manniche and Falk (1957) found the peaks to be in their late 30s and early 40s. Moulin (1955) gives somewhat higher mean ages for the Nobel prize winners from 1901 to 1950.[11] Reif and Strauss (1965) state that 'during the past half dozen years . . . mean ages at the time of the award have been between 45 and 50 years in physics, chemistry and medicine' but that 'some men [sic] were in their late twenties when they did the outstanding work leading to subsequent awards of the prizes; indeed, their work was done at an average age of less than 35 years'. Zuckerman (1977), in her comprehensive exploration of the subject, would appear to dissent from this view, concluding that: 'Among Nobel laureates at least, science is not exclusively a young person's game; evidently it is a game the middle-aged can play as well.'[12]

Future generations of numerologists will doubtless continue to crunch out statistics, culled from diverse databases and generated from mutually incompatible assumptions, in the hope of producing a final, definitive statement on the relationship between age and productivity. Those lacking such inclinations, however, may conclude that there are too many complexities in all this to allow for more than a brace of unequivocal claims: first, that whatever the realities of the situation, the legend will die hard that subject areas making strong demands on abstractly symbolic or heavily quantitative reasoning are the main province of younger intellects; and, second, that for the rest, if custom has the scope to stale, yet age must lack the power to wither the propensity for intellectual excellence.

Personal matters

One of the self-imposed limitations of the original empirical research for this book was that it did not enquire into the lives of respondents as private individuals. None the less, respondents were invited to comment on issues relating to professional commitment and job satisfaction. The responses on these points, though they have no direct bearing on the shape and development of academic careers, deserve a brief resumé.

It was typical of the active researchers who constituted the initial sample that they admitted to a strong sense of personal involvement in their work. However, the form that involvement took varied somewhat from one knowledge area to another. The academics who were subjected to the strong competitive pressures of urban research seemed to find it hardest to 'switch off'. In some areas of physics, to survive, you have to be 'dedicated and determined', 'monomaniac' and 'obsessed'. Several interviewees found it difficult to leave their work behind: 'I live my physics.' There are departments where the labs are seldom empty.

The patterns among engineers and biologists seem less consistent. A number of the former, especially in the hotter areas of the subject, spoke of their 'total absorption' in their research interests: 'It amazes me how much time people spend working – at least that's true if you're active; and if it's not true it means you've opted out.' One respondent went on to describe how his wife had instituted a customs-type search of the car to impound all contraband work from the holiday baggage. Others, however, had schooled themselves against 'getting overwound and overdoing things'. Again, while some biologists admitted that their professional concerns took up a large part of their lives ('you can't help carting your work round with you'),[13] others considered it essential to 'know when you have to stop working', and to avoid too much emotional intensity by the deliberate cultivation of other interests. By comparison, one respondent observed, 'physicists are more motivated and involved'.

There were fewer comments along these lines from those in the softer knowledge fields, though there remained a clear tendency to view the world from one's own disciplinary perspective. Much as a physicist might 'see everything from a physics point of view, 24 hours a day', or a biologist could discern 'a biological analogy in almost every situation', a number of historians claimed that their subject gave them a special understanding of life, 'a better feel for what is going on'; and a human geographer remarked that 'geography gives you a way of looking at the world: I can't imagine how I could stop being a geographer, especially when I'm in the countryside – seeing is an important part of geography to me'. But those who worked in disciplines concerned with human affairs were not perhaps as conscious of the dividing line between their occupational and their everyday lives, and seemed to adopt a more relaxed attitude towards their intellectual commitments.

The sense of personal pleasure to be derived from research activity was widely acknowledged, and there was not a single interviewee who confessed to being 'turned off' by, or uninvolved in, even its more routine aspects (it may be that, as one respondent suggested, most academics seem to end up in a field in which they find even the 'busy work' enjoyable, where others might consider it tedious). This is not to say that there are no boring or unsatisfactory facets of an academic life. The most common candidates under this heading were administration, committee work and marking undergraduate essays and exam scripts (the actual process of teaching was generally held to be enjoyable and worthwhile, and could sometimes be found to have a broadening effect on one's research).[14] Many of the younger academics felt frustrated by the lack of career prospects, especially when compared with the expansionist opportunities enjoyed by their predecessors a generation before; and some of the more senior ones expressed concern that increasing professionalization, along with other forces pressing for uniformity, would rule out the making of imaginative or risky appointments, and so reward safe mediocrity at the expense of wayward brilliance.

Few of those with some years of professional experience would have wanted to live their lives differently: a finding remarkably different to Halsey's later (1992) comment that few academics who responded to his survey would recommend an academic career to their students. The difference may be attributable partly to the fact that the sample for the original study was drawn from elite individuals in elite institutions, and partly to the subsequent changes in the academic environment noted in Chapter 1. As Clark (1987a) found (unsurprisingly), people in privileged settings are far more comfortable with their lot than those in lower status positions and institutions: apart from anything else they do not suffer the role ambiguity that besets the latter.

Among the special virtues of their own disciplines – the ability, say, to immerse oneself in and come to appreciate another culture in modern language studies, history or anthropology; the engineer's pride in 'knowing how to do things'; the physicist's sense of command in knowing how things work – most of the academics interviewed would affirm the enjoyment that one expressed of 'a vivid intellectual life, full of satisfaction and exhilaration', and share with another the claim that 'I can't imagine doing anything else, or any other job where I would be paid to talk to lots of bright people and do what I want to do.'

This last point – the special opportunity that academia affords 'to exercise your own creative instincts – to be your own boss' – was a leitmotif of the testimony from virtually every discipline. There is no contesting the importance given by respondents to freedom of choice and freedom of action in their research. How far that freedom is a real one, or how far it persists only as a romantic illusion, must be a topic for the next chapter to consider.

Women's academic careers

Academic tribes, like those of other sorts, are splintered by structural inequalities, most obviously by ones associated with gender. However, because no conscious attempt was made to control the original interview sample for gender representation, and because the sample was drawn from individuals in prestigious posts in elite institutions, only 22 of the original 221 academics interviewed were women.[15] Such a small subsample could shed little light on the important systematic differences between male and female career patterns, particularly as there were no women at all from mathematics, chemistry, geography and economics (each of which included around a dozen interviewees), and only two each from modern languages and pharmacy; there were a mere three in each larger group of some two dozen from biology, law, physics and sociology; none in engineering; and even in history only 6 out of 22.

However, by the end of the 1990s there existed a fairly substantial body of research literature exploring the gendered nature of academic career patterns. Both British and American findings suggest that women in academia have been marginalized in a number of respects. Historically there have been far fewer female than male academic staff in North American and British universities, though this situation is changing. Between 1969 and 1990 the proportion of US women academics increased from around 20 per cent to just over 30 per cent. Finkelstein *et al.* (1998) report a surge in the appointment of women to full-time faculty positions across all institutional types and curriculum areas in the USA, constituting over 40 per cent of new appointments 1985–92, compared with only around 28 per cent of those appointed prior to 1985 (the new cohort of women constitutes nearly 42 per cent of all full-time women faculty). In the UK in 1997–8 women occupied 31 per cent of all full-time academic posts in the HE sector, held 34 per cent of all appointments and constituted 52 per cent of part-time and hourly paid academic staff (HESA 1999). Put another way, in the UK 21 per cent of women academics are part-time compared with 10 per cent of men (HESA 1999): in the US comparable figures are 46 per cent and 37 per cent (Nettles *et al.* 2000).

In both the UK and USA the academic appointments of women tend to be bunched in the lower-status institutions, and particularly in public rather than the private universities. In the first half of the 1990s women academics were more likely than men to work in American 2-year institutions (33 versus 23 per cent), while male faculty were more likely than women to work in research universities (20 versus 14 per cent) (Nettles *et al.* 2000). In the UK 27 per cent of the academic staff in chartered universities are women compared with 42 per cent in ex-polytechnics (HESA 1999).

Women in general receive initial appointments at lower-ranking positions; they are promoted more slowly and achieve tenure at a later age. As a result fewer women than men in the US have tenured positions – 42 per cent versus 66 per cent (NCES 2000). Again, women in American universities spend more time than men on teaching as against research (Nettles *et al.* 2000).

Women academics' salaries are lower than those of men at the same academic rank, even in women-friendly disciplines (Bett 1999; Sax *et al.* 1999; NCES 2000; MacLeod 2000b). At the same time women give more time to their institutions (Carnegie Foundation 1990; Bagilhole 1993). Women professors in the early 1990s worked a 64.5 hour week in the UK as compared with their male peers' 58.6 (Davies and Holloway 1995).

Female academic profiles tend not to be as high; they are less well qualified; a smaller proportion than men have doctoral degrees (40 per cent of women compared with 58 per cent of men in the USA in 1992 – Nettles *et al.* 2000). Women academics are more likely to be involved in teaching than men and are given heavier tutorial loads (Bernard 1964; Deem 1996; Barnes-Powell and Letherby 1998). They are less likely to reach the higher levels of the academic profession: HESA statistics for 1997–8 give a total of 847 posts occupied by females with the title of 'professor' compared with 8750 for males (HESA 1999). In the USA the percentage of female full-time faculty who held the rank of full professor was less than half the percentage of men (15 versus 39 per cent, respectively: Nettles *et al.* 2000).[16]

There are different demographic patterns for male and female academics between different subject fields.[17] In 1997–8 women in the UK were poorly represented in the hard pure and hard applied disciplines (physics 10 per cent; engineering 12 per cent) but better represented in the soft pure and (especially) soft applied areas (social studies 35 per cent; education 46 per cent): data from HESA (1999). Similar patterns can be found elsewhere, including the USA. Predictably, the feminization of subjects such as engineering has been less marked than, for example, law, the humanities or, particularly, the health-related fields. Women are more numerous in disciplines with low status both within the university and beyond: but even here the senior posts are likely to be held by men: according to a 1994 AUPSW survey only 12 per cent of professors in social work were women.

Women are very well represented in non-academic university posts. In the UK, while only 25 per cent of senior staff are female, women constitute 88 per cent of the clerical grades in chartered universties, 67 per cent of the administrative and clerical grades in unchartered universities and 62 per cent of all university manual staff (Bett 1999). However, within all these staff groups there are proportionately fewer women than men at higher grades.

Not surprisingly in the light of this data women academics (particularly in Germany, Australia, USA and UK) are less likely than their male colleagues to be satisfied with their job security and less likely to consider themselves to have academic autonomy in terms of research (Sheehan and Welch 1996; Adams 1998).

Explaining these differences is more difficult than describing them. Liberal feminists point to subtle and pervasive considerations rather than deliberate discriminatory behaviour against women: 'a reflection of larger social differentiation'; the outcome of 'intermittent, mild, largely unconscious prejudice' (Blackstone and Fulton 1975); a consequence of 'accumulative disadvantage' (Cole 1979). The institutional and social context may itself create conflicting demands, as for example when institutions offer no child care facilities and recurrently hold meetings during the evening (Connell 1987; Acker 1994; Munn-Giddings 1998).

For women, who are on the whole expected to take responsibility for many aspects of domestic life, the work-home linkage creates special, and sometimes discipline-specific, challenges. The NewU study (Trowler 1998a) indicated the difficulties women faced because of the domestic expectations imposed on them and the resultant role conflict. One described herself as 'a one man band [sic], doing three jobs' with only half an hour to relax in the evening before she began lecture preparation, which continued until midnight. For some these pressures had led to health problems. These domestic responsibilities also meant that women were more reluctant to attend conferences or meetings away from home. Finding large uninterrupted batches of time free of responsibilities to their partners or their children was generally more difficult for women than for men. In disciplines such as astronomy, physics and some areas of the social sciences in which data collection, analysis or write-up call for sustained concentration women were clearly at a disadvantage in terms of their ability to promote their academic interests. Other considerations include careers interrupted for childbirth or hampered by other family obligations (Spurling 1990), together with the relative immobility of married women tied to husbands' workplaces (Bernard 1964).

The linkage between the domestic responsibilities ascribed to women and the roles imputed to them in their professional lives extends beyond this, of course. Sex-role spillover (Gutek and Cohen 1992) means that women in general are expected to do more 'smile work' and 'mom work' (Tierney and Bensimon 1996) in order to fit in and get on in departments with a tradition of male dominance. Smile work involves the symbolic management of behaviour to present oneself in an agreeable way. Mom work is another form of accommodation and describes the imposition of nurturing and caretaking roles on women. Tierney and Bensimon's study of socialization in 12 different North American HE settings found that male-dominated departments tended to elicit one or other of these responses in women: 'There is a substantial number of [male] faculty around here who remember when they were masters of the universe . . . and they are still living in that culture' (quoted in Tierney and Bensimon 1996: 83).

In relation to scientific fields in particular, Zuckerman and Cole (1975) identify a 'triple penalty' for women: the definition of science as an inappropriate female career (reducing recruitment); the stereotyping of women as less competent at quantitative reasoning than men (reducing motivation); and 'some evidence for actual discrimination against women in the scientific community'. Thomas (1990) has pointed to the incompatibilities between gender identity and the characteristics of particular disciplines and domains of study. Disciplinary stereotypes are not culturally neutral: certain areas of enquiry are widely believed to possess qualities connoting either masculinity or femininity. A woman specializing in a discipline with a masculine gender identity such as physics therefore has to contend with a situation in which she (unlike a male physicist) has a dual identity, one aspect of which challenges conventional ideas about gender roles.

Radical feminists see gender conflict of this kind as an inevitable consequence of the patriarchal nature of HE. Slaughter and Leslie (1997: 172) note that while a female lecturer may find science 'alienating', this obscures the way in which male ambitions reinforce the disciplinary gender identity to 'construct a milieu that [is] uncomfortable for women'. For radical feminism, the consequence is that 'mainstream' is 'malestream' in a patriarchal society. This has repercussions in many dimensions of life: the very experience of working in a patriarchal environment imposes pressures and constraints on women that men do not face (Acker 1994; Newman 1995). For Cockburn (1991) men 'get in the way of women' by using various strategies to enmesh them in the 'feminine' aspects of the organization's work on which they confer lower value (Cockburn 1991: 63–4). Coate (1999) examines epistemological hegemony, arguing that feminist knowledge has been 'silenced' in the academy by men. According to Dominelli, women in feminized disciplines such as social work embedded in a male-dominated institution suffer low status and other disadvantages: because 'men dominate in the upper echelons of the academy, men's agendas will once again determine the parameters within which social work will be evaluated and may mean that the discipline . . . will lose out' (1998: 42). Certainly American female academics perceive the HE climate as less congenial than do males (Sax *et al.* 1999: 19).

Poststructuralist feminist writers have debated the tension between recognizing the fractured nature of the category 'women' while retaining the analytical perspective which that category affords on, for example, the way structured inequalities in terms of gender interact with such other inequalities as those associated with race, social class and disability. We turn to consider one of these, race, next. As we see in the next section, the more obviously fractured nature of the concept 'minority ethnic group' limits its explanatory power in a much clearer way than is the case for 'women' as a category.

Race, ethnicity and academic careers

The term 'race', because it is open to a wide range of implicit meanings, has to be interpreted within metaphorical inverted commas. Nonetheless, it has no adequate synonym that dispenses with its ambiguities, and is hard to replace as a term in common usage. While wishing to dissociate ourselves from its value connotations, we shall therefore employ it *faute de mieux* in the discussion that follows.

As with gender, the structured inequalities associated with race and ethnicity in the wider society can also be discerned in the academy. Much the same overall patterns exist in the USA and the UK and elsewhere in terms of these inequalities, though there are fewer academic members of minority ethnic groups (MEGs) than there are academic women, and many subdivisions and much diversity within the overall category. The academic profession remains predominantly 'white' in both the UK and USA. In the USA there was little change in the last decade of the twentieth century: a fraction over 90 per cent of academic staff in US colleges and universities were white/Caucasian (Sax *et al.* 1999). Generally in the USA the lower the status of the institution the more members of MEGs are to be found on the staff: the figures are higher in 2-year as against 4-year colleges and in public as against private universities. There are, however, internal differences among the constituent minority groups: for example a higher percentage of Asian and Asian American staff in 4-year than 2-year colleges (Sax *et al.* 1999). In the UK the statistics are called into question because large numbers of respondents refuse to give information about their ethnic origin and because of limitations in the categories they use (Modood and Acland 1998;

Singh 1998). However, of those UK academic staff providing the relevant information, 92 per cent were 'white' while those putting themselves in the Indian, Asian other and Chinese categories greatly outnumbered other minority groups. The lower status post-1992 universities in metropolitan locations tended to have larger proportions of staff from MEGs than the older chartered universities. Middlesex University was at the upper end of representation with a reported 130 staff (15 per cent) belonging in the 'minority' category while the comparable figures for many chartered universities were around 5 per cent of staff and only around 1 or 2 per cent for some smaller, specialized institutions (HESA 1999).

There are also differences by discipline: in the UK much higher proportions of at least some MEGs are found in business and management, nursing and paramedical studies and electrical, electronic and computer engineering than in geography, the humanities or design and the creative arts (HESA 1999). Very similar patterns pertain in the USA, with only minor changes over time but considerable variation across the different categories of ethnic origin (Kirshstein *et al.* 1997).

As might be expected the distribution of members of MEGs across the academic ranks mirrors that noted in relation to gender. In both the UK and the USA most academics from MEGs are to be found in the lower grades of lecturing and research appointments and among those on short term or part-time contracts, with this pattern being most pronounced in the higher status institutions (Kirshstein *et al.* 1997; HESA 1999). Partly as a result of this, average salaries are lower, though in the USA Asian/Pacific Islander and Hispanic faculty constitute an exception (Nettles *et al.* 2000). In sharp distinction from women, there are few members of minority groups in the UK on teaching-only contracts, and a comparatively high proportion engaged only in research (the majority with non-tenure contracts) or in both teaching and research roles (HESA 1999): though again, however, this varies according to the particular minority group considered.

The patterns of causal factors lying behind these phenomena are complex. The Higher Education Research Institute report (Sax *et al.* 1999) identifies the importance of continued under-representation of minority groups among doctoral degree recipients, but this is simply another phenomenon to be explained. The findings of industrial tribunals point towards the existence of some real discriminatory practices in some parts of the UK HE system (Singh 1998).

Singh quotes a finding against an English chartered university in a racial discrimination case. The tribunal found the university 'negative, inadequate and hostile' in its treatment of the law lecturer involved (1998: 145). This can have important implications for the identity of staff members from minority ethnic groups too, as this native American Canadian respondent in the new academics study (Trowler and Knight 1999) shows:

> I went to the Dean and 'I said I don't want to be socialized into this system. I don't know how long I'm going to last here because there are

so many things that are against who I am, in conflict with who I am as an individual' . . . [There are areas in which I] can't say the kind of things I really want to. If I really start on the meat and potatoes, the real essence, the core where some of this stuff is coming from, then it's like all of a sudden the person is gone.

(Respondent 17, female, teacher education, Canadian university)

Institutional policies, or the lack of them, concerned with promoting awareness of racism and procedures for monitoring recruitment, selection and promotion practices are a significant concern (Modood and Acland 1998). While universities simply mirror the discriminatory tendencies in the larger society, their cultures, curricula and pedagogical practices are in some cases unsympathetic to those who are not from the dominant ethnic backgrounds. Esmail and Dewart (1998) investigated the fact that in 1994 all ten students who failed the clinical practice element of Manchester University's medical course were males with an Asian heritage. They identify a number of crucial factors in explaining this. These included the fact that assessement was face-to-face, exclusively involved white examiners and patients, lacked clear assessment criteria, and that examiners were not teachers but practicing medics. In addition the prevailing stereotype of Asian medical students was that they quickly 'hit the books', were good theoretically but weaker in clinical practice. In combination these factors all contributed to these students' failure according to Esmail and Dewart. This case highlights both generic factors and those unique to a particular course of study that may be detrimental for particular groups. It also shows the danger of isolating race alone as the key factor in disadvantage: the Asian women students were as successful as their white counterparts.

Allen (1998), looking more generally at the culture of the academy, suggests that the 'ivory tower' marginalizes the black perspective, black researchers and the black experience making it a very uncomfortable environment for black students and the few black staff found there. While students can create their own 'black space' the tower itself needs to become 'blacker in culture, blacker in ethos and blacker in understanding' (Allen 1998: 95).

However, even in universities that recognize and respond to issues of race and ethnicity problems remain. Padilla (1994) points to the burden of 'cultural taxation', which uniquely affects minority faculty:

> 'Cultural taxation' is the obligation to show good citizenship toward the institution by serving its needs for ethnic representation on committees, or to demonstrate knowledge and commitment to a cultural group, which may even bring accolades to the institution but which is not usually rewarded by the institution on whose behalf the service was performed.
>
> (Padilla 1994: 26)

This indirect form of discrimination was evident among Tierney and Bensimon's sample of academics. It meant that maintaining a research agenda in their discipline and to achieve tenure or promotion on the basis of it was considerably harder for minority faculty than it was for their white colleagues. They also note another form of cultural taxation: the 'commodification of race or ethnicity to make an institution look good' (Tierney and Bensimon 1996: 117).

The underlying attitudes that contribute to the current situation can only change in the long term, and the improvements Allen would like to see will inevitably be slow in coming. However shorter term changes to, for example, induction and other organizational practices can have an impact (Trowler and Knight 1999). In particular they can stop, or at least slow down, the 'revolving door' into universities for minority academic staff (Cross 1991).

It needs, finally, to be reiterated that accounts which treat race, gender and other aspects of socially structured inequalities as separate categories tend to play down their complex and potentially significant interconnections, as do data collected and presented in terms of one category at a time. As Acker points out (1994: 143), 'we have no easy way of assessing the combined effects of class, sex, "race" and other characteristics . . . on subject specialties, promotion prospects, or any other aspect of being an academic'. Such factors can, moreover, operate in contradictory ways, making it difficult to develop policies to counteract them. As one black female academic quoted by Morley (1994: 199) notes:

> 'We [black women] get tokenized and exploited by white women too . . . many of whom describe themselves as feminists . . . I have lost count of how many times I have been asked to contribute to books and conferences at the eleventh hour, that is, when they've suddenly realised the "black perspective" is missing'.

Notes

1. In this connection, Mulkay (1977) observes that 'graduate students, who naturally find it difficult to compete with mature scientists, are often given research topics which are somewhat peripheral and which are, therefore unlikely to attract the attention of older and more experienced researchers.'
2. Knorr Cetina (1982) argues that the exploitation here, as in the case of research students, is mutual. She cites the case of a postdoctoral researcher who complained that he was 'being used' by the head of his laboratory:

> The post-doc conducted all the research in a project [acted as overseer to] students and technicians, and came up with ideas . . . His name appeared on papers but not on patents which resulted from the research, and it was the head of the laboratory who decided when and where to publish, and who presented the work at conferences. However, while the head of the laboratory was using the post-doc to 'run' the project, the post-doc was using the head of the laboratory to promote his own career. He came to the laboratory to get access to journals, research money and 'hot' research

topics; and he thought that his affiliation with a prestigious institute would enable him to get a high-paying, high-prestige position.

3. 'A scientist rarely makes a career decision more consequential than the selection of a problem for research' (Gieryn 1978).

4. Thagaard (1987), by way of illustration, writes: 'According to my interviews with physicists and chemists it was emphasized that 10 years (including the graduate study) was necessary in order to qualify for work at the research frontier.'

5. As one biologist in the sample observed, 'it can be traumatic to go back to being a student when you've earned a reputation in your field'. Another remarked, 'if you invest a lot of effort in learning a difficult technique, you naturally want to use it to the maximum advantage – you have to think twice about picking up a different one'.

6. It is interesting to note how closely these (epistemologically based) comments echo the (sociologically based) assertion by Griffith and Mullins (1972), quoted on p. 93, that the typical lifespan of a successful 'coherent social group' in science is 10–15 years.

7. In his study of 'specialization and change in academic careers', Ziman (1987) argues that 'most scientists do in fact change their research specialties substantially in the course of their lives', but adds that they 'actually change . . . quite gradually . . . Again and again, scientists described the evolution of their research interests as an unplanned process of gradual drift.' His sample was, however, wider than that of most writers on the topic, in that it included career scientists in freestanding research establishments, government laboratories and private industry, along with a small minority holding academic posts.

8. A view that received authoritative endorsement from G.H. Hardy in his well-known and widely-read *A Mathematician's Apology* (1941). The claim is directly contradicted, on the basis of citation analysis, by Stern (1978): 'no clearcut relationship exists between age and productivity, or between age and quality of work. The claim that younger mathematicians (whether for physiological or sociological reasons) are more apt to create important work is, then, unsubstantiated.' Stern attributes an apparent dip in productivity in the 45–49 age group to increased administrative responsibilities at that career point.

9. This is surprising, insofar as the chemists among the respondents tended to the view that chemical physicists reached the end of their useful lives earlier than natural product chemists, but that in the case of the latter (to mix a metaphor) 'people usually blossom by their mid-thirties and then reach a plateau'. Comments were that 'there is no very obvious mid-career crisis – some people do allow themselves to become a bit out of date and old-fashioned but there is always new stuff to assimilate and nothing to keep you from doing research', and that 'some people are productive to incredible ages'.

10. Lehman claims that these 'early maxima' are steadily decreasing. The peaks in most fields tend to occur at younger ages in the twentieth century than they did in the eighteenth or nineteenth.

11. More specifically, he quotes the average age for physicists as 45–6 and for chemists as about 50. The youngest prize winner in physics was 25, and the youngest in chemistry 35. A total of 31 per cent of the physicists were under 40; the corresponding figure for chemists was only 13 per cent.

12. This is not altogether consistent with her earlier acquiescence with Lehman that the highest productivity is to be found in the 30s (see the chapter on 'Age, ageing and age structure in science' in Merton 1973).

13. Terman (1954) notes that the physical scientists who formed part of his study frequently cited their work as their greatest source of life satisfaction. Mitroff (1974) concurs with Roe (1953) that all eminent scientists seem to have a strong devotion to their work, and that this spills into their weekends, holidays and all the time available.
14. A typical comment was that of a physicist interviewed for this study: 'Teaching is one of the best ways to familiarize yourself with a new area of science which you aren't currently researching.'
15. The proportion was roughly comparable with contemporary statistics for the UK universities as a whole, which showed the percentage of women full-time staff on academic and related grades as some 17 per cent of the total, and the percentage 'wholly university financed' as about 10 per cent (University Grants Committee 1987). Historically, the comparable US figures were much higher, fluctuating between 20 and 28 per cent for the HE system as a whole between 1889 and 1959 (Bernard 1964).
16. These considerations may help to explain the small proportion of women interviewed in the initial sample of elite academics.
17. McDowell (1984) advances an ingenious argument suggesting that women may be attracted into disciplines in which the obsolescence of knowledge is relatively low, and which therefore exact fewer penalties on interrupted careers.

8
The Wider Context

The academy in the marketplace

So far, the considerations that have been advanced – apart from those in Chapter 1 – have rested on a particular, restricted view of the world of learning. We have set out in Chapters 2–7 to explore a problem that lies at the margins of the sociology of knowledge and the study of HE; namely, how the nature of knowledge is related to the cultures of those who explore it. To make sense of the complexities that beset this issue, we have pushed into the background those contextual factors which, however intrinsically important, seem to bear on it only indirectly. In attempting at this point to set the findings into a wider framework, we again pose a deliberately limited ambition, invoking the broader questions of knowledge and society only insofar as they seem relevant to the themes already addressed. The question of how individual academics relate to the larger society they inhabit offers a suitable point of departure for the *tour d'horizon*.

One hackneyed image of the world of learning – for a variety of reasons less in vogue now than it was in bygone times – is that of the ivory tower. There is of course some comfort as well as some scholarly benefit to be drawn from a cloistered withdrawal from the everyday world. Though dons might be written off as 'remote and ineffectual' – as Hilaire Belloc once scathingly dubbed them – on another reading, any such sense of isolation has always been more illusory than real. As Barnett (1988) maintains, 'higher eduction in the modern world is inescapably bound into its host society'. Rothblatt (1985) is equally unequivocal in repudiating the notion of academics:

> as busily pursuing their work with no other consideration but the intrinsic pleasure of the intellectual task itself. That there is an intrinsic pleasure I will not deny, but that the pursuit of knowledge can be discussed apart from all the other pressures that affect human activity even of the most cerebral sort no one, I am certain, would defend. In

this the economists have a point. Intellectual work must be supported
by an economic surplus. How that surplus is sought and allocated is of
great significance in discussing the autonomy of intellectual work.

Academics no longer have a choice: whether they like it or not the market
and the state intrude in a variety of ways into their lives and work. For many
there is a fundamental conflict between quality audits and entrepreneurial
pressures on the one hand and academic norms and values on the other.
Rothblatt (1985) goes on to refer to:

> two different sets of pressures . . . The first . . . consists of outside demands
> for a wide range of scientific services [originating] in government, in
> the military, in industry, or more vaguely from the public . . . The
> second set of pressures . . . derive[s] from the internal constitution of
> science, from its cultural or value system and from the institutions that
> scientists themselves have built or have cooperated in building in order
> to maximise the conditions under which their work is performed.

Gibbons (1985), in his approach to the same issue, writes of:

> the tension between the way science (or knowledge) is used in our
> societies and the way in which it is supposed to be generated. The
> tension arises because it is not clear whether the knowledge that is
> generated is being used properly or whether if it were to be generated
> properly it would be usable.

Something of this tension between intrinsic and extrinsic considerations
was touched on by J.D. Bernal as long ago as 1939. But it has come more
sharply into view among sociologists of science more recently 'at a time
when science has become more capital intensive while economic policies
call for constraints and cutbacks in various sectors in society' (Elzinga 1987b).
The increasingly political and commercial orientation of science is not,
however, in Elzinga's (1987b) view, a purely one-way process. He rejects
the notion advanced by Weingart (1974) and others that 'external social
influences are translated into cognitive developments and these, in turn,
are translated into society' in favour of a more strongly reciprocal 'process
of mutual accommodation and mediation'. The view he favours is of 'a
complex interrelation of deinstitutionalization or reinstitutionalization of
science on the one hand, and a scientification of society on the other'. As
Elzinga (1987b) goes on to argue:

> social and cognitive regulative structures interplay with each other.
> In practice it is often impossible to draw a clear-cut line between the
> two. Truth-claiming activities are at one and the same time social
> power claiming activities in the real world of science in society . . . As
> power- and knowledge-claiming structures in society change and
> become more reliant on basic research, knowledge- and power-claiming
> activities in science become at the same time selectively facilitated and
> constrained.

The mutuality of the relationship between cognitive developments and social influences is perhaps at its most evident in the domains of the natural sciences and the science-based professions. Certainly, a major part of what has been written on the topic has been couched in terms of scientific and technological issues. It is even easier, therefore, to overlook the rather different sets of considerations that relate to the humanities and social sciences on the one hand and the social professions on the other. We attempt where possible in the ensuing discussion to take them into account. However, we are not in a position to give more than a brief mention to the equally important but distinctive interplay between undergraduate teaching and external demands because it lay outside the scope of the initial enquiry.

Academics as social animals

Rothblatt's (1985) contention that 'Intellectual work must be supported by an economic surplus' applies in a direct and obvious way to the individual academic. The general economic climate is one of the main factors conditioning whether HE is in a period of growth, stasis or contraction. In the boom years of the 1960s, HE in many countries expanded: academic jobs were plentiful and there were good prospects of early advancement and promotion. In the recession of the 1970s and the relative stasis of early 1980s, the opposite was the case: tenured posts were hard to come by, the competition for them fierce and the waiting period in some disciplines long; senior positions were not always replaced after their incumbents retired; and career opportunities were relatively limited. In the UK the shift to 'mass' HE, which began in the late 1980s, led to a resurgence in appointments to academic posts, though not in keeping with the increase in student numbers because student–staff ratios fell as student numbers rose (NCIHE 1997).

There are other less immediately evident but nonetheless important ways in which an academic's professional life may affect, and be affected by, the wider social environment in which he or she works. In some cases, the research an academic does may have significant implications for the world outside the scholarly cloister. Many of the now taken-for-granted improvements in the quality of human life, and many of the benefits of technological advance, can be traced back to their origins in academic enquiry and exploration. On the darker side, physicists may share a particular sense of responsibility for the creation of atomic and nuclear weapons, and engineers for the dubious blessings of nuclear power. Chemistry has given rise to its own forms of weaponry; biology to the possibility of bacteriological warfare and, along another pathway, to the ethical uncertainties of genetic engineering. The pure and applied sciences are not alone in their openness to such accusations. The appeal to history lies behind some of the most bitter territorial and racial disputes; sociological theorizing has given birth to powerful and sometimes destructive ideological movements; economics shares some of the blame for disastrous financial policies as well as some of the credit for successful ones. All in all, the outcome of research must be rated as a mixed blessing to humanity.

But this kind of argument allows for two possible responses, and which one is adopted remains a matter of individual conscience. Some academics may be ready to go along with the general concern that their research has real or potential negative effects; others will wish to dissociate themselves from the implications of their work, arguing that whether and how it is exploited is a matter for collective social responsibility. Thus, while there are those among the older generation of physicists who seek expiation in the wake of Hiroshima by what one of respondents dubbed as 'indulging their social consciences', the engineers – in keeping with their pragmatic tradition – tend to stand aside from the politics of protest about Chernobyl and its counterparts, their natural line of argument being that if a thing works it must be good, and that one day it will be rendered foolproof. 'Engineers', remarked one of them, 'have no social conscience, though some pay lip service to the idea that they should.' Again, the ancestral philosophers whose ideologies were used to justify the Nazi movement might well, had they been alive at the time, have denied responsibility for the particular ways in which their views were interpreted and put into effect.

The decision to engage in social action or to avoid it extends also to those problem areas to which research may seem to offer some answer or amelioration, whether or not they were the original concern of academics. Not many of the UK biologists in the initial sample chose to involve themselves in ecological or other pressure groups, not only because they were generally seen as too time-consuming, and because their members were inclined to take an over-simple view of the issues, but also because such activity 'adds nothing to your professional prestige'. On the other side of the Atlantic, respondents commented on a growing interest in matters of social moment – but there, too, 'there are still plenty of biologists who don't give a damn'. On the whole, it is wiser simply to steer clear of controversial issues. Again, academic pharmacists are not often in the front line of those engaged in tackling drug abuse. The more ambitious and successful economists, one informant noted, are attracted by intellectual rather than by social and political issues – they take the view that ethical considerations are 'not my problem'. Historians commonly prefer to avoid relating their scholarly concerns to contemporary affairs, on the grounds that generalization from one situation to another is highly suspect. Sociologists, in contrast, have fewer inhibitions in connecting their academic stances with their attitudes towards wider political issues, though they may prefer to do so from the comfort of the armchair than in the rough-and-tumble of the hustings or the demonstration rally.[1]

Alongside the cases we have considered so far, of research that has helped to generate a particular set of social issues, or which may have a relevant response to a particular set of social demands, there are instances in which academic work may in its turn be affected by external factors. The values, causes and philosophies that academics as individuals espouse will often have their biographical origins outside the library or laboratory. Their most obvious manifestations are likely to be in knowledge areas which are themselves value-laden. The findings of the study confirm that economics and sociology are disciplines in which a practitioner's value position may show up in his or her work: right-wing economists tend to espouse one set of theories and left-wing economists another, and quite a few sociologists would regard themselves as 'being on the side of the underdog'. Historians, in common with sociologists, would seldom contemplate using 'biased' as a term of criticism, because 'it is taken for granted that every historian is biased in one way or another'. Nevertheless, a distinction may be drawn here between being committed to a set of values (and perhaps allowing them to influence one's choice of specialism), and letting them 'impose a pattern on the past', or 'distorting evidence to fit preconceptions', as is arguably the case with at least one English historian's notorious dismissal of the holocaust. The position of academic lawyers is more complex. According to the informants, there is 'a craft tradition of constructing arguments from different sets of values', in a profession in which a well-formulated legal argument is considered as being independent of the side of the case it takes. Traditionalists 'pretend to be practising a Weberian, value-free science', and 'would regard the use of the law as a left-wing or right-wing weapon with total horror'. Reformists, on the other hand, see room for a critical function within legal studies: 'there can certainly be bad ideological law, but there can also be good'. Other social professions, such as education, social work and community nursing, allow a more direct, and sometimes painful, relationship between personal belief and occupational practice.

Some fields of enquiry would appear less open than others to the influence of external ideology and less hospitable to imported values. It may be over-simplistic to equate this difference to the distinction between disciplines concerned with things and disciplines concerned with people. In a sense, engineering is concerned with both, but academic engineers as a group tend to portray their work as value-free and apolitical. Even so, none of the mathematicians, physicists or chemists interviewed for this study could identify any part of their practice as subject to outside doctrinal influence, except in the very general sense that someone's world-view might influence his or her professional judgement – though a predilection for one theory against another was not, it was pointed out, immune to the subsequent demonstration of falsity. Although, among many others, Rose and Rose (1974) argue in convincing terms against the supposed neutrality of science, it is perhaps significant that they choose neurobiology as their subject, and show its rival approaches to reflect particular views about human beings.

The relationships here may sometimes be as profound and elusive as the workings of the Zeitgeist itself. As Foucault's (1970) influential study of *The Order of Things* implies, what people see and understand is conditioned by the contemporary intellectual climate.[2] Values may be unconsciously as well as consciously assimilated: academics 'may find themselves subject to "sea changes in social thought" running through society', as Henkel (1987) observes. Perhaps it is this phenomenon which lies behind her suggestion that 'academic values are being transformed . . . an inevitable process as academics are exposed to more external norms and influences'. More specifically, in relation to history, Wesseling (1985) remarks on the 'vague and unconscious' response of researchers to 'what actually goes on in society', adding that 'rather more unconsciously than consciously, society has an influence on what kind of historical research tends to be undertaken'.

The process of internalization of values may in some instances be calculated rather than inadvertent. Henkel (1987) remarks that:

> Academics are not, for the most part, helpless pawns in others' games. They are reading the changes and adapting in order to sustain their positions. Where they can, they are coopting external funders and strengthening their currency in the institutional and student market place.

Writing about the same study ('the responsiveness of higher education to external influences'), Kogan (1987) makes a related point, quoting one academic as saying 'we often work not with direct knowledge of what the external pressures are but with our own constructions and myths of what they are and what they might be'; and 'the important thing is the internal perception of what the exogenous pressures are'. But there is evidence also of resistance, of a reluctance or refusal to go along with external trends. Another of those interviewed saw it as possible for academics to remain as 'specialists not much touched by pressure from outside influences', and a third claimed that 'The threats from the environment are translated into justifications for what they are already doing.'

In Trowler's study of NewU (1998a) it became clear that some academic staff were interpreting and using the 'requirements' of professional bodies to support a position which they already held. Moreover research into policy implementation suggests that important interpretive processes occur as policy is received at the ground level, leading to the phenomenon of 'policy refraction' (Lingard and Garrick 1997). Again, Trowler's study indicated that a number of factors were influential in this process, including academics' interpretations of epistemological constraints as well as external cultural and ideological influences. A useful metaphor here is that of a tidal river. There is an inward and outward flow as well as movement within; impediments (rocks in the river, contentious issues within the institution) cause eddies and channel the current into new configurations. Over time the flow may re-align or even erode, the impediments. Cultural flow into and through each institution is dynamic and complex: close attention must be paid to the important streams if the researcher hopes to come close to understanding its nature and impact in any particular context. In considering the influence of external forces Kogan (1987) concludes:

> managerial, centralising and instrumental rhetoric [has] had some effects on structure and on the disposition and content of courses. It is

not evident, however, that the underlying knowledge rules or intellectual ambitions . . . have changed. Teaching in this respect may change whilst research and scholarship continue to change less in response to system demands . . . It is fair to assume that when change is imposed from the outside for reasons which the academy may not always share, the rhetoric of change will overreach its actuality.

This may be to overstate the case. While Trowler's study of the discourse and epistemological assumptions that underpin managerialism and the New Higher Education (Trowler 2001) questions an unalloyed notion of 'discursive capture' (the notion that individuals' view of the world is limited by dominant discourses), it notes that considerable effort has to be expended to resist dominant discourses. Similarly the Lancaster University project on new managerialism in HE found extensive use of new managerialist discourse among managers in the study. Sometimes this was used unreflectively or even positively; sometimes ironically or as part of a 'bilingual' performance (Deem 1998). Craig Prichard (2000) uses the concepts of 'managerial station' and 'locale' to illuminate this issue: the managerial station refers to managerialist discourse and ideology while the concept of locale highlights the situationally contingent reception to it on the ground. While there is an attempt by a combination of forces with similar interests (the 'power bloc') to impose the managerial station through a variety of mechanisms, there is resistance, reinterpretation and reconstruction at locales at the ground level. Similar processes, were mapped in Trowler's NewU study.

Faced with this multiplicity of considerations, only two general points may confidently be made. The first is that certain significant differences continue to manifest themselves between different knowledge fields (though, as an aside, the picture is complicated here as elsewhere by the fact that a particular subject area may embrace not only topics which are discernibly of social relevance and ones which are not, but also both relatively value-free and heavily value-laden elements). The second is that the pattern of involvement of academics with political and social issues outside academe can be seen to stem in part from their personal or professional concerns, but in comparably large part from extraneous considerations.

Outside influences on specialist groups

New considerations arise in turning from an assessment of how the outside world impinges on the aspirations and values of individual academics to a review of its effects on specialist groups, and in particular on the structure of their communication networks and the organization of their research activities.

Viewed in collective terms, research on a given topic may be enhanced by intellectual and technological developments outside its confines. As we have already seen, theories and techniques generated in one milieu may turn out to be productively applied elsewhere; instrumentation developed in one setting may be the occasion of significant advances in another. Computing provides a clear example of a facility that has affected the shape of many research fields. Contributions of this kind, while external from the perspective of a particular specialism, remain for the most part internal to the academic world as a whole.

The availability in practice of expensive equipment, and of the technical support that goes with it, must however be a reflection of economic circumstance. As Henkel (1987) notes, 'the capacity . . . to attract [research contracts] is an important criterion of evaluation . . . particularly where the acquisition of modern equipment, often essential even for keeping pace with a fast developing subject, depends upon it'. Thagaard (1987), in turn, emphasizes the importance of underpinning of this kind in many areas of pure and applied science, reminding us that 'Research instruments do not only influence the choice of research problems but also the organisation of research. Advanced and expensive machinery requires large-scale organisation of scientific work' – thus depriving the individual academic of some measure of freedom of choice (Ravetz 1971; Ziman 1981).

Economic constraints bear more harshly on the urban, capital-intensive areas of 'big science' than on the rural, labour-intensive pastures of the humanities and social sciences. But other types of sanction may affect hard and soft, pure and applied areas alike. Lay questioning of, or even in some cases formal legislation against, academic practice may be manifest in such ethically sensitive areas as genetic experimentation, the treatment of laboratory animals, the study of sexual behaviour, the critical acknowledgement of pornographic literature, or mental testing research which appears to contravene the requirements of racial equality. Political hostilities may be aroused outside as well as within academia at the promulgation of what may be labelled as seditious or blasphemous views, or at the apparent endorsement of socially – or morally – subversive writings. On the wider scene, as we saw in Chapter 1, demands for greater social and economic relevance in research and calls for increased academic accountability have accompanied the rise of neo-liberal politics; meanwhile the new managerialism raises concerns about organizational efficiency and the ability of HE to offer taxpayers and other 'consumers' good value for money.

Reflecting this change, national HE policies in the UK, the USA and elsewhere have been moving with apparent inevitability both towards an emphasis on a particularly utilitarian version of 'knowing how', performative knowledge (Barnett 2000), rather than 'knowing what', propositional knowledge, and towards a concurrent demand for economic relevance. This was particularly evident during the Thatcher years in the UK: the 1991 White Paper *Higher Education a New Framework* (later to reach legislation as the 1992 Further and Higher Education Act) was described by Martin Trow (1994: 13) as 'a document of hard managerialism'. It underlined the human capital functions of universities as against their liberal ideals, and stressed efficiency and economy in provision.

There is alongside this a growing tendency for political and media interests to combine in promulgating moral panics about one profession or another, usually instigated when one 'bad apple' hits the headlines (Becher 1999). That particular case is then used to indict a whole profession and so to justify further regulation of it, in a 'panic-then-control' cycle identified and theoretically elaborated some years ago by the Birmingham Centre for Contemporary Cultural Studies (Hall 1978). This process has already begun in relation to the academic profession in the USA (Altbach 1997: 315) and seems likely only to further intensify and spread.

We need to return later to the call for relevance, since this poses a fundamental problem in relation to the autonomy of research communities. It may be useful first, however, to look at another less clearly visible form of inhibition on research activity, namely the way in which academia is itself predominantly organized. One of the physicists interviewed expressed a concern, on the basis of his personal experience, at the way in which a promising research topic could 'fall into the cracks' of the specialist areas recognized as legitimate by the established academic peer groups and the funding agencies acting on the basis of their expert advice. One effective way round this difficulty, Geiger (1987) suggests, has been the development of 'organized research units' (ORUs) set up within universities to accommodate forms of research that 'did not fit into the departmental structure, usually for reasons of size, duration and/or purpose'. He shows ORUs to be an important component in the recent development of academic research:

> the American university department, despite its considerable flexibility, is an inherently conservative institution when it comes to assimilating new forms of knowledge, particularly when this depends upon making additional appointments. In terms of conducting research . . . ORUs exist to do what departments cannot do: i.e. to expand into interdisciplinary, applied, or capital intensive areas in response to social demands for new knowledge.

Similarly Henkel (1997) notes the development of a 'centralized decentralization' with devolved budgeting and decision making accorded to such centres but within tight, centrally-controlled parameters. Clark (1998) in turn contends that the characteristics of entrepreneurial universities include an expanded developmental periphery and a stimulated academic heartland which, together with other characteristics, lead to 'concentric entrepreneurialism'. Dooris and Fairweather (1994) also cite these trends, but caution that the effectiveness of ORUs depends on their compatibility with existing structures and academic cultures: in its absence their potential to bring about institutional change in directions desired by institutional managers can be quite limited.

In his 1987 study Geiger introduces the distinction between interested and disinterested research: the 'concern of the investigator' in the latter being 'with the validity of the knowledge contribution, not with whatever use might be made of it', and the former being typically initiated by a sponsor whose financial support would be 'predicated on the probability that the investigator's knowledge contribution would, at least in the long run, have utility'. Geiger emphasizes that 'the basic-applied axis of research [is] by no means coextensive with the interested-disinterested axis': funding agencies may have an interest in basic research in the expectation that it could ultimately have some practical pay-off, and some applied research activities may be undertaken for their own sakes and not with an ulterior end in view.[3]

Elzinga (1987b) provides a detailed exploration of the way in which fundamental research may be supported for extrinsic reasons:

> Support to basic research has become selective, and the criteria of selection are ultimately tied to an industrial economic policy or social policy agenda in society. Basic research that can rapidly be exploited or which holds potential for future technological markets tends to be favoured. Thus demands of societal relevance are transferred from the field of applied science into fundamental research ... Legitimations of decisions in academic research are increasingly involving such 'externalist' considerations as social relevance, utility and appropriateness that were traditionally reserved for mission-oriented and sectoral research projects and programs.

Accordingly, Elzinga suggests, 'it has become difficult to separate basic science from applied science, because the political goal-setting and prioritising perspective has come into the picture so centrally'. What this amounts to is a process of 'epistemic drift', which he defines variously as 'a shift from a traditional reputational control system associated with disciplinary science to one that is disengaged from disciplinary science and, thus, more open to external regulation by governmental and managerial policy impositions' (Elzinga 1985); and 'the tendency whereby knowledge structures and social structures within the university system tend to become reorganised into dysfunctional patterns when research communities come under strong external pressures of relevance and accountability' (Elzinga 1987a).

There are, as Elzinga (1987a) sees it, two distinct causes of epistemic drift:

> a continuing pressure of mandating science in line with political and bureaucratic decision-making institutions, and via the pressure of market forces at a time when emerging technology clusters like microelectronics, biotechnology and advanced industrial materials have to be based on strategic reserves of basic research.

The first of these tends to push research towards 'politicization' or 'socialization' – 'state dirigisme or orientation deriving from government'. The resulting 'externally based regulatives and controls ... may crystallise around sectoral functions of knowledge utilisation (housing, defence, development aid, health care, social problems, etc.) ... or it may be around social and political movements (environment, women, black studies, etc)'. The second, market forces, tends to pull research towards 'commercialization' or 'privatization'; hence the phenomenon of 'science and technology parks, . . . little "Silicon valleys", cropping up around . . . universities' (Elzinga 1987a) – 'a case of multi-national capital buying itself a ringside seat in the arena of Big Science' (Elzinga 1987b).[4]

The vulnerability to epistemic drift is not of course confined to hard pure areas. Among soft pure academic communities, those in the social sciences are also susceptible to industrial sponsorship and consultancy, although the direction their research takes is, in general, more likely to be dominated by state agencies and government-funded research councils with a bias towards enquiry which can be represented as socially useful. There appears to be an increasing emphasis on the political acceptability of research results in these disciplines, with funding agencies stipulating ever-closer controls on dissemination of the results (Maguire and Ball 1994; Halpin and Troyna 1994).

Research in the humanities, however, is more immune from these pressures, both because the contribution it is able to make to the wider society is less directly utilitarian, and because – for the reasons explored in earlier chapters – scholarly enquiry of this kind is neither readily amenable to large-scale collective activity nor for the most part financially demanding. But *ipso facto* its comparative freedom from the fetters of government and commerce is won at the expense of a philistine perception that it is marginal and irrelevant as well as small-scale and trivial. The notion of epistemic drift is also less obviously relevant to research in the technological or social professions, though for a very different reason. They, it is commonly assumed, have nowhere left to drift to, being in part beholden to the larger professional groups whose research and training interests they represent, and for the rest under the sway of private and governmental industry (including defence) in the case of hard applied research groups and of the relevant ministries and social welfare agencies in the case of soft applied ones.

Organized research units, as Geiger (1987) shows, can play an important part as intermediaries between sponsors and the specialist communities whose know-how they seek to commandeer: 'the utilization of ORUs has allowed American universities to expand selected parts of their research commitments without significantly affecting their fundamental instructional mission as represented in academic departments'. In more abstract terms, van den Daele *et al.* (1977) refer to 'new forms of institutionalization and new communication structures', adding that 'The external problems set by science policy programs become foci for the formation of new communities.' They dub these 'hybrid communities', because they typically comprise researchers from a variety of different specialisms, together with non-scientists. Hybrid communities, they go on to assert, develop their own 'evaluation standards, reputation structures and career patterns'. Whitley (1982) takes up the argument, noting that 'scientific ideals and goals become altered to accommodate themselves to these new relations [with the medical, business and political establishments], as new reputational communities have established themselves around non-academic or quasi-academic goals'. The contrast is sharpened by Elzinga (1987a):[5] 'Traditional systems are ones where reputation accrues through internal recognition and peer review; in the new reputational systems reputation may be linked to recognition of services to an external economic or political elite.'

Elizinga here returns to his earlier contention that the relationship between 'social and cognitive regulative structures' is by no means unidirectional: 'External processes of stimulation, professionalization, sectoralization, etc. do not effect organizational and epistemic structural changes directly in higher educational systems, but rather by mediation, for example by hybrid communities and broker communities'; and at the same time 'a good "hybrid research community" that is associated with a particular field of research is one that is also successful in representing the interests of the research community and getting money, positions and resources'. Rip (1981), in his critique of the earlier account of hybrid communities by van den Daele *et al.* (1977), agrees that 'the appearance of hybrid communities is an indicator for an attempt at political direction of science, while its success depends on the institutionalization of the external regulatives in a manner compatible with the internal regulatives'. He also endorses a further important point:

> the cognitive state of a discipline and the nature of its internal regulatives are independent variables determining the attitudes of scientists towards external orientation. This implies that resistance of scientists cannot always be reduced by the institutional measures that administrators can take (e.g. money, opportunities, career structure), and that science policy has to take the cognitive aspects of its policy object into account.
>
> (Rip 1981)

In other words, too exclusive a concentration on the (admittedly intriguing) processes of negotiation between specialist research communities on the one hand and the paymasters who wish to harness them to secular goals on the other plays down two fundamental points: first, that it is knowledge, viewed as a commodity, that forms the object of their shared concern; but, second, that knowledge is more than a mere commodity, subject to paper transactions. Much of the previous discussion has been concerned to establish that its development cannot be represented simply as a by-product of, or (as the relativists would have it) a chimera created by, social, economic and political considerations within and outside academia.

Disciplinary status and power

We now consider disciplines as a whole, rather than as conglomerates of individuals or specialist groups. One useful approach to their relationship with their environment is to consider how they are brought into being, the conditions for their survival, and what happens to them in decline.

There seems to be agreement on two distinct modes of genesis, though the variations on both modes are presented in a plurality of guises (compare Blume 1985; Elzinga 1987a; Becher and Kogan 1992). In the most basic terms, there are those disciplines that owe their origins to internal causes, and those which come into being for reasons that lie outside the sphere of purely academic influence. Disciplines that are internally generated need not concern us here. It may nevertheless be remarked in passing that Becher and Kogan see them as stemming either from fission, the process by which a large and increasingly independent specialism breaks away from the parent discipline to establish an autonomous existence (as in the secession of computing from mathematics), or from fusion, the mechanism that governs the amalgamation of two overlapping specialisms from different disciplines and their subsequent emergence as a new field (as in the birth of biochemistry from a fertile liaison between biology and chemistry). Blume refers instead to differentiation (a concept close to, if not identical with, fission) and extension, which he describes as 'the attempt to extend the scope of science to cover areas of experience, phenomena, where previously there was no science', giving as instances psychoanalysis as developed by Freud and the origination by I.A. Richards of practical criticism in literature.

Externally generated disciplines provide a clear example of the interaction between academia and the world that lies beyond its confines. Becher and Kogan draw attention to a single pattern of origination, namely that stemming from potential market demand. They characterize the responsiveness to market considerations as 'particularly marked in relation to vocational courses', such as accountancy and nursing, whose establishment depends on their being seen both as 'academically acceptable and as viable in terms of student numbers'. The same process is identified by Blume as professionalization. He gives engineering education as an example, drawing attention to the 'intellectualizing dynamic', which leads to 'greater autonomy, more theoretical instruction, and higher entry requirements . . . the movement to a gradually more theoretically-based curriculum at the expense of earlier practical emphases'. But Blume adds a further 'mode by which new fields of research become established in the university', which he calls external stimulation: 'the development of a technical field [which] begins when someone perceives the potential utility of a particular phenomenon (a natural process or an effect) for serving a particular social function'. Examples of this process would include aeronautical engineering, biotechnology and medical physics, all of which involve 'the reorganization of existing knowledge and the generation of new problem hierarchies . . . around a technical concept or set of such . . . concepts'.

Clark (1996b) and Elzinga (1987a) adopt a more eclectic approach to the emergence and establishment of new disciplines, allowing both for internalist and externalist, and sociological and epistemological accounts of the same phenomenon. We saw in Chapter 1 that Clark's distinction between the processes of subject parturition, subject dispersion, programme affiliation and subject dignification involves both internalist and externalist processes: the first pair being internalist in character while the second pair are externalist. Elzinga's main concern is with external factors of change. Taking up Blume's categories, he argues that external stimulation should include 'the non-technological sciences and varieties of learning', in that the social sciences have administrative uses and the humanities may serve ideological ends: 'Indeed it is not unusual to find new fields of investigation crystallising around . . . new administrative practices, welfare needs or an ideological discourse in society.' The last of these may be exemplified by peace and conflict research, environmental research and women's studies, though Elzinga notes that 'as movements' demands are taken up and trans-lated into researchable problems . . . the research may become encapsulated and lose its radical sting', as a result of its having 'to suit the definitions of corporativist funding bodies'. His general conclusion is that:

> we find in the emergence of some new disciplines a confluence of various different, sometimes contradictory interests and stakes: popular grass root movements, academic disciplines or rather their traditional knowledge 'bearers' with their own disciplines to defend; professionaliza-tion of specific groups of highly qualified or skilled persons in society; and a variety of corporativist interests. Many of the new disciplines that emerged in the seventies . . . did so on the basis of external corporativist or professional stimulation, or else thanks to pressures from below, from popular movements. In both instances it is thus more a question of external motive factors than internal ones.
>
> (Elzinga 1987a)

These comments are reminiscent of Elzinga's previously quoted account of the process of epistemic drift at the level of research specialisms. The comparison is underlined in a further reference (Elzinga 1985) to Blume's four sources of disciplinary origination:

> Blume's conceptual framework allows the successive policy shifts from the 1960s onwards to be interpreted as shifts in focus from cognitive to social factors as central for policy considerations; from having been largely based on or involving a consideration of internalist regulatives, science policy doctrines have come to reflect more strongly the factors belonging to the two externalist processes: socio-economic stimulation and professionalization.

Whatever their origins may be, emergent disciplines must face the competit-ive demands of those which are already established. Crane (1972) observes that, in the development of a new field, 'the existing academic system must be capable of expansion, of creating new positions and new departments in order to absorb the innovation and permit it to develop'. If the newcomer is seen as a threat to established interests, or as a rival claimant for the available resources, its development is likely to be inhibited (Spiegel-Rösing 1974).

From a particular sociological perspective, disciplines may be viewed as engaging in a constant Darwinian struggle for power and status, in which the hardiest and most adaptable flourish while the weakest go to the wall. Henkel (1987) is not alone in discerning the attractions of 'the evolutionary analogy and the concept of the survival of the fittest'. But it also has to be recognized that the competitiveness here is in large measure occasioned by the dependence, noted earlier, of intellectual work on external economic support and on the means by which that support is acquired and distributed. Freedom of research is in general limited by the need to persuade others that the necessary resources should be provided. Unless, as rarely happens, money is available in sufficient abundance to dispense with any competition for it, disciplines are forced into the position of rival interest groups. Their quest for status, which one might see as in some respects analogous with the individual academic's concern with reputation, is stimulated not merely by an intrinsic tribal pride but by an extrinsic need to justify their existence and maintain their collective livelihood. Or as Spiegel-Rösing (1974) puts it, the subjective attribution of status can have objective consequences: status brings the resources essential for the cognitive development of a discipline.

Henkel (1987) points out that disciplines 'may find themselves having to select and adapt strategies on the organisational, normative and political front in order to deal with their changing environment and to compete successfully with rival interests'. The nature of such 'disciplinary strategies of status maintenance' is examined closely in Spiegel-Rösing's discussion of the subject: here, we shall concern ourselves only with a selected few.

One common approach has already been identified in the earlier examination of epistemic drift: the establishment of a claim to external utility. In the exploration by Kogan, Henkel and others of 'the responsiveness of higher education to external influences', Henkel (1987) observes that, with certain important exceptions, 'the power of individual disciplines . . . increasingly depended on their perceived contribution to the economy'. When that contribution must – in the very nature of the subject in question – be indirect at best, the issue can only be argued in more or less far-fetched terms. Thus, a justification may be sought for apparently disinterested research, such as that in particle physics into the ultimate constitution of matter, in terms of the eventual possibility that it will yield applicable results. Such claims are so manifestly implausible in the case of many humanities subjects that the attempt is rarely made to advance them: though Kogan (1987) notes the case of a history department – not, it must be said, in an elite institution – whose continued survival depended on the modest contribution it was able to establish to the study of tourism.

Even in the most crassly utilitarian social climate, however, the external standing of a discipline is at least in some measure independent of its proven economic worth. It was contended, in the discussion of disciplinary pecking orders in Chapter 5, that within the academic world itself hard knowledge domains are regarded more highly than soft ones, and pure than applied. This perception is to a certain extent shared by outside observers of the academic scene, who will tend, independently of calculations of utility, to show a greater sense of awe towards research in biochemistry and physics at the one extreme than to studies related to education or social work at the other. The establishment of a strong academic image is therefore by no means irrelevant as a move in the game for external credibility and status.

Spiegel-Rösing (1974) distinguishes in this connection between strategies for image improvement as such and those that are also directed towards more fundamental changes in substance. The former may rest on careful reinterpretations of a discipline's history or on modified claims about the nature of its prevailing mission. Changes of nomenclature may themselves prove significant. One of the biology respondents in the initial study noted that a number of botany departments had judged it worth relabelling themselves as departments of plant science; another suggested that analogously, at the specialist level, functional morphology had acquired a more vigorous image when it was renamed biomechanics. In mathematics, too, one informant remarked, 'people play word games to improve their status. For instance, the group that originally called themselves analysts then took on the name classical analysts, then became functional analysts, and now call themselves hard analysts'. Elzinga (1987a) notes that the establishment of nursing studies as a field of applied research has been characterized by 'quibbles about whether to call part of the new subject "nursing care" generally, or "health care research", or again "ward oriented research"'. Similar terminological battles have more recently raged about whether 'information science' should be associated with the words 'library', 'management', 'knowledge' and 'studies' in the designation of the subject's name. What is at stake here is more than a mere choice of name: 'the quibble about the terminology . . . is not neutral. Rather it reflects strong vested interests on the parts of different actors' (Elzinga 1987a) and underlying disagreements about what form of knowledge is to occupy the prime focus of attention. The change of nomenclature in an established discipline can in its turn stem from more than a social concern with 'impression management'; it may, as suggested above, involve a cognitive change in substance, signalled by an identifiable shift in paradigm, the viewing of familiar phenomena through new eyes. The same is, one may note, true of the application of the word 'university' itself: after the 1997 Dearing report had noted the proliferation of its use, subsequent legislation in the UK limited the sorts of institutions eligible to employ it. Elsewhere the adoption of that title has not been limited to HE colleges seeking promotion of status: there has also in various parts of the world been extensive re-labelling of commercial training and development organizations to include the word 'university', as in the instance of The Disney University.

The viability of a discipline is also closely bound up with its capacity to attract students, which is not necessarily commensurate with its ability to guarantee them subsequent employment. The student recruitment market is as unpredictable and as subject to the capriciousness of fashion as the market for graduate labour, as can be seen by the substantial variations over time in the power and resources which a particular discipline can command. In its heyday, the study of the classics stood at the pinnacle of scholarly prestige among the non-vocational disciplines, as did divinity among those predominantly concerned with training for a profession. Now, both struggle for survival in the absence of any substantial student demand for places in even the most long-established and well-regarded departments. More recently, analytical philosophy has seemed to purvey a more faded glory than it did in the post-war generation; and linguistics, perhaps an overpriced stock a decade or two ago, seems to have fallen back to reflect a more modest market valuation.

The most apparently self-confident and respected disciplines are not immune to external influences of this kind. Many of the economist respondents in the intial study reported a decline in morale within their intellectual community, largely related to the failure of economic measures to cope with the world recession of the early 1970s. Henkel (1987) reports that:

> Both history and physics were found in our study to be under threat in different ways . . . Physics is suffering from poor school teaching of the subject, retraction of research funding for big science and competition with engineering for students and for institutional support. Historians were being forced to make statements about the relevance and value of their subject to employers.

The vagaries of disciplinary fortune can, then, be seen as a further manifestation of the complex relationship between academia and its wider environment. One much-quoted thesis, which passes under the name of finalization theory, links the vulnerability to external influence of scientific disciplines with the stages of their evolutionary cycle. Böhme *et al.* (1976), following Kuhn (1962), argue that any science must pass through a three-phase sequence: from pre-paradigmatic to having provisional paradigms, and thence to the establishment of clear, mature paradigms. In the second of these phases, when the preoccupation is with theoretical development, a discipline is more or less impervious to attempts at outside interference. In the first, however, it is vulnerable to invasion by extraneous considerations because there are no strong internal regulatives that can contest them. And in the third, also sometimes referred to as the post-paradigmatic phase, there is no further theoretical expansion; internal regulatives cease to operate as the prime motor of research; and thus the mature science becomes again open to political and economic intervention. As Rip (1981) explicates: 'The river of science has, as it were, reached its delta and can now be made to change its course very easily. The internalization of external goals is called *finalization*,[6] and the resulting specialized developments are called finalized specialties or disciplines.'

This attractively simple account of the disciplinary equivalent of epistemic drift at the specialist level, though it made a considerable impact on the sociology of science when it was first advanced, has subsequently been questioned on a number of counts. Besides the vagueness of the notion of maturity, as Rip points out, it involves a strongly reductionist assumption that all science follows the model of physics (in the context of which the theory was evolved). It also shares the deterministic overtones for which Kuhn's work has been criticized, implying an inevitability of evolutionary pattern for which counter-examples can readily be found. Elzinga (1987a) adds two further indictments. First, 'the case studies that have been carried out have not succeeded in demonstrating how social factors influence "truth" in fields of knowledge. Indeed this very thesis has helped to fan the flames of relativism.' His second objection is perhaps more fundamental:

> Even if we were to agree that certain fields of research become mature in the sense that no further theoretical developments are needed or possible, it does not follow that the researchers' right and responsibility ceases regarding the need to translate practitioner problems into research problems. This is not an automatic process. Also the researchers' responsibility for maintaining high standards and choosing methodologies or basic concepts, accepting or rejecting hypotheses, or publishing their results for scrutiny in the scientific community, all this does not cease to hold.

Whatever the merits or demerits of the doctrine of finalization, its applicability outside the field of hard science in however modified a form remains to be argued. But enough has perhaps already been said about the ways in which non-scientific subjects in their turn cannot escape the necessity to interact with the outside world and to accommodate to its demands. The case seems unarguable against any extreme form of disciplinary isolationism: even an ivory tower is not immune from environmental influences, be they the gales of natural happenstance or the man-made depredations of atmospheric pollution.

Knowledge domains and social relevance

A map of the world meets a purpose different from, and in some respects more useful than, a one-inch survey map of a limited piece of terrain. In a somewhat similar fashion, the four contrasting knowledge domains identified in Chapter 2 (hard pure, soft pure, hard applied and soft applied) serve at a macroscopic level to consolidate the diverse features identified at the microscopic levels of the individual and the specialism and at the intermediate level of the discipline. This process of consolidation, though it inevitably blurs the subtle variations that can be observed in close perspective, has the advantages of simplifying, and hence to some extent clarifying and underlining, the salient features of the map of knowledge.

With much of the detail already explored, relatively little remains to be said about the interplay between knowledge domains, viewed as aggregates, and the socioeconomic climate in which they have to justify their existence. This section will accordingly serve as a brief resume of what has gone before, while also attempting to draw out its main implications.

Hard pure knowledge tends to carry high prestige, involving as it does the search for the general laws governing the areas of human understanding with which it is concerned. It is commonly held to be intellectually demanding, and is seen as attracting individuals of high ability. The purity and elitism are, however, mitigated by the promise that it may, in possibly unexpected ways, have beneficial application. These features help to explain the substantial sums that society seems prepared to invest in problem-centred enquiry concerned with causal explanation of a general kind. The funding of 'big science' calls for a particularly effective professional-political lobby, which is fostered by strong, well-organized and closely knit specialist associations. Even in less costly areas of investigation, grantsmanship is an art to be cultivated by the successful careerist: the earning of outside funds is a positive influence in the process of professional recognition and advancement. Overall, the substantial dependence of hard pure research on external sponsorship opens the way to political and commercial intervention, and may lead in some situations to a heavy emphasis on work considered to be socially applicable, at the expense of those areas of enquiry whose direction is determined by predominantly epistemological considerations.

In hard applied areas, where the prime function of knowledge is the generation of product-oriented techniques, and more directly of products as such, the profile is different. Effort tends to be spread across a wide front rather than clustered round a limited number of problems. It is therefore less easy for a single interest group to coalesce and to present a coherent, united case for funding. The difficulty may be compounded by the utilitarian criteria invoked in assessing research promise. In particular, the views of non-academic, professional practitioners in the field of application are likely to have some influence, clouding the simpler, more domestic processes of peer-group judgement. The value attached to directly useful knowledge is related to broader cultural considerations, and varies over time and place. In Western and Central Europe there has been a tradition of according social esteem to practice-related enquiry, as may be seen in the strong infrastructure of technological and applied institutes within their educational systems as a whole. In Britain, on the other hand, less positive social attitudes have been fostered by the equation of elitism and theoretical purity with the gentry, and practical application with the working classes (see Wiener 1981; Barnett 1986). It has taken unremitting political insistence on promoting contract-based, utilitarian research to shift the balance in the direction of favouring application. But there are countervailing tendencies among elite applied scientists towards achieving independence from external influence by favouring the more theoretical, less instrumental aspects of the domain – a particular form of 'academic drift' (Neave 1979; Clark 1983), which is the alter ego to the epistemic drift already identified in hard pure enquiry.

Both hard pure and hard applied knowledge involve their champions in active competition for research funds and a corresponding dependence on the goodwill of both the public and private sectors of the economy. Pressure of this kind is noticeably less intense at that end of the soft pure domain, which deals with inapplicable, largely atheoretical knowledge, involving the study of the particular rather than the general and the search for empathetic understanding rather than causal explanation. The view from the external world of this form of knowledge is ambivalent. On the one hand, scholarship is a respected attribute and activity; on the other, it is open to the hostile accusation of being arcane, inbred and largely pointless. Postmodernity itself has the characteristic of undermining the authority of particular forms of knowledge, and the propositional knowledge that has typified university learning is no exception: it too can become simply one choice among many (Bloland 1995). What has at times been proudly designated by academics as the pursuit of learning for its own sake may understandably be written down by the laity as not possessing any wider social justification, and hence as having little if any call on the public purse. It seems too personal and specific to merit large investment, and is in any case too cheap to need it, involving as it typically does one or at most two people rather than a substantial research team, and demanding no more than access to source material, modest funds for books and the cost of occasional travel. Because fund-raising is not a significant activity, the specialisms concerned have no pressing need for strong promotional public relations. This, coupled with the individualism that is one of the inherent features of soft pure research, means that their professional organizations, viewed as groups representative of their interests to the outside world, are relatively weak.

The soft pure knowledge domain is perhaps even more heterogeneous than its counterparts, in that it also embodies areas of enquiry that aspire to something of the generality of hard pure research and that may offer some potentiality of application. Economics is a discipline that straddles the boundaries of hard and soft, pure and applied: 'What is, or is not, an economic problem is largely determined by the analytical framework of neoclassical economics but external influences do affect the range of issues tackled and policy demands lead to extensions of that framework to the new areas which were not previously considered appropriate' (Whitley 1984); 'The claim is . . . for unifying as well as more sophisticated theories. [The] preoccupations are largely internalist, although the externalist influences upon a subject so enmeshed in society are powerful' (Henkel 1987). Sociology, too, displays elements of a quest for grand, over-arching theories in awkward conjunction with a tendency towards policy-oriented enquiry: though here, the influence of research on practice is seldom a very direct one, and may be argued to take the form of a general enlightenment – a modification of commonly held concepts – rather than of effective prescription for social amelioration or improvement (Weiss 1977; Thomas 1985). In the social sciences generally, the role of outside political agencies would appear to be stronger than it is in the humanities, the natural sciences or the technical professions.

The predominant feature of soft applied knowledge is the susceptibility of its research agenda to dictation by non-academic interests. Because of their close links and overlapping membership with the academic community, the relevant professional practitioners' associations will often have a strong say in identifying issues and approving strategies of enquiry, as in the cases of nursing and social work. Government ministries will tend, by their control of sectoral research budgets, to promote developmental activities alongside investigation into 'useful' topics (Kogan and Henkel 1983). Client groups may also seek to exert their influence. As Whitley (1984) observes, 'where the central phenomenon of a field is largely defined by powerful non-scientific [i.e. non-academic] groups . . . its autonomy is very limited and subject to invasion in the name of "relevance"'.

The implication of this analysis is that even when aggregated at a broad general level, different epistemological categories can be seen to be associated with distinctive sets of relationships between the academic communities concerned and the wider contexts in which they subsist. No part of the world of learning is immune from interaction with its environment, but the form that interaction takes will both reflect and influence the nature of the knowledge domain in question.

Notes

1. The issue is perhaps more complicated than this makes it seem. One sociologist remarked that 'many sociologists have strong feelings of social justice, but most sublimate them into research rather than translating them into action'. But the comment of another that 'the kind of sociology one practices is seen as a political and an existential statement', allows a different interpretation.
2. Elzinga (1987b) gives a nice illustration, depicting the way in which intellectual fashions have changed in the sociology of science. He argues that 'Merton's sociological scheme and Popper's philosophical one' (see Merton 1973, on the norms of science, and Popper 1979, on the principle of falsification) sought to portray science as functionally autonomous and cognitively authoritative, and hence as 'relatively immune and independent of societal influences'. In 'some of the newer trends . . . facts are sometimes seen not to be formed primarily or at all by confrontations with objective realities, but by the social mediation and cultural weave in which researchers work . . . the boundaries between science and non-science are said to be dependent on negotiation and power struggles, both at the micro and macro levels.' Accordingly, 'contrasting the newer imagery with the traditional one that has legitimated traditional academic science, the defrocking of the priesthood of science may serve to legitimate pragmatic science policy doctrines . . . which form the basis of mission orientation and politicization of science'.
3. This claim perhaps amounts to no more than a further indication of the diversity within superficially homogeneous disciplinary areas. The phrase 'disinterested applied research' could reasonably be used to refer to predominantly theoretical

work in such fields as pharmacy and mechanical engineering. A contrast might be noted here with what is sometimes called 'applicable mathematics'; that is, research topics within the disciplinary confines of pure mathematics that promise to be capable of exploitation in applied subject fields.

4. The dependency can cut both ways. Henkel (1987) observes that:

> There are fields in which industry is at the leading edge of knowledge. Examples in physics are digital electronics and opto-electronics . . . some teachers in higher education were using their links with industry to gain knowledge of current developments in opto-electronics for transmission to students.

5. And blunted again by Knorr Cetina (1982), who argues that even in apparently disinterested pure science 'the arenas of action within which . . . inquiry proceeds are transepistemic – that is, they in principle include scientists and non-scientists, and encompass arguments and concerns of . . . a "non-technical" nature'. These transepistemic arenas are 'the locus in which the establishment, definition, renewal or expansion of resource-relationships is effectively negotiated'.

6. ' "Finalization" is a process through which external goals for science become the guide-lines of the development of the scientific theory itself' (Böhme *et al.* 1976).

9

Implications for Theory and Practice

Tidying up the categories

The initial research on which this exposition was based was shaped and directed by one underlying assumption: namely, that there are identifiable patterns to be found within the relationship between knowledge forms and their associated knowledge communities. However, inside the limits of this defining framework, we have attempted to avoid any firm preconceptions about the nature of the information to be sought, allowing the data themselves to yield up consistencies and to dominate the forms of explanation offered to account for them. A 'grounded' approach of this kind (Glaser and Strauss 1967) offers more assurance than does a theoretical stance based on a particular set of axioms that the range of evidence taken into consideration will not be intentionally or subliminally restricted (see Pantin 1968): that the resulting theoretical account will be faithful to a wide spectrum of data, and not merely one that is only preselected by the theorist's own assumptions. We recognize that implicit sets of assumptions will guide selectivity in such a way as to render no approach truly 'grounded' (Alvesson and Skoldberg 2000): but as against that, such an approach is less likely, except where the phenomena under review are themselves very simple and straightforward in character, to generate the illusion of a powerful and apparently all-embracing explanatory structure.[1]

There are other reasons why the emergence is not to be expected of a single theory that could account for all the considerations which have so far been advanced. Leaving aside the contention that human affairs – allowing as they do for intentionality – are too complex to be amenable to the lawlike regularities to be discerned among natural phenomena, it has already been acknowledged that academic communities are subject to influences from the wider society as well as from the inherent nature of the epistemological issues on which they are engaged: educational ideologies, understandings of profitability of actions for the self and one's community, cultural influences such as those associated with gender, and the like (Trowler 1998a).

We do not argue, therefore, for a neat one-to-one correspondence between forms of knowledge and the characteristic cultures of those who engage in them.

Nonetheless, there remains scope for a tidying-up operation of the kind we now attempt. In seeking identifiable patterns in the data and advancing recognizably related explanations for them, we begin by looking again at some of the main categories employed in the course of the exposition and attempting to clarify and systematize the connections between them.

Much of the preceding discussion has been conducted in terms of disciplines and specialisms, seen as marking two different levels of specificity. Each of these concepts has the property of combining, in ways that are not easily separable, both cognitive and social characteristics. Thus, when we speak of a discipline, or of a specialism, we tend to run together the notions of a particular field of knowledge and an associated group of academics: people belong to a discipline, or embrace a specialism, but that discipline or specialism is defined in terms of its intellectual content as much as by its adoptive community.

When it becomes necessary, for the purposes of conceptual clarification, to distinguish the two aspects – epistemological and sociological – we are forced into an artificial form of categorization, in that a natural one is not readily to hand. For present purposes, we will use the term 'subject' to refer to the cognitive component of a discipline, and the term 'segment' to designate the corresponding component of a specialism. Their social counterparts will be labelled 'disciplinary community' and 'network', respectively. We here need to re-emphasize the elusiveness of the distinction: we acknowledge that constructions of disciplinary epistemology, socially derived, are at least as important as 'real' differences in the knowledge characteristics of the disciplines, that the 'social construction of reality' (Berger and Luckmann 1966) can be as real in its effects as epistemological 'reality' itself. Thus, to return to an analogy used in Chapter 1, the perceptual 'scape' in landscape is as important as the solid 'land'.

With this said subjects and segments are to be seen in our explanatory framework as cognitive entities and disciplinary communities and networks as social ones, formed by the logical dissection of disciplines and specialisms. These entities possess certain important attributes, which have formed the topic of previous discussion. Segments, as well as subjects, may be hard or soft, pure or applied. Both sets of dualities in practice allow for gradation; neither hardness nor softness, purity nor application, should be seen as absolutes, but as end-points of continua. So too, networks and disciplinary communities may be characterized as highly urban or pre-eminently rural in their patterns of interaction, or as lying somewhere between the two extremes. Disciplinary communities may in varying degrees be seen as convergent; that is, manifesting a sense of collectivity and mutual identity, or divergent; that is, schismatic and ideologically fragmented.[2]

It is important to observe the asymmetry in this exercise in conceptual mapping. Subjects and segments share both sets of their cognitive attributes;

disciplinary communities and networks do not. That is to say, the notion of convergence, which is roughly analogous with the sense of nationhood attributable to sovereign countries (but not to their member states, counties or departments), can be applied at the level of a disciplinary community but not at the level of a network. Both networks and disciplinary communities may be more or less tightly knit; but the sense in which this epithet is applied differs between the two, and the distinction helps to highlight the contrast between the convergent/divergent spectrum on the one hand and the urban/rural spectrum on the other.

Networks are at least in certain respects homogeneous and coherent by definition, where communities may or may not be so as a matter of contingency. To say that a disciplinary community is tightly knit is to say something about the *Weltanschauung* (compounded by folklore, mythology and hero-worship) that binds its constituent networks to one another; to say that it is loosely knit is to imply a collectivity held together not by a strong sentiment of cultural affinity but by the weaker bonds of historical or social circumstance.[3] But to say that a network is tightly knit is not to say anything new about the mutuality of its members' scholarly interests and concerns, since all networks, whether tight or loose, owe their very existence to such characteristics; rather, it is to say something about its predominantly urban mode of existence, about the intensity and nature of the interaction between the individuals who comprise it. Putting it differently, tightly knit convergent disciplinary communities are characterized normatively, in terms of a commonality of intellectual values and a coherence of cultural assumptions among the networks and individuals within their jurisdiction; tightly knit urban networks are identifiable operationally, in terms of the types of activities and practices in which those who belong to them engage.

We may wish for certain purposes (as in Chapter 2) to denote subjects as hard or soft, pure or applied, while recognizing that they are in reality an admixture of segments with different combinations of characteristics. The amalgam may be predominantly pure (as in chemistry) while some parts of it are clearly applied, or predominantly hard (as in mechanical engineering) while some parts of it are clearly soft. Similarly, when we choose to designate disciplinary communities as urban or rural, we are in practice identifying a predominance among what is often a heterogeneity of urban and rural networks. But to say of a disciplinary community that it is convergent or divergent is to refer to the nature of the relationships between its networks, not to the predominance of one type of network over another (since degrees of convergence are not, within the meaning of the term, accorded to networks as such).

The basic dimensions

Some further issues need to be clarified before we turn to consider the implications of applying this taxonomy to the knowledge forms and knowledge communities which have been the subject of the enquiry. In the first place, Pantin's (1968) distinction (see Chapter 2) between the restricted and unrestricted sciences has been subsumed in passing under that between hard and soft knowledge areas. The correspondence deserves now to be underlined, so that it is clear that we are not required to deal with a further distinct set of categories.

Briefly, restricted knowledge has clearly defined boundaries; the problems with which it is concerned tend to be relatively narrow and circumscribed. It focuses on quantitative issues, and tends to have a well-developed theoretical structure embracing causal propositions, generalizable findings and universal laws. It is cumulative, in that new findings tend to be linear developments of the existing state of knowledge. That is to say, it shares the defining properties of hard pure knowledge identified in Chapter 2. Unrestricted knowledge has the opposite characteristics: unclear boundaries, problems that are broad in scope and loose in definition, a relatively unspecific theoretical structure, a concern with the qualitative and particular, and a reiterative pattern of enquiry. It is thus cognate with soft pure knowledge as also characterized in Chapter 2.

We have already established the sense in which convergent disciplinary communities are equivalent to tightly knit ones, and the different sense in which urban networks may also be said to be tightly knit, thus disposing of another analytically redundant set of terms. This leaves us with four basic sets of properties: hard/soft and pure/applied in the cognitive realm; convergent/divergent and urban/rural in the social. It should be noted that these properties are not only relative rather than absolute, but that their attributions may change over time and space. To give some instances, a subject that at one stage appears predominantly soft (as economics did before it became more strongly theory-orientated and mathematically sophisticated) may at a later stage seem noticeably harder. Conversely a predominantly hard subject or segment may become soft, as has happened in the case of educational administration, which moved away from a highly quantitative approach influenced by positivist thinking (Greenfield and Ribbins 1993). One which takes a strongly applied form in one kind of situation ('mechanical engineering' at an English unchartered university) may emerge as comparatively pure elsewhere ('engineering science' in an elite research university): the 'institutional logic' and other factors are at work here. A disciplinary community that is identifiable at a particular moment as convergent (e.g. linguists in the 1950s) may subsequently diverge; and another (comprising, say, physicists) which looks predominantly urban in one country (the USA) may have a more rural profile in another (Latin America). Moreover the spread of critical theory and of postmodernist thinking across the disciplinary landscape has led to a fracturing of paradigms and disciplinary cultures in many places, as Toma (1996: 4) points out:

> Scholars in several academic fields, including law, increasingly employ
> different varieties of critical theory or interpretive models as the

foundation for their work. The rise of these alternative inquiry paradigms to positivism and postpositivism has been unsettling. Scholars
working within the same disciplines increasingly construct and consider
knowledge and inquiry differently and no longer share common philosophical traditions and distinct academic cultures.

The characteristics of the four basic dimensions have been explored at
various points in previous chapters. However, it may be helpful here to
bring together and underline a few points of substance that have arisen
in the course of the discussion, without any pretence at offering a comprehensive review. On the cognitive side, the notions of contextual imperatives and contextual associations, the first a feature of hard knowledge
areas and the second of soft, proved useful in Chapters 6 and 7 in showing how the cumulative, sequential nature of hard pure knowledge limits
the range of currently relevant topics and reduces the degree of explanatory preamble necessary in setting out an argument. Another way of
indicating the difference is to note that in hard, restricted fields, the
available methods tend to determine the choice of problems; in soft,
unrestricted ones, it seems rather that the problems determine the methods.[4] A further important dichotomy, this time between the two ends
of the pure/applied continuum, was identified in Chapter 8, where it was
noted that pure knowledge, though increasingly vulnerable to epistemic
drift, is essentially self-regulating, and that applied knowledge, though
occasionally prone to academic drift, is in its nature open to external
influence.

As far as social distinctions are concerned, convergence can be related
to the maintenance of reasonably uniform standards and procedures,
and the existence of 'intellectual control' and a 'stable elite' (Mulkay 1977;
see Chapter 5). Divergent communities lack these features, tolerating a
greater measure of intellectual deviance and in some cases degenerating
into self-destructive disputation. In contrast, the defining feature of the
rural/urban dimension, as delineated in Chapter 6, is the people-to-
problem ratio: the number of researchers engaged at any one time on a
particular problem or constellation of problems. Urban researchers tend
to occupy a narrow area of intellectual territory and to cluster round
a limited number of discrete topics that appear amenable to short-term
solutions. Their rural counterparts span a broader area, across which
problems are thinly scattered and within which they are not sharply distinguished: articulating the solutions to such problems is often a lengthy
business.

The purpose of elaborating these distinctions is two-fold. First, it draws
attention to the range and variety of academic activity and to certain systematic differences relating to that activity. Second, it provides an analytical
framework for exploring the connections between the epistemological attributes of subjects and segments and the sociological properties of disciplinary
communities and networks.

Applying the taxonomy

The conceptual scaffolding, which was put in place earlier has served its purpose and may therefore be dispensed with. Having made the necessary theoretical distinctions between hardness and softness, and purity and application, as related to the cognitive aspects of disciplines and specialisms, and convergence and divergence, and urban and rural research styles, as related to their social aspects, it is no longer necessary to preserve the figurative boundary, erected as an expository device, between subjects and segments on the one hand and disciplinary communities and networks on the other. Now that the two sets of entities have been shown as logically separable in analysis, their factual interconnections can be explored more rigorously in synthesis.

From this point onwards, therefore, we refer directly (and quite properly) to disciplines and specialisms as combining within their essential natures both epistemological and sociological aspects, and use the conjunction to identify the nature of the links between the two. The first move towards this end is to apply our four-dimensional taxonomy to the 12 individual disciplines that have formed the main subject of our investigation and to some of their component specialisms (the exercise has of course to be seen as one conducted within the context of leading research departments, related to a particular point in history, and carried out at a fairly high level of generality).

Along the hard/soft dimension, physics, chemistry, pharmacy and mathematics are predominantly hard; biology and mechanical engineering less evidently so. Economics and geography may be classed as borderline disciplines on the other side of the divide; history, modern languages, sociology and law lie firmly at the soft end of the scale. But we have noted, in passing, that there are also physicists who study the more complex and far from clear-cut areas of the subject such as meteorology and cosmology, and a number of applied branches which lack the conceptual sharpness and mathematical underpinning that would characterize them as unequivocally hard knowledge areas. Demographic and economic history are relatively hard branches of their discipline; modern languages embraces the harder areas of textual analysis and classical philology alongside critical theory and other soft specialisms. Within those disciplines that occupy the middle ground – biology and economics among them – one similarly finds a mixture of hard and soft elements (microbiology as against ecology; macroeconomics as against developmental economics).

At the disciplinary level, only three of our 12 disciplines (engineering, pharmacy and law) can readily be classed as applied: the other nine are predominantly pure. But a number of the latter include areas of application, just as certain applied subjects contain relatively pure elements. Chemistry, for example, comprises not only the pure field of physical chemistry but also synthetic organic chemistry, which has numerous commercial applications. Economics is concerned not only with mathematical theory but also with industrial organization. Similarly, mechanical engineering has areas of overlap with physics, especially in its more theoretical aspects. And in academic law, the study of jurisprudence represents a pure component, whereas family law is nothing if not applied.

Turning to the social aspects, it is evident that some disciplines enjoy a high level of convergence. The most obvious perhaps is physics, where the sense of commonality is powerful in spite of the existence of numerous and sometimes mutually incomprehensible specialisms. Respondents in the subject commented on an overriding sense of collective kinship, a mutuality of interests, a shared intellectual style, a consensual understanding of 'profound simplicities', and even 'a quasi-religious belief in the unity of nature'.

History, for very different reasons, may also be classed as a convergent discipline. Its diversity of coverage is much greater than that of physics, in that its subject matter knows few restrictions. It is not characterized by any dominating conceptual structure, nor by any strongly developed techniques or methods of enquiry (indeed, historians tend to describe their discipline as a craft, to assert that it is 'rooted in evidence, not based on theories', and to comment that 'history has sources but no methods'). Nonetheless, there is, as among physicists, a sense of inhabiting 'a particular and definable world', a sharing of 'common assumptions and styles of thought', and a strong tradition of intellectual kinship. 'Most historians', said one, 'see themselves as part of the same fraternity'; more historians used the phrase 'community of scholars' than did respondents in any other discipline.

Two other strong candidates for convergence among the 12 disciplines that formed the basis of this study are mathematics and economics. The former is characterized by its practitioners as having 'common modes of discourse'; universal agreement on 'the notions of proof and definition, and on the criteria for acceptability'; and 'the need for a special talent'. The latter, economics, embodies 'a clear consensus about method and judgement', 'a common basic training', and a sharing of 'the same fundamental principles'.

There are three of our 12 areas of enquiry that can be seen as occupying the intermediate ground between the convergent and the divergent. One of these is law, another chemistry, and the third biology. What disables academic lawyers from unequivocally convergent status is a continuing dispute about the nature of the subject. Although they have 'the same basic intellectual know-how', 'a common core of technique', 'a shared database', and 'the same forms of thought and rules in formulating arguments', they are nonetheless divided in their views about whether law departments ought to concentrate on the content of their subject (black letter law), or should aim to place it in its social context (the socio-legal approach), or indeed to view it from a predominantly sociological perspective (the sociology of law movement).[5] This uncertainty over what the discipline is or ought to be makes it inappropriate to categorize academic law as a highly convergent field. Biologists convey a similar ambiguity. They are 'very heterogeneous'; in particular, there is 'a mutual antagonism' between those who study structures and processes and those whose concern is with organisms or communities. But the subject is not prone to 'deep and permanent divisions'; there is 'more intellectual unity than the structural diversity of the subject suggests'. Again, chemists have 'many shared assumptions, and a common basis in the study of molecules', but it is 'hard to think of it as a unified discipline'. Chemists 'tend to cut each other down', and 'slanging is more common among chemists than among other scientists': 'When under attack, chemists draw their wagons into a circle, and then start firing into the middle. People tend to be highly critical of each other, rather than supportive. They don't hang together, because the field itself is so fragmented.' So chemistry too has to be located some way towards the divergent end of the scale.

This categorization leaves five divergent disciplines among the original 12. The collective identity of mechanical engineers suffers from their being diffused across a wide field and lacking a central core of theory. On their own testimony, 'We don't have a corporate image or a collective view, and we don't close our ranks'; and 'there is envy and a competition among engineers which physicists don't have'. In applications for grant funds, mechanical engineers 'can't get their act together in the way the physicists do'. Sociology is seen as fissiparous and fragmented: 'insofar as it is a family, it is a fractious family'. It is 'a discipline with not much unity or much agreement on perspectives and problems': one might even say, as did two sociologists interviewed (one English, one American): 'it is not really a discipline'. Its lack of candidature for convergent status is borne out by references in the literature: 'Sociology is a multiple paradigm science' (Ritzer 1975, 1979, 1980); 'The attempts to order sociology by ideology and by paradigm compound its confusions' (Martindale 1979). Modern languages might be designated as a cluster of related disciplines, rather than a single unity, but it is arguable that each of its constituent communities is split, not only between literary critics and linguistic scholars, but also within the former between advocates of conflicting theories – the psychoanalytic approach, deconstruction, structuralism, and the like. Against this background, no sense emerged from the interviews of any commonality of intellectual perspective or any closely shared set of disciplinary values. Finally, geographers and pharmacists identify themselves as 'highly multidisciplinary', having numerous overlaps with neighbouring subject groups and a heterogeneous set of professional concerns. Papers in these two fields frequently appear in the journals of other disciplines, with the result that the journals dedicated to their own disciplines tend to be weakly supported and lacking in prestige. Accordingly, it seems reasonable to categorize geography and pharmacy, alongside mechanical engineering, sociology and modern languages, as instances of divergence.

We come, finally, to the urban/rural dimension. It is a curiosity that, although much of the writing in the sociology of science has focused on urban research activity, its actual incidence in the academic workplace is quite limited. The only discipline in the initial study which could be designated as substantially urban in research style is physics. Outside that sample, biochemistry may offer another case in point. Chemistry, contrary perhaps to its external image, must be classified as rural in its aggregate make-up: it is uncommon for researchers to compete in 'a fight for the finish'; publication delays can be quite lengthy in most subdisciplines, and the circulation of preprints is noticeably less prevalent than in physics; laboratory investigation 'doesn't involve expensive machines, experiments on a large scale, or collaboration in a global sense'; and the community 'thinks small – it is a cottage industry'. Some groups of mathematicians meet the criteria of general gregariousness and occasional disputes over priority, but the pressure for publication is not high, the choice of problems at any given time usually rather wide, and the people-to-problem ratio is normally rather low. Across the landscape as a whole, urban research can be seen to take place only in scattered pockets, engaging a few networks within the confines of a limited number of disciplinary communities (microbiologists; control engineers; a number of specialties in pharmacy and more generally in biomedical science). There are few if any urban groupings to be found in history, modern languages, economics, sociology, geography or academic law.

Connections between categories

This venture in categorization need not be seen as an end in itself. It can be put to good purpose in helping us to identify some of the significant, if only partial, interconnections between cognitive and social characteristics. To take a fairly evident trend revealed in the course of the exercise, it would appear that instances of urban research are to be found exclusively in hard – and predominantly in hard pure – knowledge fields. This is not surprising, in that it is in such fields that the research front is sufficiently narrow and the problems sharply defined enough to encourage academics to cluster round a limited area of intellectual territory.[6] As we have noted, however, only a subsection of hard specialisms generates an urban style of research; others are rural, or at best suburban, because the possible themes of enquiry are numerous, the extent of overlap between individual research interests is small and the publication delays are long.

One might expect this link at the level of segments and networks to be reflected in a similar relationship between the degree of convergence of disciplinary communities and the cognitive attributes of academic subjects. It would seem probable that tightly knit, cohesive academic clans would be promoted by the shared study of a restricted, densely structured and clearly bounded area of knowledge; equally, one might regard subject areas with these characteristics as reflecting the shared definitions imposed by tightly knit academic groups. By the same reasoning, loosely knit communities would seem to be the likeliest products – or producers – of an unrestricted, incohate and relatively permeable disciplinary field. However, the correspondence here is not as close in practice as it might promise to be in principle. Some predominantly hard disciplines (physics, mathematics) enjoy a high degree of convergence, and most soft ones (modern languages, sociology, law) a low one; biology occupies an intermediate position on both scales; and the match for geography and economics is perhaps near enough. But the two hard applied disciplines in the sample (mechanical engineering and pharmacy) are misfits. So, noticeably, are chemistry and history; the former as a hard pure but relatively divergent subject and the second as a soft pure but convergent one.

Two possible reasons for these anomalies are that external influences operate, especially in areas with numerous applications, to loosen the ties between communities and the forms of knowledge they study; and that the cognitive properties of disciplines are in any case no more than aggregations of their epistemologically heterogeneous specialisms. Applied subjects, both hard and soft, are, as we have noted in Chapter 8, particularly amenable to outside intervention, and appear liable accordingly to lack the sense of collectivity that convergence requires.[7] Further special considerations apply to chemistry and history. In the case of the former, the coherence of its disciplinary community may be weakened both by its sizeable dependence on industrial sponsorship and by the highly atomistic and fragmentary character of its subject matter. History, though predominantly soft, seems in an apparently paradoxical way to have achieved its convergent status by virtue of its very open-endedness, all-embracing catholicity of coverage and relative absence of theoretical divisions (in that it manages to remain largely atheoretical).

The visceral, complex connections at a very general level between knowledge forms and knowledge communities are reinforced by many linkages of a more limited and specific kind. Previous chapters have identified two main types of association: those that bear on the collective activities of academics and those which affect them as individuals. Among the first, we have noted differences in the validation process associated with particular knowledge areas, together with variations in the degree of importance attached to refereeing and citation; diversities in the ways in which reputations are established, disciplinary elites are identified, eminence recognized and power exploited; contrasts in the sources of, and shapes taken by, intellectual fashion in different domains of enquiry; and distinctions in the impact made by radically new ideas. We have also observed systematic deviations in language and style, modes of competitiveness, the nature and incidence of collaboration and the consequences of controversy. In terms of individual experience, as against group behaviour, we have been able to identify characteristic divergences in recruitment and initiation, choice of specialisms, form of doctoral supervision, mobility between research fields, peaking in productivity and achievement, and intensity of involvement in work. In Chapter 8 it was suggested that the interplay between academic communities and their external environment also follows disparate patterns in one cognitive context as against another.

Such considerations, taken together, seem to offer a fair degree of support to the thesis that fields of enquiry and academic cultures are closely interconnected. Nevertheless the central focus on fields of enquiry has allowed only limited attention to other factors that condition academic cultures, both at the level of community and network and in terms of their articulation in individual behaviour, attitudes and values. This alternative approach is exemplified in at the local level by practice-based theory (discussed, for example in the papers in *Organization*, 7(2) 2000), which explores the ways in which technologies, discourses and recurrent practices operate in micro-social situations and interact with identities and the social construction of reality there (Trowler 2001). At a different analytical level also evident are approaches to the study of organizations that stress their dialogical nature; that is, which see them as the locale for multiple cultures and discourses which are in not necessarily compatible configurations (Alvesson 1993; Trowler 1998a; Parker 2000).

A further note on status

Even if it is conceded that there are more densely woven and more systematically patterned ligaments connecting forms and communities of knowledge than is generally recognized and that a closer examination of them may help to enhance our understanding of the physiology of the academic enterprise, there remains a legitimate question to be answered. What, it may be asked, follows from all this? Does the investigation, analysis and argument that has gone into the attempt to establish the nature and extent of such relationships amount to anything other than an elaborate intellectual exercise; is it any better than a mere conceptual crossword puzzle whose solution has no results of real consequence? We can do no more than sketch an answer here, beginning with a further consideration of the issue of intellectual status and going on briefly to explore some of the implications of diversity.

The disparities that have been identified within subjects and segments, disciplinary communities and networks have significant effects on judgements of academic quality, and in particular on the standing accorded to disciplines and specialisms in virtue of their epistemological and sociological attributes. This is a matter of some practical concern. HE is suffused with considerations of value and almost obsessively taken up with the identification of excellence; grading of a more or less rarified kind is endemic. The placing of both knowledge fields and those that profess them in a finely tuned order of merit has to be recognized as contributing to a much wider process of appraisal, a process that stretches all the way from the ranking of academic institutions to the classification of students' work.

The degree of convergence of a discipline, for example, has evident political implications. Convergent communities are favourably placed to advance their collective interests (since they know what their collective interests are, and enjoy a clear sense of unity in promoting them), if necessary at the expense of other, less fortunately endowed groups of colleagues.[8] They also tend to command the respect, admiration and envy of divergent disciplinary communities, and thus to be identified as members of the academic elite. To reinforce their advantages, they are further liable to be regarded by viewers outside the academic world as having privileged status. Thus physicists, historians, mathematicians and economists (among other elite groups, such as medical academics, outside the present sample) are in a position to enjoy considerable power both within the intellectual sphere and beyond its boundaries. Conversely, disciplines at the opposite end of the convergent–divergent spectrum are seen internally as politically weak and externally as lacking in good intellectual standing. This is particularly the case when postmodernist or other comparable influences cause a discipline to question the validity and status of the forms of knowledge it generates: as Trow (1994) has pointed out, such loss of self-confidence has rendered the social sciences especially vulnerable to attack from unsympathetic external forces. This perception is heightened if one of the disciplines in question allows a domestic quarrel to erupt into public view: at that point, there may well be a damaging loss of both academic and public credibility, which in turn reinforces a tendency in 'postmodernity' to challenge orthodoxies and the privileging of knowledge (Bloland 1995).

At the level of individual specialisms, there is a finer set of distinctions to be made. As noted in Chapters 5 and 8, the most favoured specialisms are those that are pure; not only pure but hard, and not only hard but urban. In other words, good standing accrues on each scale at the end that emphasizes the theoretical, the quantitative and the sharply defined. This of course leaves a wide scatter of areas of enquiry that have a reasonably high reputation because they meet a significant proportion of such requirements. Examples from different fields might include theoretical welfare economics, demographic history, fluid dynamics and physical chemistry. Other areas, because of their particular constellation of properties, seem doomed to a place relatively far down the academic pecking order. Thus food chemistry, plant physiology, regional geography, social psychology, literary history, alongside many other specialisms in the chemical, biological and social sciences and the humanities, tend to be given a lower intellectual rating than their practitioners might find acceptable, because they do not meet sufficiently the favoured criteria: hardness, purity and an urban research style.

As with many exercises in social discrimination, this one is to some degree dependent on wider national values. The UK (see Chapter 8) is held to be peculiarly subject to anti-utilitarian snobbery, to the extent that the UK intelligentsia has traditionally downgraded socially relevant technologies such as pharmacy and engineering – though medical science, perhaps because of its apparently convergent status, enjoys considerable prestige. The general climate in Continental Europe and the United States seems more favourable to hard applied subjects at least, but there remains a common tendency for practitioners in fields that are academically well-entrenched and established to look sideways at soft applied researchers (those in public administration, social work, education and the like) because their disciplines are viewed as lacking in proper rigour.[9]

It would seem in some respects unfair that – in large part because of the intrinsic nature of their subject matter – certain academic communities are able to exploit their social and cognitive advantages while others – perhaps through no fault of their own – are not. After all, even the stigmas associated with factionalism and family disputes often appear to be a consequence of the shape of the knowledge base (for instance, biology is perhaps necessarily divided between the study of systems and a concern with whole organisms, modern languages between linguistic research and literary scholarship, and geography between investigations of physical and social phenomena). To those denied it, the ascription of privilege may seem like that of class in England or of caste in India – simply a characteristic feature of the academic scene, having no necessary connection with either merit or worth, but nonetheless enabling the chosen groups to enjoy superiority and command deference. Those who are so privileged would doubtless reply that their subjects are intellectually more than usually demanding, call for a particular clarity of thought and expression and, because they impose clear and unequivocal criteria of merit, exercise a firm control on quality. (In contrast, as one mechanical engineer remarked, 'engineering is more pedestrian and there are less breakthroughs – the signs of brilliance are less pronounced and less evident'.)

It is not surprising in the circumstances that groups of academics in disciplines lacking high prestige have occasionally initiated reforms designed to increase the degree of hardness of certain specialisms and (it may be hoped), in association with this, the degree of convergence of their community as a whole. To take a few cases in point, a coterie of behavioural psychologists, in the early decades after the Second World War, set out to develop highly quantitative techniques in an effort to create a science of behaviour based on mathematical models. Similarly, advocates of the 'new geography' in the early 1960s argued that the adoption of numerical approaches would help to push the subject 'back into the mainstream of scientific method' (Slaymaker 1968, quoted in Goodson 1983). At one stage in the development of political science, 'The use of statistical methods became more complex and sophisticated, mathematical and quasi-mathematical formulations were frequently used, and vocabularies became increasingly technical and esoteric' (Waldo 1975, quoted in Ruscio 1986). In none of these instances did the revolution take hold sufficiently to create a new disciplinary image, because, it could be argued, the knowledge domain in question was not in essence sufficiently amenable to the imposition of the techniques and methods of hard science or because the dominant paradigm was too deeply entrenched. 'Academic drift' (see Chapter 8) nonetheless continues to exercise a strong attraction for those who are too low in the pecking order for their own comfort.

Diversity and its consequences

Although one of the central purposes of the research has been to emphasize the existence and to begin to identify the nature of the connections between fields of study and those who work in them, it has (like many such investigations) had other incidental outcomes. In particular, the examination of the cognitive and social aspects of intellectual enquiry has highlighted a remarkable diversity in the activities that go to make up the academic enterprise. Knowledge areas, professional networks and individual career patterns can be classified, and operationally distinguished one from another, in a multiplicity of different ways. On this reading, it would seem that variety is not merely the spice but the very essence of scholarly life.

Insofar as the distinctions are accepted as observational substantives rather than theoretical artefacts, they can be argued to have significant implications for the management of HE and the policies of individual institutions within it. The current political trends within many, if not most, national systems reflect a concern to tidy up and rationalize – to render both more efficient and more economical – what is seen, in organizational terms, as a ramshackle and unnecessarily Byzantine structure: this is one aspect of the technical-rational thinking evident in, for example, QAA disciplinary benchmark standards in the UK. Such sentiments are understandable in the light of the massive growth of post-secondary provision witnessed in most countries inside a single generation, the accompanying escalation in costs, and the coincidental pressures of worldwide economic recession. They have, however, tended to be given expression through the adoption of a simplistic view of HE itself. It appears to have been derived from the conventional stereotype of an urban research community whose activities are conducted on a sizeable scale, based on well-organized teams, highly competitive one with another, and heavily dependent on external funding from industry and government. It is consequent on this interpretation that any academic department that does not measure up to such requirements is considered to be too small to be viable, managed in an amateurish fashion, insufficiently motivated to earn its keep within the ranks of the intellectual elite, and undeserving of resources for anything other than undergraduate teaching: 'a low tech cottage industry managed by amateurs' as Michael Thorne, Vice-Principal of Napier University, put it (MacLeod 2000b: 1).

The implications of such a perspective sit uneasily with the actualities of current practice, as a number of previous studies have emphasized. For example, Lodahl and Gordon (1972) noted that their findings:

> strongly argue against some current tendencies to view university problems in terms that are too simple to match the demands of technology and the associated realities of attitudes and activities found within scientific disciplines. Our results seem to indicate that there are differences between disciplines that go to the heart of teaching, research, and student-faculty relationships.

Along similar lines, Trowler's conclusions regarding the implementation of the credit framework in one university called for an appreciation by managers of the diversity of the disciplinary landscape and an awareness of the inappropriate imposition of modularity in some disciplines. Some were seen by their practitioners as appropriate candidates for a modular curriculum, given careful planning of the structure: physics was in this category. For others, however, a modular structure represented a Procrustean bed, which resulted in all kinds of discipline-specific problems (Trowler 1998a: 90–3). In the arts in particular such an attempt amounted, in the words of one art and design specialist, to 'trying to force a square peg into a round hole'.

Similarly, attempts to tackle issues related to teaching and learning that are not informed by an understanding of the diversity of the academic tribes and their territories are likely to prove problematic. While the links between pedagogy and the disciplines are both complex and under-researched (Donald 1997), it has been clear since Shulman completed his work (in 1986 and 1987) that they nonetheless exist and are important. In this regard the contributors to Hativa and Marincovich's (1995) volume conclude that:

- Teaching behaviours such as clarity, expressiveness and interaction with students vary by disciplinary category, but there are no disciplinary differences in terms of the ratings attached to the importance of these variables by the students themselves.
- As a result, there are disciplinary differences in overall ratings of instructor effectiveness by students, with those in the humanities, fine arts and health-related professions rated more highly in general; at the same time faculty members in soft disciplines are more likely to implement measures to improve teaching.
- Academics' understanding of their disciplinary subject matter can be seen to influence the approach they take to teaching it: there are distinct ways of thinking about, talking about and acting on teaching, which vary according to discipline.
- Academics in different disciplines place differing stress on the goals of education as between (1) knowledge acquisition, (2) knowledge application and (3) knowledge integration. Faculty in hard disciplines stress the second more than their colleagues; those in non-life soft fields stress the first and third more than colleagues in hard disciplines; faculty in life-systems hard and soft fields give the same weighting to these two goals. Teachers in some academic disciplines continue to stress simple transference of knowledge, despite the rhetorical emphasis in recent years on higher order skills.

The findings from a study based on the testimony of students by Astin (1997) finds important disciplinary differences among learners also, with majors in humanities, physical and social science and in psychology reporting satisfaction with their teaching and generally perceiving their faculty as student-oriented: less positive findings were reported among business and engineering students. Ylijoki (2000) suggests from research into computer science, library science and informatics, public administration and sociology and social psychology that different 'moral orders' of studying develop among students in these disciplines. Essentially the moral order represents a dimension of disciplinary culture into which students are socialized. As Ylijoki demonstrates, its consequences for quality assessment and the development of university teaching are both numerous and signficant.

Likewise Braxton and Hargens (1996), in a review of the literature on variations between disciplines in their orientations to teaching, similarly observe that high-consensus fields are likely to be more oriented to research, while chairs of low-consensus disciplines are more likely to emphasize teaching. Disciplines in the latter category tend to be more oriented to student-centred learning and student development, more ready to foster critical thinking, and more inclined to favour student self-assessment.

Other disciplinary contrasts include the relative difference in staff approaches to student assessment (Smart and Ettington 1995; Warren Piper *et al.* 1996), with a leaning towards short answer papers and multiple choice questions in hard pure fields and a greater openness to continuous assessment, long essay questions and in some cases oral examinations in soft-pure subjects. There are contrasts in the preferred learning skills of students (Nilson 1998), with those following hard-pure courses being 'required to apply hard facts and reliable data to a problem-solving situation . . . student opinion has little or no place' (p. 145), while for those studying soft pure programmes such as literature 'personal opinion is an integral aspect of interpretation . . . But more than in other fields . . . the writing style [is highly important]' (p. 146).

Perhaps unsurprisingly there are important disciplinary differences to be found in job satisfaction, career aspirations and motivation in general (Clark 1987b; Opp 1992) The implication is that attempts to introduce change also call for sensitivity to disciplinary differences.

Institutional context is important too, with those in US liberal arts colleges placing more emphasis on knowledge acquisition, for example, than those in other types of institution, while knowledge application is more stressed in US 2-year institutions. Braxton and Hargens (1996) note that faculty from high consensus disciplines find it easier to adjust to working in a teaching-only college than do low consensus faculty to a research university. Characteristics of the academic staff as a whole in a given institutional context may serve to counteract the influence of disciplinary cultures (Kempner 1990). Lattuca and Stark thus rightly note the interaction between institutional context (the institutional logic as Raffe *et al.* 1994, put it) and disciplinary factors:

> those who attempt to lead curricular reform may be more successful if they recognize both the strength of disciplinary culture and the campus contextual factors that make faculty redefine discipline cultures to meet local needs.
>
> (Lattuca and Stark 1995: 340)

As Bloor and Dawson (1994), Trowler and Turner (2001) and Knight and Trowler (2001) demonstrate, the interactions between professional and organizational cultures, personal and professional identities, Great Culture (national-level norms, values, assumptions) and participation in working groups are not only complex, but highly relevant for those seeking to introduce change.

To pursue these considerations as far as we can in the light of the present study, it must first be remarked that a large majority of academic departments are expected to maintain teaching programmes across a wide spectrum of the subject areas they represent. This means that, unless they are relatively large, their staffing policies have to be geared to the provision of several different specialisms, and hence that their academic membership can usually include no more than one or two people within any given specialism. There is, in other words, seldom a critical mass of researchers with cognate interests, such as would make it easy for departmentally based research teams to be established, let alone to make an identifiable impact.[10] There are some obvious exceptions to this generalization. Some departments, for instance, manage to build up viable (if unstable) research groups through the recruitment, on grant funds, of doctoral students and postdoctoral fellows. Others consciously narrow their undergraduate programmes, cutting out whole areas of the subject concerned, in order to concentrate research as well as teaching effort within a limited number of specialist fields. And quite large departments are able to operate on a generous enough scale to build up areas of research specialization within their tenured faculty while still maintaining a broad teaching provision. The difficulty is also ameliorated by the fact that some academics are involved in more than one research field at any given time and many teach in more than one topic area.

Even so, the overall picture is of academic institutions made up of basic organizational units whose constituent faculty members have relatively little mutuality of research interest. Given that different categories of specialism (pure and applied, hard and soft, urban and rural) may well coexist within the confines of a single small department, it also follows that there must be several distinct career patterns, reputation-building strategies, forms of external relationship, and the like. From this perspective, departments have indeed a noticeable resemblance to holding companies for their members, much as institutions can be portrayed as holding companies for their basic units (Halsey and Trow 1971; Becher and Kogan 1992).[11]

The absence of internal research communities has more direct implications for those working in urban contexts than for their opposite numbers engaged in rural enquiries. As we have seen, they gain clear professional advantages by establishing collaborative research programmes. Accordingly, they often find it necessary to link up with colleagues who are geographically scattered (one striking example, cited in Becher 1987b, was of a co-publication by authors in Kansas, Aarhus and Calcutta). Those who are highly active will tend to identify more strongly with external colleagues in their professional networks than with internal colleagues with whom they

may have much less in common. They are, in Gouldner's terms, cosmopolitans, as against the locals who remain committed to rural specialisms
(Gouldner 1957) and for them the invisible college (Crane 1972) has an
enhanced significance compared with that of their own university.

Such observations have a bearing on the comparisons between different
departments in the same institution and similar departments in different institutions. Some, as we have noted, may enjoy a higher status than their
competitors for no better reason than that they are affiliated to disciplines
that manifest a high degree of convergence; others, in contrast, are marked
down for their lack of intellectual coherence because their parent disciplines are divergent and fragmented. Academics in convergent departments
with predominantly urban characteristics are likely to accumulate more
prestigious honours and awards, and a larger volume of grant funding, than
those in divergent disciplines with predominantly rural research patterns.
Departments with a preponderance of urban researchers will often enjoy a
reputation for higher productivity than departments in the same field with
a majority of rural researchers, even though the output of the latter may be
well above average for their particular spread of specialisms, and the output
of the former may in their context be substantially below average. There is
no intrinsic scholarly merit in hard as opposed to soft, urban as opposed to
rural, or pure as opposed to applied, research: yet 'objective' criteria – at
least those of a strictly academic, rather than an entrepreneurial kind – will
tend to favour the first of each of these categories because they seem to
lend themselves to simple and uncontentious measurement as against complex and contestable judgement.

Individual academics differ in comparable ways, according to their type
of specialization. Those in urban networks, because of the greater intensity
of their involvement in their research, may appear to be more hard working
and more dedicated than their colleagues with rural lifestyles. They are also
likely to be well placed in their ability to earn outside funds and in the
frequency of their publication. These are basic criteria for determining
academic worth and eligibility for promotion: as in a number of other
respects, urban researchers are liable to be favoured at the expense of rural
ones if such yardsticks are too literally and crudely applied.

These arguments suggest that it is unjust and inappropriate to lump
together for administrative purposes different institutions, different subject
departments and different individuals, taking little or no account of the
variety of characteristics that they may between them quite reasonably display. Bureaucratically inspired measures of performance, which may be
seen as one by-product of a demand for efficiency and accountability in
HE, offer a striking instance of this tendency. They are typically designed
for imposition with equally blind impartiality across the whole range of
academic endeavour. But however carefully chosen the individual criteria
that make up such composite instruments may be, it is not difficult to
demonstrate the unevenness of their application and their varying relevance
to different subject fields. An example may serve to illustrate the point.

Consider an agency for academic management that chooses to allocate resources to departments, or a newspaper or other organization compiling a league table of departments and universities on the basis of the following mixture of internalist and externalist requirements: the annual level of outside research funding; the volume of refereed research publications (which, together with research funding, is likely to have some correlation with postgraduate student numbers); the ability – suitably quantified – to recruit good undergraduate students (which is likely to be linked to the staff:student ratio); and the subsequent employment statistics of those who have graduated. Each of these seems a perfectly reasonable measure of departmental competence. It may be useful to see what ratings, taken together, they are likely to yield for departments commonly held to be of good academic standing in four different disciplinary areas – physics, history, engineering and law.

Even the best physics departments, in the present context, have a relatively poor undergraduate recruitment (and a correspondingly low staff:student ratio), related, it is often said, to deficiencies in secondary schooling. The employment prospects for their graduates, according to recent statistics, are not particularly outstanding. They promise to come out well, however, on research grants and on refereed publications. Prestigious history departments will almost certainly do well on undergraduate recruit- ment (and on economical staff:student ratios), relatively poorly on graduate employment, only moderately well on publication (at least, in comparison with physics; see Chapter 6) and very poorly on grant earnings. The profiles of leading engineering departments are likely to be different again: a reason- ably high level of outside funding, a modest publication record (coupled with a dearth of postgraduates), a comparatively weak calibre of undergradu- ate student, but excellent employment prospects. Law departments of high standing are destined to offer an equally patchy performance, doing well only in those areas in which physics departments do badly, and badly in areas in which they do well: healthy recruitment, good employment statistics, negligible grant funding and a poor publication record (together with few postgraduate students).

There are bound to be inherent limitations in any attempt to apply such quasi-objective 'performance indicators' to an organization as complex and diverse as a university. The persistence with which central funding bodies, organizations seeking to increase the transparency of the HE market, and sometimes university bureaucracies themselves, espouse such simplistic devices may arise as much from a desire to appear to be fair and unbiased as from a less scrupulous wish to make managerial life easier. But once any recognition is allowed to the need to disaggregate the component elements in the organization, and to consider them in their particularity, rules of thumb of this kind must nonetheless be seen as totally inappropriate.

Nor do the considerations advanced earlier make it seem any more rea- sonable, despite its evident administrative attractions, to attempt to simplify and streamline the criteria for career progress within the institution as a whole: the distinctions between individuals' activities are sufficiently diverse to require some degree of subtlety, flexibility and openness alike in initial appointment, granting of tenure and promotion to higher rank.

A more fitting strategy for the assessment of academic worth would call for the detailed and reasonably sensitive case-by-case approach adopted in English common law, as against the rule-bound features generally held to be more appropriate in criminal proceedings. That is to say, it would almost certainly be the wisest policy to make do with the familiar system of peer group judgement whose inadequacies (see Chapter 5) are well acknowledged, but whose overwhelming advantage lies in its responsiveness to the variety and idiosyncrasy of all that counts as a legitimate form of intellectual endeavour. In the UK the Research Assessment Exercise and the Quality Assurance Agency's procedures have been the better for basing themselves on this approach.

In summary, it can be argued that a horticultural analogy is more appropriate than an industrial one in the advancement of learning. A market garden is successful insofar as it cultivates a variety of produce to meet its clients' disparate needs. To drive a bulldozer through it in the interests of greater efficiency and higher productivity makes sense only if one wishes to transform it into a cornfield. Corn grows easily, but too assiduous a concentration on producing it will – as we now know to our cost – create a massive and useless surplus of one particular commodity, and a corresponding scarcity of those whose cultivation, though beneficial in its own right, happens to be more demanding, more labour-intensive, and generally less easy to govern.

Managerialist intervention and academic autonomy

The imposition of managerialist values is not the only threat that academia faces. The discussion in Chapter 8 highlighted the extent to which research communities form part of a wider social environment on whose support they depend and to whose interests they are accordingly required to subscribe. Such obligations pose a problem whose resolution can differ in practice between one country and another and between one historical period and the next. The problem, however, is perennial, and the tension to which it gives rise inevitable. 'This tension in the political or policy sphere', Elzinga (1987b) writes, 'between utility and freedom, between steering and serendipity, runs parallel to the tension in the economic sphere between bounded resources and unbounded needs in research and development.'

Many commentators agree that the inroads on academic autonomy have increased significantly in recent years: but from a historical perspective (as Rothblatt 1985 demonstrates), the scope for outside intervention has been there from the earliest establishment of the academic profession. The role of those from whom the wherewithal comes – the direct agencies of government, the quasi-independent research councils, the independent grant-awarding foundations and the commercial and industrial sponsors concerned to buy knowledge and know-how – is crucial, and can be argued to carry certain moral obligations to preserve the integrity of the intellectual enterprise. Gibbons (1985) refers to 'the fear that, as a commodity, science will be manipulated for their own ends by those who allocate resources for research', adding that 'Given the economic and military potential of contemporary scientific knowledge, such manipulation cannot be regarded with equanimity.'

Leaving aside the issues that bear with particular insistence on hard pure knowledge, many other aspects of academic life have been affected by 'the trend towards more centralized bureaucratic control ... accompanied by greater emphasis on socially determined research objectives' (Geiger 1985). The considerations advanced in the previous chapter suggest, moreover, that 'grassroots movements' and professional lobbies may also attempt to shape the direction, and sometimes to censor or suppress the outcomes, of research: government and 'the military-industrial complex' are not alone in their concern to harness academic activity to suit their sectional interests.

The more narrowly functional the intellectual climate becomes, the greater the danger that 'The less seemingly applicable sciences, zoology, animal behaviour, plant physiology, or entomology – all fields which have made significant contributions to knowledge – could be permanently shrunk with little likelihood of attracting gifted young scientists' (Zinberg 1985). The relatively inexpensive disciplines outside science, however well they are regarded, may run the risk of similar impoverishment, as Kogan's (1987) study of history departments in contemporary UK HE underlines.

Developments of this kind lead inevitably to a defensive concern that something must be allowed to survive in the way of enquiry which is not blatantly the creature of outside circumstance. But the more emotive arguments – the appeals to the time-worn principles of academic freedom, the dire warnings of a crisis of civilized values – are unlikely to cut much ice among those enemies of an enlightened culture who were long ago pilloried by Matthew Arnold as barbarians and philistines. Rothblatt (1985) suggests that even 'the historic argument on behalf of pure science, namely, that it will one day result in applied science and technology, is largely unproven'. Although there are instances where this has happened (apparently arcane 'pure' research in mathematics, conducted long before the advent of modern computer technology, was found to be crucial in its development, for example) advancing an argument on the basis of a series of unique historical instances is both tricky and unconvincing.

One of the physicists interviewed for this study was emphatic in his acknowledgement that society, acting through the government funding agencies, had an absolute right to channel research in the directions it considered most appropriate. He was equally clear that it was counterproductive for this right to be exercised, in that to do so could eventually undermine the very foundations from which intellectual enquiry drew its stability and strength. The government, he contended, would best serve the interests of the public by facilitating basic research while minimizing attempts to direct it.

Geiger (1985) argues in essentially similar vein:

> reliance upon the internal mechanisms of science and the scientific community would ultimately be more conducive to furthering constructive types of adaptation. The essential work of science – hypothesising, testing, challenging, and reinterpreting knowledge – imports an inherent dynamic to its cognitive foundations. The basic institutional resources for the organization and funding of university research, then, ought to be designed insofar as possible to complement and facilitate the natural processes of adaptation and change that are continually at work in science. In the final analysis only such an approach seems capable of coping with the inescapable uncertainties that the future most certainly holds.

The argument for unpredictability is one cogent line of attack on instrumentalism, since even applied research is not immune from an uncertainty of means, if not of ends in view. However well-formulated its goals, the intellectual understanding that may be needed before those goals can be achieved is not so easily legislated in advance.

Another powerful rationale developed in support of academic autonomy relates to the inherent authority of specialized knowledge. As Rothblatt (1985) reminds us, too liberal a degree of outside involvement in the determination of research activity serves to undermine academics' professional expertise, posing:

> challenges in the way in which they govern themselves, ask questions, decide the research agenda, identify and reward success . . . Once the authority of the expert is rejected, standards are difficult to establish. There is no arbiter to distinguish the degree of scientific achievement.

A different, if equally dangerous, limitation may be imposed by outside interests on those areas of knowledge predominantly concerned with human affairs. The freedom to question established values is not the sole prerogative of centres of learning, though that may be strongly implied in some of the more high-minded discussions of the role of the university.[12] A spirit of free intellectual enquiry nonetheless seems an essential ingredient of any society which aspires to the virtues of democracy, and needs for that reason to be judiciously preserved. Social and political pressures, if allowed too easily to exert themselves, can have the effect of stifling critical discussion, especially in those areas of the humanities and social sciences that lend themselves to challenging received orthodoxy. For politicians in power to be able readily to command that particular academic departments should be open to external inspection, because they have been alleged to display 'Marxist bias', is not an unimaginably long step away from giving sanction to the infamous purges associated with Senator McCarthy in the early postwar years in the USA; nor, of course, to those of a different colour, but an even more devastating kind, perpetrated by the Stalinist regime in the former USSR. Within universities the same argument applies: Willmott (1993) has pointed to the dangers of cultural corporatism in a university environment and shown how the attempt to impose a managerial monoculture would effectively kill academic creativity, with all its consequent costs. One of the HE managers interviewed by Prichard (2000) recognized the need to 'tolerate' academic diversity:

> As far as I can see if you want to be a major research university you have got to have something like the traditional untidy structure of dean councils and senates with a fair amount of departmental autonomy ... if you want to be a major research university you have to tolerate a certain amount of chaos and anarchy.
>
> (Pro-Vice Chancellor, 'Harbourside' University, quoted in Prichard 2000: 137)

As Prichard notes, the way this is phrased firmly locates this manager within the managerialist 'station', while recognizing in amelioration that imposing an artificial orderliness is likely to prove counterproductive.

On the basis of a survey of 2630 academics in eight Australian universities, Winter notes that large-scale 'reforms' across the system, including those that can be categorized as managerialist, have had a major impact. In an attempt to reduce costs universities have engaged, to use the relevant jargon, in delayering, downsizing and outsourcing policies. These have indeed achieved savings, but at significant human cost. As an end result: 'An adverse behavioural consequence of managerialism may be academics exhibiting low levels of commitment to their institutions. Ultimately, low levels of commitment translate into organizational rigidity and a culture of stifled learning and creativity' (Winter *et al.* 2000: 9).

Elzinga (1987a) succinctly sums up the position in relation to academic knowledge as a whole: 'The principle of autonomy cannot be ditched; on the contrary, strong relevance and accountability pressures ... must be met with increased consciousness concerning the internalist mechanisms for quality control in the knowledge process.' He goes on to remark that:

> Arguments for autonomy may be based on (a) moral principles such as the need for critical research potential; (b) pragmatic principles that stipulate how good research results are only forthcoming if quality control criteria are upheld; and (c) epistemological claims concerning internal regulatives and their characteristic status of independent variables determining the attitudes ... towards external orientation, be it under pressure of sectoral policies, commercialisation or medial penetration. The third type of argument if it can be developed is a very strong argument for autonomy.

It is the establishment of this 'third type of argument' which we would take to be one of the main outcomes of this enquiry. Much as it can be shown that ecological environments establish a homeostasis which may be disrupted in quite unanticipated ways by external intervention, so too it can be argued that cultural systems depend on a delicate mutual adjustment of interests which, if insensitively encroached on, can result in their disintegration. We have sought to show that the ideals and the practices of academic communities and the nature of the knowledge they pursue are intimately connected. On the social dimension, too forceful a superimposition of the extrinsic values of accountability and relevance on the intrinsic values of reputation-seeking and quality control by peer-group judgement can only lead to intellectual subservience, and thence to academic sterility. As Clark (1997: 40) notes 'Those who seek to replace professional commitment with the nuts and bolts of bureaucratic regulation run down the calling . . . Wise academic leaders and sophisticated critics sense that only professional norms and practices are ingrained, person by person, in every activity to constructively shape behavior and steer motivation'. On the cognitive side of the equation, knowledge itself, viewed as a cultural resource, demands good husbandry and steady replenishment. It cannot, except in the short term, be constantly subjected to the stripping of its more marketable assets or the repression of the more challenging insights that it yields.

Mutual understandings and common causes

In an effort to preserve even a modest degree of intellectual integrity the enemy within should not remain unnoticed. Barnett (1988) underlines the danger of internal rivalry and dissension, pointing to 'a fairly unprincipled struggle' between competing interest groups, 'particularly evident at times of institutional threat but present all the time nevertheless'. In consequence, because the professional identity of academics 'lies with their own discipline, there is a general failure to notice those larger threats to academic freedom which affect the academic community as a whole'.

Barnett goes on to suggest that it is 'the fragmentation of the academic community into discrete disciplinary sub-cultures' which is to blame for 'reducing the internal sense of community across academic fields'. If he is right in his diagnosis, the condition would seem to have no easy remedy. The argument in the preceding pages has implied that knowledge has its own internal dynamic, and one which seems to demand an increasing level of specificity and specialization as enquiry proceeds. It is not so much an ingrained wilfulness that drives academics into exploring the deep and narrow parts of the territory they inhabit, but rather that – even if its boundaries are always subject to change, and new perspectives on it may occasionally be discerned – the broader, more open landscape is already well mapped.

It was suggested in Chapter 2 that knowledge is itself diverse and disparate, and in Chapter 4 that its piecemeal character gives rise to the very fragmentation of which Barnett complains. Clark (1983) rounds off his notable conspectus of the world of learning with a similar conclusion:

> It is around the formidable array of specific subjects and their self-generating and autonomous tendencies that HE becomes something unique, to be first understood in its own terms . . . Knowledge will

remain a divided and imperfect substance. In its fissions and faults we come closest to a root cause of the many odd ways of the HE system.

But Clark also remarks, in the course of his account, that all academics 'are part of a single "community of scholars", sharing an interest that sets them apart from others'. And Bailey (1977) reminds us that, from an anthropological perspective, the notion of group identity is context-dependent: what looks from one standpoint to be 'an arena of disputing factions' can be seen from another as 'a single culture which directs interactions between the many distinct and often mutually hostile groups'. He writes, too, of 'that sense of likeness with other members of the [academic] community and difference from outsiders, empirically present and not to be ignored', and of the 'community of culture . . . the whole set of tribes possess in common'. While it is clear that we need to use the plural form in talking about academic cultures and communities, there are good reasons for looking for commonalties across them.

The problem remains of how to bridge the evident divisions and thus to promote that recognition of commonality which seems essential to the maintenance of some measure of collective independence. Another anthropologist, in advocating 'an ethnography of the disciplines', has sketched the outlines of a possible solution:

> The problem of the integration of cultural life becomes one of making it possible for people inhabiting different worlds to have a genuine, and reciprocal, impact upon one another . . . the first step is surely to accept the depth of the differences; the second to understand what these differences are; and the third to construct some sort of vocabulary in which they can be publicly formulated.
>
> (Geertz 1983)

It is primarily towards taking the first and second of those steps that the present enquiry has been directed. Paradoxically, the more it becomes necessary to recognize the academic scene as disjointed and compartmentalized, the more essential it becomes to turn towards an apprehension of that scene in its entirety. The tribes, after all, share the same ethnicity; the territories they occupy are part of the same land mass.

If this, and other studies of its kind, can begin to succeed in constructing 'some sort of vocabulary' that enables academics in different fields better to understand each other – and hence perhaps to enhance their appreciation of their own particular share of the enterprise – it may be hoped that further benefits would ensue. An enhanced recognition of mutuality could serve as a better defence against the intrusive managerialism which seeks to impose a crude form of accountability, based on false assumptions about the nature of intellectual endeavour, and bolstered by insensitive and often spurious 'indicators of performance'. It might even help to persuade the wider society, on whose patronage the pursuit of knowledge ultimately depends, to maintain for academics a reasonable liberty – if one which remains well short of licence – in their choice of what to study and how to study it.

Notes

1. It might be added that (as Kuhn's 1962 analysis has made plain) the more universal a theory appears to be, the more vulnerable it is in the long run to contradictory evidence. Explanations which are generated from, and are firmly grounded in, a broad span of empirical data are less likely to be toppled; but only at the expense, in Kuhn's terms, of failing to present a sufficiently clear paradigm to allow for revolutionary conflict.

2. The convergent-divergent distinction is comparable along the social dimension (as is the hard-soft distinction along the cognitive dimension) with Kuhn's (1962, 1970) contrast between paradigmatic and pre-paradigmatic disciplines; and, following him, the dichotomy marked by Lodahl and Gordon (1972) between high and low levels of paradigm development. However, since these authors elide the social and cognitive aspects, their analysis implies that all hard disciplines are necessarily convergent (and vice versa) and all soft disciplines necessarily divergent (and vice versa). And this, as will shortly be argued, is a misleading simplification, since it allows no scope for convergent communities to be associated with soft knowledge and divergent with hard.

3. The point is not an easy one to make with clarity, and perhaps deserves elaboration. There are some countries that possess a unified national ideology, or at least a sentiment of shared identity of a kind which others do not. This is sometimes the case even when there are strongly marked internal divisions (linguistic, tribal, ethnic, political, religious, or a mixture of these) within the population as a whole. To take some examples, among the countries with a marked sense of nationhood, one might include Israel (with its multiplicity of political schisms) and the USA (with its polyglot population), alongside such more apparently homogeneous nations as Japan, Sweden, France, Libya or Iran. Countries that are visibly fragmented would include the Lebanon, Sri Lanka, Northern Ireland and Ruanda together with currently peaceable countries such as Belgium or Cyprus (in both of which two or more historically and culturally separate groups now happen more or less successfully to coexist). In similar ways, some disciplinary communities, such as physicists and economists, may have diverse constituent networks while clearly subscribing to the same overall cultural norms; others, such as sociologists or scholars of English Literature, may seem no more internally differentiated but may nonetheless be lacking in collective coherence.

4. Closely comparable problems would seem a less pervasive phenomenon across epistemological boundaries than mutually applicable techniques. This leads on to the speculation that disciplinary imperialism – the invasion and attempted colonization of others' territories – is typically a product of the transferability of methods from one set of problems to another, and therefore more commonly originates from a hard than a soft knowledge base.

5. The distinctions between the latter two perspectives are neatly delineated by Campbell and Wiles (1976). Their article also provides some useful insights into the development of the social sciences in Britain in the 1960s and 1970s.

6. This observation parallels the relationship hinted at in Chapters 4 and 5 between well-defined, closed segments and cohesive networks on the one hand, and

between segments with permeable boundaries and loosely knit networks on the other.

7. The suggestion here may be, however, an artefact of the limited representation in the sample of hard applied disciplines. Further investigation might accord convergence to academic medicine, accountancy, and perhaps to others among the technical professions.

8. In a remark tinged with envy, one of the botanists interviewed commented, 'The unity of biochemistry is a useful slogan, which has helped the subject to advance.'

9. As an interesting sidelight on the issue of socio-academic status, it would seem that lower-ranking and applied disciplines accord more recognition to consultancy activities than do higher-ranking and predominantly pure ones. Thus, informants in economics and physics, a number of whom undertook private work for outside contractors for a fee, were adamant that such work would not be mentioned in any application for career advancement (unless perhaps, one or two conceded, it was done for a prestigious agency of national or international government); but the geographers, lawyers, engineers and pharmacists suggested that consultancies were in their communities regarded as a proper, and indeed significant, feature of any curriculum vitae.

10. 'The department qua department is less significant for the furtherance of its members' research than it is as a centre of graduate training and the academic career ... The true research communities are the 'invisible colleges' – the handful of people around the world working in some subdiscipline or line of inquiry' (Trow 1976b).

11. One might indeed wonder how the average basic unit manages to be kept together, given that almost every constituent member has his or her individual profile of activities and concerns. Two answers, among other possible ones, may be noted. The first invokes disciplinary loyalties, which, particularly in convergent communities, can be counted on to override the more temporary affiliations to specialized research areas. The second draws on the analysis by Trow (1976b) in which, in the related conflict of interests between teaching and research, he argues that an emphasis on:

> the dominant norms and functions of university academic departments simplifies and distorts reality by implying that all the members of a department are oriented primarily ... to research, and fill their departmental functions in similar ways. In fact, there is a very considerable division of academic labour, both within and between departments. But this arises informally, and not through a formal assignment of roles and functions to different departmental members. Thus, the formal characteristics (and the equality) of departments and their members are preserved, while a considerable variability in individual talent, preference and disposition allows people actually to distribute their time and energy very differently among the various functions of the department ... The academic division of labour ... allows the academic department ... to perform in actuality a wider range of functions than would be possible if its members were more homogeneous in orientation and personal preference.

12. To the contrary, a sceptical observer might conclude that the majority of academics are depressingly ready to conform to current social expectations.

Appendix:
Data for the Initial Study

Subject coverage

This enquiry is based both on a scrutiny of the relevant research literature (see Bibliography) and on the material derived from interviews with practising academics in a dozen disciplines. The discussion that follows concentrates on the latter. In alphabetical order (with numbers in parentheses of those contributing) the disciplines covered are:

Biology: botany and zoology (27)*
Chemistry (15)
Economics (13)
Geography (12)
History (22)*
Law (24)*
Mathematics (13)

Mechanical engineering (22)*
Modern languages: French, German, Spanish, Italian (12)
Pharmacy (16)
Physics (23)*
Sociology (22)*

The asterisks indicate the subjects which provided the central body of data; those without asterisks were tackled in less depth, and could in that sense be classified as subsidiary. Altogether I conducted 221 interviews across the 12 disciplines. The shortest lasted half an hour and the longest nearly 2 hours. The average length was somewhere between an hour and an hour and a quarter.

Methods of data collection

The interviews were of a type characterized in the social sciences as semi-structured and in-depth. The first term means that the interviewer has a general checklist of points to be raised, but allows the respondent's interests and the resulting shape of the discussion to dictate the order and form in which these points are introduced. The second implies that the duration of the interview should be extensive enough and the degree of rapport strong enough for respondents to discuss complex and perhaps sensitive issues if they are so inclined.

A particular variant on standard interviewing techniques was adopted. Because the emphasis was on exploring as many aspects of disciplinary communities as possible, as against collecting statistically based information on a narrower range of topics, it was not considered essential for every interview to span the complete agenda: some respondents could take the opportunity to focus in detail on particular issues, while others could be invited to concentrate on the items which had hitherto been neglected. Moreover, since unforeseen points of a kind worth exploring further might be expected to crop up in the course of any given set of interviews, room needed to be provided for topics to be added between one interview and another. They could also of course be deleted if sufficient clarification had already been achieved.

Rather than being conceived of as a small-scale social survey, therefore, the study could be seen as analogous with a detective investigation, in which significant clues could be followed up and interesting testimony corroborated with (or contradicted by) other witnesses. It was nearly always possible, as the interviews in any particular field proceeded, to find corroboration from at least one other respondent – often more – about key aspects of the disciplinary culture.

In practice, the basic checklist did not change very significantly from the start of the first interview cycle in January 1980 to its completion in April 1987. That is to say, the main categories – the structure of the discipline, the pattern of academic careers in the field, the nature of professional life, forms of communication and publication, and relevant value issues – remained more or less constant, even though a number of subsidiary themes needed to be modified systematically between one discipline and another as well as individually between one respondent and another.

Wherever it proved feasible, those who agreed to make themselves available for interviewing were sent a brief note in advance explaining the purpose of the study and outlining the topics with which it was concerned. The note, in the form in which it had evolved by 1986/7, read as follows:

A study of the cultures of disciplines

Introduction
This note is meant to set the background for a series of open-ended interviews with practitioners in various academic disciplines. It is assumed that those who have agreed to participate are interested in a reflective discussion of their own subject specialism, and are willing to make their views known to an interested, but uninitiated, enquirer.

Context
The enquiry – of which it is hoped that the proposed discussion with you would form a part – is directed towards substantiating, or repudiating, the hunch that the members of different disciplines differ from one another in systematic and discernible ways. It is the nature rather than the causes of these differences that provides the immediate focus: but it could well turn out that some of the more significant contrasts relate to epistemological issues – that is, to the forms of knowledge characteristic of particular areas of intellectual investigation.

It is not intended to elicit any information about the personal, is opposed to the professional, lives of those interviewed. (Whether, e.g. biologists drive faster cars than historians may be an interesting issue, but it is no concern of the present proposal.)

Content and format
There are likely to be six main areas for discussion (see below) though I am anxious
not to be rigid about these, and would like to leave scope for others to be raised
according to individual interest. Whether or not all six are covered will be a matter
for individual informants to decide.

I would hope, in the normal course of events, to interview each informant in his
or her own room, at a mutually convenient time. The length of the session would
again be a matter of the informant's own choice, but – on the basis of experience –
I would expect the timespan to lie somewhere between an upper limit of an hour
and a half and a lower limit of half an hour. The normal conventions of anonymity
and confidentiality would of course be strictly observed.

Some possible themes for discussion

The structure of the subject
External and internal boundaries; extent of overall cohesion/fragmentation; relationships with neighbouring fields, etc.

Epistemological issues
Nature of evidence; forms of controversy; scope for ideology; verification/confirma-
tion procedures, etc.

Career patterns
Modes of recruitment; initial barriers to tenure; choice of specialization; mobility
between specialisms; extent of emigration from/immigration to other disciplines,
etc.

Reputation and rewards
Criteria for professional recognition; terms of praise and blame; nature and existence of disciplinary heroes; marks of distinction, etc.

Aspects of professional practice
Individual scholarship versus teamwork; types of professional association; varieties of
communication; publishing patterns; purposes of citation; availability of outside
funds; characteristics of competition, etc.

Costs and benefits of disciplinary membership
Pros and cons of professional career; qualities fostered; predominant values; enjoyment, frustration and boredom in work, etc.

In almost every case, recipients commented that this note had given them a reasonable idea of what kind of discussion to expect: although they were offered a specific
opportunity to raise any preliminary queries, very few wanted to do so. The implication is that the academics concerned felt generally at ease with the themes of the
interviews. As might have been expected from their professional skills and background, they were invariably both articulate and lucid in their responses, to an
extent which made interviewing them pleasurable as well as not too demanding (see
Platt 1981 for some detailed comments on academics as interview subjects). A

sizeable proportion of respondents remarked at the end of the session that they had enjoyed the opportunity to talk about their work; some went on to voice their regret that opportunities of this kind were so rare.

Variables in the research design

At the outset, a careful attempt was made to span the full range from senior to junior members of any department visited. That is to say, doctoral students and untenured research fellows were sought out as well as mid-career academics and those approaching retirement. However, no systematic difference was discernible in the responses of any of these categories: though views within a given community might differ, they did not appear significantly to do so in terms of age and experience. Accordingly, though the later interviews continued to involve academics of

Table A.1 Institutions visited in relation to the disciplines in the study

Discipline	UK	USA
Biology	Bristol, Reading	California (Berkeley)
Chemistry	Southampton	California (Berkeley, Santa Barbara, Los Angeles), Stanford
Economics	Cambridge	California (Berkeley, Santa Barbara, Los Angeles), Stanford
Geography	Cambridge	California (Berkeley, Santa Barbara, Los Angeles)
History	Exeter, London (University College)	California (Berkeley)
Law	Kent, London (LSE), Southampton	California (Berkeley)
Mathematics	Southampton	California (Berkeley, Santa Barbara, Los Angeles), Stanford
Mechanical Engineering	Birmingham, London (Imperial)	California (Berkeley)
Modern Languages	Cambridge	California (Berkeley, Santa Barbara, Los Angeles), Stanford
Pharmacy	Brighton Polytechnic London (Chelsea)	California (San Francisco)
Physics	Bristol, London (Imperial)	California (Berkeley)
Sociology	Essex, London (LSE), Kent	California (Berkeley)

Note: Pilot interviews for biology, history, law, mechanical engineering, physics and sociology were carried out in Sussex varying degrees of seniority, this was less a matter of deliberate design than had been the case earlier on.

Two concerns in drawing up the sample were, first, to be able to offset the particular characteristics of individual departments, and, second, to see how far national idiosyncrasies might play a part in the picture which emerged of one discipline or another. Together, they implied the need not only to widen the enquiry beyond a single department but also to extend it if possible outside the UK. The one requirement was taken into account by ensuring that every main discipline at least should be represented by two or more departments in UK universities; and the other by adding a modest-sized US dimension to the enquiry. A list of the institutions visited in relation to each discipline is set out in Table A.1. Their choice was determined partly by geographical considerations. All those in the UK were within relatively easy reach of the University of Sussex; in the US, most of the interviews were conducted at Berkeley (where the interviewer was a Visiting Fellow for 3 months in 1980 and a further 3 months in 1986) and the remainder in universities reasonably accessible to it.

As already remarked, the interviews in California were intended mainly to gain some impression of how British academics might differ from their American counterparts. In the event it transpired that the differences were, save in a few cases, negligible. Nevertheless the transatlantic study was pursued in part because of the possibility of catching more contrasts, but also because it provided an opportunity to extend the data base. The increase in spread of US universities (from one for the six main disciplines to four for the subsidiary ones) again made little difference: the chemists, the modern linguists and so on in one institution were very much like those in another.

Bibliography

Acker, S. (1994) *Gendered Education.* Buckingham: Open University Press.

Acker, S. and Feuerverger, G. (1996) Doing good and feeling bad: the work of women university teachers, *Cambridge Journal of Education,* 26(3): 401–42.

Acker, S., Black, E. and Hill, T. (1994) Research students and their supervisors in education and psychology, in R.G. Burgess (ed.) *Postgraduate Education and Training in the Social Sciences,* pp. 53–74. London: Jessica Kingsley.

Adams, D. (1998) Examining the fabric of academic life: an analysis of three decades of research on the perceptions of Australian academics about their roles. *Higher Education,* 36: 421–35.

Allen, P.M. (1998) Towards a black construct of accessibility, in T. Modood and T. Acland (eds) *Race and Higher Education,* pp. 86–95. London: Policy Studies Institute.

Allison, G.T. (1971) *Essence of Decision: explaining the Cuban missile crisis.* Boston: Little, Brown.

Allison, P.D. (1980) Inequalities in scientific productivity, *Social Studies of Science,* 10: 163–79.

Altbach, P. (1997) An international academic crisis? The American professoriate in comparative perspective, *Daedalus,* 126(4): 315–38.

Alvesson, M. (1993) *Cultural Perspectives on Organisations.* Cambridge: Cambridge University Press.

Alvesson, M. and Skoldberg, K. (2000) *Reflexive Methodology: New vistas for qualitative research.* London: Sage.

Andreski, S. (1972) *Social Science as Sorcery.* London: Andre Deutsch.

Anthony, L.J., East, H. and Slater, M.J. (1969) The growth of the literature of physics, *Reports on Progress in Physics,* 32: 709–67.

Arnold, M. (1894) *Culture and Anarchy.* Uniform edition. London: Smith and Elder.

Association of University Professors of Social Work (1994) *AUPSW List.* Dundee: University of Dundee Department of Social Work.

Astin, A.W. (1997) *What Matters in College? 4 critical years revisited.* San Francisco, CA: Jossey-Bass.

Bagilhole, B. (1993) How to keep a good woman down: an investigation of the role of institutional factors in the process of discrimination against women academics, *British Journal of Sociology of Education,* 14(3): 261–74.

Bagilhole, B. (1994) Being different is a very difficult row to hoe: survival strategies of women academics, in S. Davies, C. Lubelska and J. Quinn (eds) *Changing the Subject.* London: Taylor & Francis.

Bailey, F.G. (1977) *Morality and Expediency.* Oxford: Blackwell.

Ball, S.J. (1982) Competition and conflict in the teaching of English, *Journal of Curriculum Studies,* 14(1): 1–28.

Ball, S. and Lacey, C. (1995) Revisiting subject disciplines as the opportunity for group action: a measured critique of subject subcultures, in L.S. Siskin and J.W. Little (eds) *The Subjects in Question: departmental organization and the high school,* pp. 95–122. New York: Teachers College Press.

Ball, S.J. (1997) Policy sociology and critical social research: a personal review of recent education policy and policy research, *British Educational Research Journal,* 23(3): 257–74.

Ballantyne, R., Bain, J. and Packer, J. (1999) Researching university teaching in Australia: themes and issues in academics' reflections, *Studies in Higher Education,* 24(2): 237–57.

Barber, B. (1961) Resistance by scientists to scientific discovery. *Science,* 134: 596–602.

Barber, B. (1968) The functions and dysfunctions of fashion in science, *Mens en Maatschappij,* 43(6): 501–14.

Barnes, B. and Dolby, R.G.A. (1970) The scientific ethos, *European Journal of Sociology,* 2: 3–25.

Barnes-Powell, T. and Letherby, G. (1998) All in a day's work: gendered care work in higher education, in D. Malina and S. Maslin-Prothero (eds) *Surviving the Academy: Feminist Perspectives,* pp. 69–77. London: Falmer.

Barnett, C. (ed.) (1986) *The Audit of War.* London: Macmillan.

Barnett, R. (1988) Limits to academic freedom, in M. Tight (ed.) *Academic Freedom and Responsibility.* Milton Keynes: Open University Press.

Barnett, R. (1997) *Higher Education: A Critical Business.* Buckingham: Open University Press.

Barnett, R. (2000) *Realizing the University: in an age of supercomplexity.* Buckingham: Open University Press.

Barry, B. (1981) Do neighbours make good fences? *Political Theory,* 9(3): 293–301.

Baruch, J. (1984) The cultures of science and technology, *Science,* 244: 7.

Baudrillard, J. (1985) The ecstasy of communication, in H. Foster (ed.) *Postmodern Culture.* London: Pluto.

Bazerman, C. (1981) What written knowledge does, *Philosophy of the Social Sciences,* 2: 361–87.

Bazerman, C. (1987) Literate acts and the emergent social structure of science, *Social Epistemology,* 1(4): 295–310.

Becher, T. (1987a) The disciplinary shaping of the profession, in B.R. Clark (ed.) *The Academic Profession.* Berkeley, CA: University of California Press.

Becher, T. (1987b) Disciplinary discourse, *Studies in Higher Education,* 12(3): 261–74.

Becher, T. (1990) The counter-culture of specialisation, *European Journal of Education,* 25(3): 333–46.

Becher, T. (1994) The significance of disciplinary differences, *Studies in Higher Education,* 19(2): 151–61.

Becher, T. (1997) The hunting of the gilt-edged degree, in J. Brennan, P. de Vries and R. Williams (eds) *Standards and Quality in Higher Education,* pp. 157–69. London: Jessica Kingsley.

Becher, T. (1999) *Professional Practices: Commitment and Capability in a Changing Environment*. New Brunswick: Transaction Publishers.

Becher, T. and Kogan, M. (1992) *Process and Structure in Higher Education*, 2nd edn. London: Routledge.

Becher, T., Henkel, M. and Kogan, M. (1994) *Graduate Education in Britain*. London: Jessica Kingsley.

Becker, H.S. (1982) *Art Worlds*. Berkeley, CA: University of California Press.

Becker, H.S., Geer, B. and Hughes, E.C. (1961) *Boys in White*. Chicago, IL: University of Chicago Press.

Ben-David, J. (1960) Roles and innovations in medicine, *American Journal of Sociology*, 65: 557–68.

Ben-David, J. (1964) Scientific growth: a sociological view, *Minerva*, 2: 455–76.

Ben-David, J. and Collins, R. (1966) Social factors in the origin of a new science, *American Sociological Review*, 31: 451–65.

Benjamin, E. (1999) Disparities in the salaries and appointments of academic women and men: an update of a 1988 report of Committee W on the status of women in the academic profession. American Association of University Professors. www.aaup.org/Wrepup.htm (accessed 1 November 2000).

Bereiter, C. and Freedman, M.B. (1962) Fields of study and the people in them, in N. Sanford (ed.) *The American College*. New York: John Wiley.

Berger, P. and Luckmann, T. (1966) *The Social Construction of Reality*. Harmondsworth: Penguin.

Bergonzi, B. (1990) *Exploring English*. Oxford: Clarendon Press.

Bernal, J.D. (1939) *The Social Function of Science*. London: Routledge.

Bernard, J. (1964) *Academic Women*. University Park, PA: Pennsylvania State University Press.

Bernstein, B. (1971) On the classification and framing of educational knowledge, in M.F.D. Young (ed.) *Knowledge and Control*, pp. 47–69. London: Collier Macmillan.

Bett, M. (1999) *Independent Review of Higher Education Pay and Conditions*. London: The Stationery Office (Bett Report).

Biglan, A. (1973a) The characteristics of subject matter in different scientific areas, *Journal of Applied Psychology*, 57(3): 195–203.

Biglan, A. (1973b) Relationships between subject matter characteristics and the structure and output of university departments, *Journal of Applied Psychology*, 57(3): 204–13.

Blackstone, T. and Fulton, O. (1975) Sex discrimination among women university teachers, *British Journal of Sociology*, 26(3): 261–75.

Blaug, M. (1985) *Great Economists since Keynes*. Brighton: Wheatsheaf.

Blaug, M. (1986) *Great Economists before Keynes*. Brighton: Wheatsheaf.

Bloland, H.G. (1995) Postmodernism and higher education, *Journal of Higher Education*, 66(5): 521–59.

Bloor, G. and Dawson, P. (1994) Understanding professional culture in organizational context, *Organization Studies*, 15(2): 275–95.

Blume, S. (1985) After the darkest hour integrity and engagement in the development of university research, in B. Wittrock and A. Elzinga (eds) *The University Research System*. Stockholm: Almqvist and Wiksell.

Böhme, G., van den Dael, W. and Krohn, W. (1976) Finalization in science, *Social Science Information*, 15: 307–30.

Boice, R. (1992) *The New Faculty Member: Supporting and Fostering Professional Development*. San Francisco, CA: Jossey-Bass.

216   *Academic Tribes and Territories*

Boissevain, J. (1974) Towards a sociology of social anthropology, *Theory and Society*, 1: 211–30.

Boulding, K. (1956) *The Image*. Ann Arbor, MI: University of Michigan Press.

Bourdieu, P. (1979) Les trois états du capital culturel, *Actes de la Recherche en Sciences Sociales*, 30: 3–6.

Bourdieu, P. (1981) The specificity of the scientific field, in C.C. Lemert (ed.) *French Sociology*. New York: Columbia University Press.

Bowe, R., Ball, S.J. and Gewirtz, S. (1994) Captured by the discourse? Issues and concerns in researching parental choice, *British Journal of Sociology of Education*, 15(1): 63–78.

Bown, H.R. and Schuster, J.H. (1986) *American Professors: A National Resource Imperilled*. New York: Oxford University Press.

Boyer, E. (1990) *Scholarship Reconsidered: priorities of the professoriat*. Princeton, NJ: Carnegie Foundation for the Advancement of Teaching.

Boys, C., Brennan, J., Henkel, M. *et al.* (1988) *Higher Education and the Preparation for Work*. London: Jessica Kingsley.

Bradbury, M. (1977) *The History Man*. London: Arrow.

Braun, D. (1999) New managerialism and the governance of universities in a comparative perspective, in D. Braun and F-X. Merrien (eds) *Towards a New Model of Governance for Universities?*, pp. 239–61. London: Jessica Kingsley.

Braxton, J.M. (1995) Disciplines with and affinity for the improvement of undergraduate education, in N. Hativa and M. Marincovich (eds) *Disciplinary Differences in Teaching and Learning: Implications for Practice*, pp. 59–64. San Fransisco: Jossey-Bass.

Braxton, J.M. and Hargens, L.L. (1996) Variation among academic disciplines: analytical frameworks and research, in J.C. Smart (ed.) *Higher Education: Handbook of Theory and Research*, vol. 11, pp. 1–46. New York: Agathon.

Brookman, J. (1992) Same song but with a different tune, *Times Higher Education Supplement*, 2 October: 21.

Brooks, A. (1997) *Academic Women*. Buckingham: Open University Press.

Brown, D.G. (1967) *The Mobile Professors*. Washington, DC: American Council on Education.

Brown, J.S. and Duguid, P. (2000) *The Social Life of Information*. Boston, MA: Harvard Business School Press.

Buchanan, J.M. (1966) Economics and its scientific neighbours, in S.R. Krupp (ed.) *The Structure of Economic Science*. Engelwood Cliffs, NJ: Prentice-Hall.

Bucher, R. and Strauss, A. (1961) Professions in process, *American Journal of Sociology*, 66: 325–34.

Bulik, S. (1982) *Structure and Subject Interaction*. New York: Marcel Dekker.

Burbules, N. (1997) Web publishing and educational scholarship: where issues of form and content meet, *Cambridge Journal of Education*, 27(2): 273–82.

Burbules, N. (1998) Digital texts and the future of scholarly writing and publication, *Journal of Curriculum Studies*, 30(1): 105–24.

Burke, P. (1980) *Sociology and History*. London: Allen & Unwin.

Burton, R.E. and Kebler, R.W. (1960) The 'half-life' of some scientific and technical literatures, *American Documentation*, 11: 18–22.

Callahan, R.E. (1962) *Education and The Cult of Efficiency: A Study of the Social Forces that have Shaped the Administration of the Public Schools*. Chicago, IL: Chicago University Press.

Cameron, K. and Tschirhart, M. (1992) Postindustrial environments and organizational effectiveness in colleges and universities, *Journal of Higher Education*, 63(1): 87–108.

Campbell, C.M. and Wiles, P. (1976) The study of law in society in Britain, *Law and Society Review*, 10: 547–78.

Campbell, D.T. (1969) Ethnocentrism of disciplines and the fish-scale model of omniscience, in M. Sherif and C. Sherif (eds) *Interdisciplinary Relationships in the Social Sciences*. Chicago, IL: Aldine.

Carnegie Commission on Higher Education (1973) *Opportunities for Women in Higher Education*. New York: McGraw-Hill.

Carnegie Foundation for the Advancement of Teaching (1989) *The Condition of the Professoriat: Attitudes and Trends*. Princeton, NJ: CFAT.

Carnegie Foundation for the Advancement of Teaching (1990) Women excel as campus citizens, *Change*, 2: 39–43.

Carter, J. (ed.) (1961) *A.E. Housman: Selected Prose*. Cambridge: Cambridge University Press.

Chubin, D.E. (1976) The conceptualisation of scientific specialties, *Sociological Quarterly*, 17: 448–76.

Chubin, D.E. and Moitra, S. (1975) Content analysis of references, *Social Studies of Science*, 5: 423–41.

Church, C.H. (1973) The professional pale, in G.P. Taylor (ed.) *History in Higher Education*. Sheffield: Sheffield Polytechnic.

Church, C.H. (1976) Disciplinary dynamics, *Studies in Higher Education*, 1(2): 101–18.

Church, C.H. (1978) Constraints on the historian, *Studies in Higher Education*, 3(2): 127–38.

Clark, B. (1963) Faculty culture, in T.F. Lunsford (ed.) *The Study of Campus Cultures*. Boulder, CO: Western Interstate Commission for Higher Education.

Clark, B. (1980) *Academic Culture*, working paper no. 42. New Haven, CN: Yale University Higher Education Research Group.

Clark, B. (1983) *The Higher Education System*. Berkeley, CA: University of California Press.

Clark, B. (1987a) *The Academic Life: Small Worlds, Different Worlds*. Princeton NJ: The Carnegie Foundation for the Advancement of Teaching.

Clark, B.R. (ed.) (1987b) *The Academic Profession*. Berkeley, CA: University of California Press.

Clark, B. (1991) The fragmentation of research, teaching and study, in M. Trow and T. Nybom (eds) *University and Society: Essays on the Social Role of Research and Higher Education*. London: Jessica Kingsley.

Clark, B. and Neave, G. (eds) (1992) Academic Disciplines and Indexes, *The Encyclopedia of Higher Education*, vol. 4, Oxford: Pergamon Press.

Clark, B. (1993) *The Research Foundations of Graduate Education: Germany, Britain, France, United States, Japan*. Berkeley and Los Angeles, CA: University of California Press.

Clark, B. (1993) The problem of complexity in modern higher education, in S. Rothblatt and B. Wittrock (eds) *The European and American University Since 1800: Historical and Sociological Essays*, pp. 263–79. Cambridge: Cambridge University Press.

Clark, B. (1995) Complexity and differentiation: the deepening problem of university integration, in D. Dill and B. Sporn (eds) (1995) *Emerging Patterns of Social Demand and University Reform: Through a Glass Darkly*. Oxford: IAU Press/Elsevier.

Clark, B. (1996a) Case studies of innovative universities: a progress report. *Tertiary Education and Management*, 2(1): 53–62.

Clark, B. (1996b) Substantive growth and innovative organization: new categories for higher education research, *Higher Education*, 32: 417–30.

Clark, B. (1997) Small worlds, different worlds: the uniqueness and troubles of American academic professions, *Daedalus*, 126(4): 21–42.

Clark, B. (1998) *Creating Entrepreneurial Universities: Organizational Pathways of Transformation*. London: Pergamon.

Clark, C., Moss, P.A., Goering, S. *et al.* (1996) Collaboration as dialogue – teachers and researchers engaged in communication and professional development, *American Educational Research Journal*, 33: 193–231.

Clarke, B.L. (1964) Multiple authorship trends in scientific papers, *Science*, 143: 822–4.

Coate, K. (1999) Feminist knowledge and the ivory tower: a case study, *Gender and Education*, 11(2): 141–59.

Cockburn, C. (1991) *In The Way of Women: Men's Resistance to Sex Equality in Organizations*. London: Macmillan.

Coffey, A. and Acker, S. (1991) 'Girlies on the warpath': addressing gender in initial teacher education, *Gender and Education*, 3: 249–61.

Cohn, B.S. (1962) An anthropologist among the historians, *South Atlantic Quarterly*, 61 (Winter): 13–28.

Cole, J.R. (1979) *Fair Science: Women in the Scientific Community*. New York: Free Press.

Cole, J.R. and Cole, S. (1973) *Social Stratification in Science*. Chicago, IL: Chicago University Press.

Cole, M. (1998) Globalisation, modernisation and competitiveness: a critique of the New Labour project in education, *International Studies in Sociology of Education*, 8(3): 315–32.

Cole, S. (1970) Professional standing and the reception of scientific discoveries, *American Journal of Sociology*, 76: 286–306.

Cole, S. (1978) Scientific reward systems: a comparative analysis, in R.A. Jones (ed.) *Research in Sociology of Knowledge, Sciences and Art*, 1. Greenwich, CN: JAI.

Cole, S. (1983) The hierarchy of the sciences, *American Journal of Sociology*, 89(1): 111–39.

Cole, S. and Cole, J. (1967) Scientific output and recognition, *American Sociological Review*, 32: 377–90.

Cole, S., Rubin, L. and Cole, J.R. (1977) Peer review and the support of science, *Scientific American*, 237 (October): 34–41.

Cole, S., Cole, J.R. and Simon, G.A. (1981) Chance and consensus in peer review, *Science*, 214: 881–6.

Collins, R. (1975) *Conflict Sociology*. London and San Diego: Academic Press.

Connell, R.W. (1987) *Gender and Power*. Oxford: Polity Press/Blackwell.

Cooper, B. (1985) *Renegotiating Secondary School Mathematics*. Lewes: Falmer Press.

Cotterill, P. and Waterhouse, R.L. (1996) I don't know how to tell you this but . . . : the invisibility of emotional labour in mass higher education. Paper presented at the Dilemmas of Mass Higher Education conference, Staffordshire University, 10–12 April.

Cotterill, P. and Waterhouse, R.L. (1998) Speaking confidentially, or how long have I got? The demise of the personal tutorial in higher education, in D. Jary and M. Parker (eds) *The New Higher Education: Issues and Directions for the Post-Dearing University*. Stoke-on-Trent: Staffordshire University Press.

Crane, D. (1965) Scientists at major and minor universities, *American Sociological Review*, 30: 699–714.

Crane, D. (1967) The gatekeepers of science, *American Sociologist*, 2: 195–201.

Crane, D. (1969a) Social structure in a group of scientists, *American Sociological Review*, 34: 335–52.

Crane, D. (1969b) Fashion in science, *Social Problems*, 16: 433–40.

Crane, D. (1972) *Invisible Colleges: Diffusion of Knowledge in Scientific Communities*. Chicago, IL: University of Chicago Press.

Cribb, A. and Bignold, S. (1999) Towards the reflexive medical school: the hidden curriculum and medical education research, *Studies in Higher Education*, 24(2): 195–210.

Crick, M. (1976) *Explorations in Language and Meaning*. London: Malaby Press.

Cronin, B. (1984) *The Citation Process*. London: Taylor Graham.

Cross, W.T. (1991) Pathway to the professoriate: the American Indian faculty pipeline, *Journal of American Indian Education*, 30(2): 13–24.

CVCP/HEFCE (2000) *The Business of Borderless Education: UK Perspectives*. London: CVCP/HEFCE.

Dahrendorf, R. (1968) *Homo Sociologicus*. London: Routledge.

Daniel, J.S. (1996) *Mega-Universities and Knowledge Media: Technology Strategies for Higher Education*. London: Kogan Page.

Darnton, R. (1968) *Mesmerism and the End of the Enlightenment in France*. Cambridge, MA: Harvard University Press.

Dasgupta, P. and David, P.A. (1985) *Information Disclosure and the Economics of Science and Technology*, publication no. 48. Stanford: Stanford University Center for Economic Policy Research.

Davidson, G. (1994) *Credit Accumulation and Transfer in the British Universities 1990–1993*. Canterbury: University of Kent.

Davies, C. and Holloway, P. (1995) Troubling transformations: gender regimes and organizational culture in the academy, in L. Morley and V. Walsh (eds) *Feminist Academics*, pp. 7–21. London: Taylor & Francis.

Dearing, R. (1997) *Higher Education in the Learning Society*. London: DfEE.

Dearlove, J. (1999) The academic labour process: from collegiality and professionalism to managerialism and proletarianisation? *Higher Education Review*, 30(1): 56–75.

Deem, R. (1996) Border territories: a journey through sociology, education and women's studies, *British Journal of Sociology of Education*, 17(1): 5–19.

Deem, R. (1998) 'New managerialism' and higher education: the management of performances and cultures in universities in the United Kingdom, *International Studies in Sociology of Education*, 8(1): 47–70.

Deem, R. and Brehony, K. (2000) Doctoral students' access to research cultures: are some more equal than others? *Studies in Higher Education*, 25(2): 149–65.

Dennis, W. (1956) Age and productivity among scientists, *Science*, 123: 724–5.

Dennis, W. (1958) The age decrement in outstanding scientific contributions, *American Psychologist*, 13: 457–60.

Dennis, W. (1966) Creative productivity between the ages of 20 and 80 years, *Journal of Gerontology*, 21: 1–8.

DES (1987) *Higher Education: Meeting the Challenge*, Cmnd 114. London: HMSO.

DES (1991) *Higher Education: A New Framework*, Cmnd 1541. London: HMSO.

DfE (1993a) *Higher Education Statistics for the UK*. London: HMSO.

DfE (1993b) *Realising Our Potential*, Cmnd 2250. London: HMSO.

DfE (1994) *Student Numbers in Higher Education – Great Britain 1982/3 to 1992/3*. Statistical Bulletin, August, Issue number 13/94. London: HMSO.

DfEE (1999) *Learning to Succeed: A New Framework for Post 16 Learning*, Cmnd 4392. London: The Stationery Office.

Dill, D. (1992) Academic administration, in B. Clark and G. Neave (eds) *The Encyclopedia of Higher Education*, vol. 3, pp. 1218–1329. Oxford: Pergamon.

Dill, D. and Sporn, B. (1995) The implications of the postindustrial environment, in D. Dill and B. Sporn (eds) *Emerging Patterns of Social Demand and University Reform: Through a Glass Darkly*, pp. 1–19. Oxford: IAU Press/Elsevier.

Dill, D. and Sporn, B. (eds) (1995) *Emerging Patterns of Social Demand and University Reform: Through a Glass Darkly*. Oxford: IAU Press/Elsevier.

Dill, D.D. (1982) The management of academic culture, *Higher Education*, 11: 303–20.

Dominelli, L. (1998) Women, social work and academia, in D. Malina and S. Maslin-Prothero (eds) *Surviving the Academy: Feminist Perspectives*, pp. 42–53. London: Falmer.

Donald, J. (1997) *Improving the Environment for Learning: Academic Leaders Talk about What Works*. San Fransisco, CA: Jossey-Bass.

Dooris, M.J. and Fairweather, J.S. (1994) Structure and culture in faculty work: implications for technology transfer, *The Review of Higher Education*, 17(2): 161–77.

Duncan, S.S. (1974) The isolation of scientific discovery, *Science Studies*, 4: 109–34.

Eisenstadt, M. and Vincent, T. (1999) *The Knowledge Web*. London: Kogan Page.

Elzinga, A. (1985) Research bureaucracy and the drift of epistemic criteria, in B. Wittrock and A. Elzinga (eds) *The University Research System*. Stockholm: Almqvist and Wiksell.

Elzinga, A. (1987a) Internal and external regulatives in research and higher education systems, in R. Premfors (ed.) *Disciplinary Perspectives on Higher Education and Research*, Report No. 37. Stockholm: University of Stockholm GSHR.

Elzinga, A. (1987b) Politicization of science and epistemic drift. Mimeo, Dalarö 1987 International Conference, Swedish National Board of Universities and Colleges, Research on Higher Education Program.

Engeström, Y. (2000) Comment on Blackler *et al.*, activity theory and the social construction of knowledge: a story of four umpires, *Organization*, 7(2): 301–10.

Erikson, K.T. (1970) Sociology and the historical perspective, *American Sociologist*, 5: 331–8.

Esmail, A. and Dewart, P. (1998) Failure of Asian students in clinical examinations: the Manchester experience, in T. Modood and T. Acland (eds) *Race and Higher Education*, pp. 134–43. London: Policy Studies Institute.

Etzkowitz, H. and Leydesdorff, L. (eds) (1997) *Universities and the Global Knowledge Economy: A Triple Helix of University–Industry–Government Relations*. London: Pinter.

Eustace, R. (1994) University autonomy: the '80s and after, *Higher Education Quarterly*, 48(2): 86–117.

Evans, C. (1983) EFCOM versus PHILIT: the politics of modern languages. Mimeo: Zeitschrift fur Hochschuldidaktic, Klagenfurt.

Evans, C. (1988) *Language People*. Milton Keynes: Open University Press.

Evans, C. (1990) A cultural view of the discipline of modern languages, *European Journal of Education*, 25(3): 273–82.

Evans, C. (1993) *English People*. Buckingham: SRHE/Open University Press.

Evans, C. (1995) Choosing people: recruitment and selection as leverage on subjects and disciplines, *Studies in Higher Education*, 20(3): 253–65.

Evans-Pritchard, E.E. (1951) *Social Anthropology*. London: Routledge.

Fairley, J. and Patterson, L. (1995) Scottish education and the new managerialism, *Scottish Educational Review*, 27(1): 13–36.

Fell, H.B. (1960) Fashion in cell biology, *Science*, 132: 1625–7.

Finkelstein, M., Seal, R. and Schuster, J. (1998) *The New Academic Generation*. Baltimore, MD: Johns Hopkins University Press.

Fisher, C.S. (1973) Some social characteristics of mathematicians and their work, *American Journal of Sociology*, 75(5): 1094–118.

Fleming, D. (1969) Emigré physicists and the biological revolution, in D. Fleming and B. Bailyn (eds) *The Intellectual Migration*. Cambridge, MA: Harvard University Press.

Floud, R. (1999) Keynote speech to the Failing Students Symposium, Lancaster University, 15–16 July.

Foucault, M. (1970) *The Order of Things*. London: Tavistock.

Fox, M.F. (1983) Publication productivity among scientists, *Social Studies of Science*, 13(2): 285–305.

Fox, M.F. and Faver, C.A. (1982) The process of collaboration in scholarly research, *Scholarly Publishing*, 13: 327–39.

Franklin, J. and Theall, M. (1995) The relationship of disciplinary differences and the value of class preparation time to student ratings of teaching, in N. Hativa and M. Marincovich (eds) *Disciplinary Differences in Teaching and Learning: Implications for Practice*, pp. 41–8. San Francisco, CA: Jossey-Bass.

Fulton, O. (1996) The academic profession in England on the eve of structural reform, in P. Altbach (ed.) *The International Academic Profession: Portraits of Fourteen Countries*. Princeton, NJ: Carnegie Foundation for the Advancement of Teaching.

Gaff, J.G. and Wilson, R.C. (1971) Faculty cultures and interdisciplinary studies, *Journal of Higher Education*, 43(3): 186–201.

Galtung, J. (1981) Structure, culture and intellectual style, *Social Science Information*, 20: 817–56.

Gaston, J. (1970) The reward system in British science, *American Sociological Review*, 35: 718–32.

Gaston, J. (1971) Secretiveness and competition for priority in physics, *Minerva*, 9: 472–92.

Gaston, J. (1972) Communication and the reward system of science, *Sociology of Science, Sociological Review Monograph*, 18: 25–41.

Gaston, J. (1973) *Originality and Competition in Science*. Chicago, IL: University of Chicago Press.

Geertz, C. (1976) Toward an ethnography of the disciplines. Mimeo, Princeton Institute for Advanced Study.

Geertz, C. (1980) Blurred genres, *The American Scholar*, 49: 165–78.

Geertz, C. (1983) *Local Knowledge*. New York: Basic Books.

Geiger, R. (1985) The home of scientists: a perspective on university research, in B. Wittrock and A. Elzinga (eds) *The University Research System*. Stockholm: Almqvist and Wiksell.

Geiger, R. (1987) Organized research and American universities. Mimeo, Dalarö 1987 International Conference, Swedish National Board of Universities and Colleges, Research on Higher Education Progam.

Gerholm, T. (1985) On tacit knowledge in academia, in L. Gustavson (ed.) *On Communication: No. 3*. Linköping: University of Linköping Department of Communication Studies.

Gerstl, J.E. and Hutton, S.P. (1966) *Engineers*. London: Tavistock.

Gerver, E. (1997) RAE 1996: the experience of the sub-panel on continuing education, *Research Intelligence*, 60 (April): 16–19.

Gherardi, S. (2000) Practice-based theorizing on learning and knowing in organizations, *Organization*, 7(2): 211–23.

Gibbons, M. (1985) Introduction, in M. Gibbons and B. Wittrock (eds) *Science as a Commodity*. Harlow: Longman.

Gibbons, M. (1997) Development of science and basic research: the implications of mode 2 science, in H. Etzkowitz and L. Leydesdorff (eds) *Universities and the Global Knowledge Economy: A Triple Helix of University–Industry–Government Relations*, pp. 90–104. London: Pinter.

Gibbons, M., Limoges, C., Nowotny, H. *et al.* (1994) *The New Production of Knowledge: The Dynamics of Science and Research in Contemporary Societies*. London: Sage.

Gibbs, G. (ed.) (1994) *Improving Student Learning*. Oxford: Oxford Centre for Staff Development.

Giddens, A. (1984) *The Constitution of Society*. Cambridge: Polity Press.

Gieryn, T.F. (1978) Problem retention and problem change in science, in J. Gaston (ed.) *Sociology of Science*. San Francisco, CA: Jossey-Bass.

Gilbert, G. (1977b) Referencing as persuasion, *Social Studies of Science*, 7: 113–22.

Gilbert, G.N. (1977a) Competition, differentiation and careers in science, *Social Science Information*, 16: 103–23.

Gilbert, N.G. and Mulkay, M. (1984) *Opening Pandora's Box: A Sociological Analysis of Scientists' Discourse*. Cambridge: Cambridge University Press.

Glaser, B.G. and Strauss, A. (1967) *The Discovery of Grounded Theory*. New York: Aldine.

Goddard, A. (2000) Britain flies the flag, *Times Higher Education Supplement*, 18 February: 6.

Goodson, I. (1983) *School Subjects and Curriculum Change*. London: Croom Helm.

Gouldner, A.W. (1957) Cosmopolitans and locals, *Administrative Science Quarterly*, 2: 281–306, 444–80.

Graham, L. (1983) Introduction, in L. Graham, W. Lepenies and P. Weingart (eds) *Functions and Uses of Disciplinary Histories*. Dordrecht: Reidel.

Grbich, C. (1998) The academic researcher: socialisation in settings previously dominated by teaching, *Higher Education*, 36: 67–85.

Greed C. (1991) *Surveying Sisters*. London: Routledge.

Greenfield, T. and Ribbins, P. (eds) (1993) *Greenfield on Educational Administration: Towards a Humane Science*. London: Routledge.

Gregg, P. (1996) Modularisation: what academics think, in N. Jackson (ed.) *In Focus: Modular Higher Education in the UK*. London: HEQC.

Griffith, B.C. and Miller, A.J. (1970) Networks of informal communication among scientifically productive scientists, in C.E. Nelson and D.K. Pollock (eds) *Communication Among Scientists and Engineers*. Lexington, MA: Heath.

Griffith, B.C. and Mullins, N.C. (1972) Coherent groups in scientific change, *Science*, 177: 959–64.

Griffith, B.C. and Small, H.G. (1983) The structure of the social and behavioural sciences literature. Mimeo, Royal Institute of Technology Library, Stockholm.

Gross, E. (1975) Patterns of organizational and occupational socialization, *Vocational Guidance Quarterly*, 24(2): 140–9.

Guile, D. and Young, M. (1998) Apprenticeship as a conceptual basis for a social theory of learning, *Journal of Vocational Education and Training*, 50(2): 173–92.

Gustin, B. (1973) Charisma, recognition and the motivation of scientists, *American Journal of Sociology*, 78(5): 1119–34.

Gutek, B.A. and Cohen, A.G. (1992) Sex ratios, sex role spillover, and sex at work: a comparison of men's and women's experiences, in A.J. Mills and P. Tancred (eds) *Mills, Gendering Organizational Analysis*. London: Sage.

Haas, J.E. (1996) The American academic profession, in P.G. Altbach (ed.) *The International Academic Profession: Portraits of 14 Countries*, pp. 343–88. San Francisco, CA: The Carnegie Foundation for the Advancement of Teaching.

Hagstrom, W.O. (1965) *The Scientific Community.* New York: Basic Books.

Hagstrom, W.O. (1974) Competition in science, *American Sociological Review*, 39: 1–18.

Hall, S., Critcher, C., Jefferson, T. *et al.* (1978) *Policing the Crisis: Mugging, the State and Law and Order.* London: Macmillan.

Halpin, D. and Troyna, B. (1994) *Researching Education Policy: Ethical and Methodological Issues.* London: Falmer.

Halsey, A.H. (1992) *Decline of Donnish Dominion.* Oxford: Oxford University Press.

Halsey, A.H. and Trow, M. (1971) *The British Academics.* London: Faber.

Hardy, G.H. (1941) *A Mathematician's Apology.* Cambridge: Cambridge University Press.

Hargens, L.L. (1975) *Patterns of Scientific Research.* Washington, DC: American Sociological Association.

Hargens, L. and Hagstrom, W. (1967) Sponsored and contest mobility of American scientists, *Sociology of Education*, 40: 24–8.

Hartley, D. (1983) Ideology and organisational behaviour, *International Studies of Management and Organisation*, 13(3): 24–36.

Hativa, N. and Marincovich, M. (eds) (1995) *Disciplinary Differences in Teaching and Learning: Implications for Practice.* San Francisco, CA: Jossey-Bass.

HEFCE (1997) *The Impact of the 1992 Research Assessment Exercise on Higher Education Institutions in England: Executive Summary.* Bristol: HEFCE.

Henkel, M. (1987) The discipline: still the dominant force in higher education? Mimeo, Dalarö 1987 International Conference, Swedish National Board of Universities and Colleges, Research on Higher Education Program.

Henkel, M. (1997) Academic values and the university as corporate enterprise, *Higher Education Quarterly*, 51(2): 134–43.

Henkel, M. (2000) *Academic Identities and Policy Change in Higher Education.* London: Jessica Kingsley.

HESA (1999) *Staff Population, 1997–8.* Cheltenham: HESA.

Higher Education Research Institute (1991) *The American College Teacher: National Norms for the 1989–90 HERI Faculty Survey.* Los Angeles, CA: UCLA.

Hillery, G.A. (1955) Definitions of community: areas of agreement, *Rural Sociology*, 20.

Hirst, P.H. (1974) *Knowledge and the Curriculum.* London: Routledge.

Hofstede, G. (1980) *Culture's Consequences: International Differences in Work-related Values.* Beverly Hills, CA: Sage.

Hofstede, G. (1994) *Cultures and Organizations: Software of the Mind; Intercultural Co-operation and its Importance for Survival.* London: HarperCollins.

Hoggett, P. (1991) A new management in the public sector? *Policy and Politics*, 19(4): 243–56.

Holloway, S.W.F., Jewson, N.D. and Mason, D.J. (1986) 'Professionalisation' or 'Occupational Imperialism'? some reflections on pharmacy in Britain, *Social Science of Medicine*, 23(3): 323–32.

Huber, L. (1990) Disciplinary cultures and social reproduction, *European Journal of Education*, 25(3): 241–61.

Hyland, K. (1999) Academic attribution: citation and the construction of disciplinary knowledge, *Applied Linguistics*, 20(3): 341–67.

ILT (1999) *Institute for Learning and Teaching: Implementing the Vision.* www.cvcp.ac.uk/ Links/LinkedActivities/ILT/ILT_Vision/ilt_vision.html (accessed 2 May 2001).

Jacobsen, B. (1981) Collection type and integration type curricula in systems of higher education, *Acta Sociologica*, 24(1–2): 25–41.

Jamison, A. (1982) National components of scientific knowledge. Mimeo, University of Lund, Research Policy Institute.

Jeffreys, M. and Elston, M. (1989) The medical school as a social organization, *Medical Education*, 23: 242–51.

Jencks, C. and Riesman, D. (1968) *The Academic Revolution.* New York: Doubleday.

Johnson, H.G. (1971) The Keynesian revolution and the monetarist counter-revolution, *American Economic Review*, 61(3, supplement): 1–14.

John-Steiner, V., Webber, R.J. and Minnis, M. (1998) The challenge of studying collaboration, *American Educational Research Journal*, 35: 773–83.

Jones, G.S. (1976) From historical sociology to theoretical history, *British Journal of Sociology*, 27: 295–305.

Jones, R.A. (1980) Myth and symbol among the Nacirema Tsigoloicos, *American Sociologist*, 15: 207–12.

Joseph, M. (1978) Professional values, a case study of professional students in a polytechnic, *Research in Education*, 19: 49–65.

Joseph, M. (1980) Professional socialisation: a case study of estate management students. Unpublished DPhil thesis, Oxford University.

Karpiak, I. (2000) The 'second call': patterns of faculty renewal and recommitment in midlife. *Quality in Higher Education*, 6(2): 125–34.

Katznelson, I. (1997) From the streets to the lecture hall. *Daedalus*, 126(1): 311–32.

Kekäle, J. (1998) The field of possibilities and academic leaders, *International Journal of Educational Leadership*, 1(3): 237–55.

Kekäle, J. (1999) 'Preferred' patterns of academic leadership in different disciplinary (sub)cultures, *Higher Education*, 37: 217–38.

Kekäle, J. (2000) Quality of research and teaching in four difference disciplines. Paper presented to 22nd EAIR Forum, Berlin, 6–9 September.

Kemp, R.V. (1977) Controversy in scientific research and tactics of communication. *Sociological Review*, 25: 515–34.

Kempner, K. (1990) Faculty culture in the community college: facilitating or hindering learning? *Review of Higher Education*, 13(2): 215–35.

Kerr, C. (1989) The academic ethic and the university teachers: a 'disintegrating profession'? *Minerva*, 27(2): 139–56.

Kerr, C. (1994) Knowledge, ethics, and the new academic culture, *Change* (Jan/Feb): 9–15.

Kickert, W. (1991) Steering at a distance: a new paradigm in public governance in Dutch higher education. Paper for European Consortium for Political Research, Colchester, University of Essex, March.

King, A.R. and Brownell, J. (1966) *The Curriculum and the Disciplines of Knowledge.* New York: John Wiley.

Kirshstein, R.J., Matheson, N., Jing, Z. and Zimbler, L.J. (1997) *1993 National Study of Postsecondary Faculty: Instructional Faculty and Staff in Higher Education Institutions: Fall 1987 and Fall 1992.* Washington, DC: US Department of Education Office of Educational Research and Improvement.

Klamer, A. (1984) *The New Classical Macroeconomics.* Brighton: Wheatsheaf.

Kleinman, S. (1983) Collective matters as individual concerns, *Urban Life*, 12(2): 203–25.

Knight, P. and Trowler, P. (1999) It takes a village to raise a child: mentoring and the socialisation of new entrants to the academic professions, *Journal of Mentoring and Tutoring*, 7(1): 23–34.

Knight, P. and Trowler, P. (2001) *Departmental Leadership in Higher Education: New Directions for Communities of Practice*. Buckingham: Open University Press.

Knorr Cetina, K. (1981) *The Manufacture of Knowledge*. Oxford: Pergamon.

Knorr Cetina, K. (1982) Scientific communities or transepistemic arenas of research? *Social Studies of Science*, 12: 101–30.

Knorr-Cetina, K. (1988) The micro-social order: towards a reconception, in N. Fielding (ed.) *Actions and Structure*. London: Sage.

Knorr Cetina, K. (1999) *Epistemic Cultures: How the Sciences Make Knowledge*. Cambridge, MA: Harvard University Press.

Kogan, M. (1987) The responsiveness of higher education to external influences. Mimeo, Dalarö 1987 International Conference, Swedish National Board of Universities and Colleges, Research on Higher Education Program.

Kogan, M. (2000) Higher education communities and academic identity, *Higher Education Quarterly*, 54(3): 207–16.

Kogan, M. and Hanney, S. (2000) *Reforming Higher Education*. London: Jessica Kingsley.

Kogan, M. and Henkel, M. (1983) *Government and Research*. London: Heinemann.

Kolb, D.A. (1981) Learning styles and disciplinary differences, in A. Chickering (ed.) *The Modern American College*. San Francisco, CA: Jossey-Bass.

Kolb, D.A. (1984) *Experiential Learning*. Engelwood Cliffs, NJ: Prentice-Hall.

Kuhn, T.S. (1962) *The Structure of Scientific Revolutions*. Chicago, IL: University of Chicago Press.

Kuhn, T.S. (1970) *The Structure of Scientific Revolutions*, 2nd edn. Chicago, IL: University of Chicago Press.

Kuhn, T.S. (1977) *The Essential Tension*. Chicago, IL: University of Chicago Press.

Kumar, K. (1997) The post-modern condition, in A.H. Halsey, H. Lauder, P. Brown, and A.S. Wells (eds) *Education, Cultures, Economy, Society*. Oxford: Oxford University Press.

Kuper, A. (1975) *Anthropologists and Anthropology*. Harmondsworth: Penguin.

Lattuca, L. and Stark, J. (1995) Will disciplinary perspectives impede curricular reform? *Journal of Higher Education*, 65(4): 401–26.

Lave, J. (1993) The practice of learning, in S. Chaiklin and J. Lave (eds) *Understanding Practice*. Cambridge: Cambridge University Press.

Lave, J. and Wenger, E. (1991) *Situated Learning: Legitimate Peripheral Participation*. Cambridge: Cambridge University Press.

Law, J. (1976) X-ray protein crystallography, in G. Lemaine, R. Macleod, M. Mulkay and P. Weingart (eds) *Perspectives on the Emergence of Scientific Disciplines*. The Hague: Mouton.

Lee, M.N.N. (1999) Corporatization, privatization, and internationalization of higher education in Malaysia, in P.G. Altbach (ed.) *Private Prometheus: Private Higher Education and Development in the 21ˢᵗ Century*. Westport, CT: Greenwood Press, 137–60.

Lehman, H.C. (1953) *Age and Achievement*. Princeton, NJ: Princeton University Press.

Leijonhufvud, A. (1973) Life among the econ, *Western Economic Journal*, 9(3): 327–37.

Lenze, L.F. (1995) Discipline-specific pedagogical knowledge in linguistics and Spanish, in N. Hativa and M. Marincovich (eds) *Disciplinary Differences in Teaching and Learning: Implications for Practice*, pp. 65–70. San Francisco, CA: Jossey-Bass.

Letherby, G. (1996) Roles and relationships: issues of self and identity at home and at work. Paper presented at the 'Dilemmas of Mass Higher Education' conference, Staffordshire University, 10–12 April.

Levine, A. (1980) *Why Innovation Fails.* New York: State University of New York Press.

Levine, A. (1997) How the academic profession is changing, *Daedalus,* 126(4): 1–20.

Levi-Strauss, C. (1978) *Myth and Meaning.* London: Routledge.

Lewis, G.C. (1849) *An Essay on the Influence of Authority on Matters of Opinion.* Reprint edition 1974. New York: Arno Press.

Lightfield, E.T. (1971) Output and recognition of sociologists, *American Sociologist,* 6: 128–33.

Lingard, B. and Garrick, B. (1997) Producing and practising social justice policy in education: a policy trajectory study from Queensland, Australia, *International Studies in Sociology of Education,* 7(2): 157–80.

Lodahl, J.B. and Gordon, G. (1972) The structure of scientific fields and the functioning of university graduate departments, *American Sociological Review,* 37: 57–72.

MacLeod, D. (2000a) Female trouble, *Guardian Education,* 4 April, 14–15.

MacLeod, D. (2000b) You've been warned, *Guardian Higher Education,* 25 January, 1.

MacRoberts, M.H. and MacRoberts, B.R. (1984) The negational reference: or the art of dissembling, *Social Studies of Science,* 14: 91–4.

Maguire, M. and Ball, S. (1994) Researching politics and the politics of research: recent qualitative studies in the UK, *International Journal of Qualitative Studies in Education,* 7(3): 269–85.

Manniche, E. and Falk, G. (1957) Age and the Nobel Prize, *Behavioural Science,* 2: 301–7.

Marquis, D. and Allen, T. (1966) Communication patterns in applied technology, *American Psychologist,* 21: 1052–60.

Martin, B. and Irvine, J. (1992) Government spending: trends in government spending on academic and related research. An international comparison, *Science and Public Policy,* 19: 311–19.

Martindale, D. (1979) Ideologies, paradigms and theories, in W.E. Snizek, E.R. Fuhrman and M.K. Miller (eds) *Contemporary Issues in Theory and Research: A Sociological Perspective.* London: Aldwych Press.

Masterman, M. (1970) The nature of a paradigm, in I. Lakatos and A. Musgrave (eds) *Criticism and the Growth of Knowledge.* Cambridge: Cambridge University Press.

McDermott, R. and Varenne, H. (1995) Culture as disability, *Anthropology and Education Quarterly,* 26(3): 324–48.

McDowell, J.M. (1984) Obsolescence of knowledge and career publication profiles, *American Economic Review,* 72(4): 752–68.

McGuinness, A.C. (1995) The changing relationships between the states and universities in the United States, *Higher Education Management,* 7(3): 263–79.

McInnis, C. (1996) Change and diversity in the work patterns of Australian academics, *Higher Education Management,* 8(2): 105–17.

McInnis, C. (2000) Changing academic work roles: the everyday realities challenging quality in teaching, *Quality in Higher Education,* 6(2): 143–52.

McNay, I. (1997) *The Impact of the 1992 RAE on Institutional and Individual Behaviour in English Higher Education: The Evidence from a Research Project.* London: HEFCE.

Megill, A. (1987) Provocation on belief: Part 4, *Social Epistemology*, 1(1): 106–8.
Merton, R. (1957) Priorities in scientific discovery, *American Sociological Review*, 22: 635–59.
Merton, R.K. (1973) *The Sociology of Science*. Chicago, IL: University of Chicago Press.
Metzger, W.P. (1987) The academic profession in the United States, in B. Clark (ed.) *The Academic Profession: National, Disciplinary and Institutional Settings*, pp. 123–208. Berkeley and Los Angeles, CA: University of California Press.
Mikesell, M.W. (1969) The borderlands of geography as a social science, in M. Sherif and C. Sherif (eds) *Interdisciplinary Relationships in the Social Sciences*. Chicago, IL: Aldine.
Milem, J.F., Berger, J.B., and Dey, E.L. (2000) Faculty time allocation: a study of change over twenty years, *Journal of Higher Education*, 71(4): 454–75.
Mitroff, I.I. (ed.) (1974) *The Subjective Side of Science*. Amsterdam: Elsevier.
Modood, T. and Acland, T. (eds) (1998) *Race and Higher Education*. London: Policy Studies Institute.
Morley, L. (1994) Glass ceiling or iron cage: women in UK academia, *Gender, Work and Organization*, 1(4): 194–204.
Morley, L. and Walsh, V. (1995) *Feminist Academics*. London: Taylor and Francis.
Morlock, L. (1973) Discipline variation in the status of academic women, in A.S. Rossi and A. Calderwood (eds) *Academic Women on the Move*. New York: Russell Sage Foundation.
Moulin, L. (1955) The Nobel Prizes for the sciences from 1901–1950, *British Journal of Sociology*, 6: 246–63.
Mulkay, M. (1969) Some aspects of cultural growth in the natural sciences, *Social Research*, 36: 22–52.
Mulkay, M. (1972) *The Social Process of Innovation*. London: Macmillan.
Mulkay, M. (1974) Conceptual displacements and migration in science, *Science Studies*, 4: 205–34.
Mulkay, M.J. (1976) The mediating role of the scientific elite, *Social Studies of Science*, 6: 445–70.
Mulkay, M. (1977) The sociology of the scientific research community, in I. Spiegel-Rösing and D. de S. Price (eds) *Science, Technology and Society*. London: Sage.
Mulkay, M.J. and Edge, D.O. (1973) Cognitive, technical and social factors in the growth of radio astronomy, *Social Science Information*, 12: 25–61.
Mullins, N. (1968) The distribution of social and cultural properties in informal communication networks among biological scientists, *American Sociological Review*, 33: 786–97.
Mullins, N. (1972) The development of a scientific specialty, *Minerva*, 10: 52–82.
Mullins, N. (1973a) *Theory and Theory Groups in American Sociology*. New York: Harper and Row.
Mullins, N.C. (1973b) The development of specialties in social science, *Science Studies*, 3: 245–73.
Munn-Giddings, C. (1998) Mixing motherhood and academia: a lethal cocktail, in D. Malina and S. Maslin-Prothero (eds) *Surviving the Academy: Feminist Perspectives*, pp. 56–68. London: Falmer.
Murray, H.G. and Renaud, R.D. (1995) Disciplinary differences in classroom teaching behaviors, in N. Hativa and M. Marincovich (eds) *Disciplinary Differences in Teaching and Learning*, pp. 31–9. San Francisco, CA: Jossey-Bass.

Murray, S.O. (1983) *Group Formation in Social Science.* Edmonton, Alberta: Linguistic Research Inc.

Nadel, E. (1980) Formal communication, journal concentration and the rise of a discipline in physics, *Sociology*, 14(3): 401–16.

NCES (1996) *Digest of Education Statistics.* Washington, DC: National Center for Education Statistics.

NCES (1997) *Instructional Faculty and Staff in Higher Education Institutions: Fall 1987 and Fall 1992.* Washington, DC: National Center for Education Statistics. Available at: www.nces.ed.gov/pubs97/97470.pdf (accessed 21 July 2000)

NCES (1999) *Digest of Education Statistics.* Washington, DC: National Center for Education Statistics.

NCES (2000) *1993 National Study of Postsecondary Faculty: Salary, Promotion, and Tenure Status of Minority and Women Faculty in US Colleges and Universities.* Washington, DC: National Center for Education Statistics.

NCIHE (1997) *Higher Education in the Learning Society* (The Dearing Report). London: DfEE.

Neave, G. (1979) Academic drift: some views from Europe, *Studies in Higher Education*, 4(2): 143–59.

Neave, G. (1997) The stirring of the prince and the silence of the lambs, in H. Etzkowitz and L. Leydesdorff (eds) (1997) *Universities and the Global Knowledge Economy: A Triple Helix of University–Industry–Government Relations*, pp. 54–72. London: Pinter.

Neave, G. (1998) The evaluative state revisited, *European Journal of Education*, 33(3): 265–84.

Neave, G. and van Vught, F.A. (1991) *Prometheus Bound: The Changing Relationship Between Government and Higher Education.* Oxford: Pergamon Press.

Nehamas, A. (1997) Trends in recent American philosophy, *Daedalus*, 126(1): 209–33.

Nettles, M., Perna, L., Bradburn, E. and Zimbler, L. (2000) *Salary, Promotion, and Tenure Status of Minority and Women Faculty in U.S. Colleges and Universities.* Washington, DC: US Department of Education Office of Education Research and Improvement.

Neumann, R. (1996) Researching the teaching–research nexus: critical review, *Australian Journal of Education*, 40(1): 5–18.

Newman, J. (1995) Gender and cultural change, in C. Itzin and J. Newman (eds) *Gender, Culture and Organizational Change.* London: Routledge.

Nicolaus, M. (1972) Sociology liberation movement, in T. Pateman (ed.) *Counter Course.* Harmondsworth: Penguin.

Nilson, L. (1998) *Teaching at its Best: Research-based Resource for College Instructors.* Boston, MA: Anker Publishing Co.

Opp, R.D. (1992) Disciplinary differences in faculty career satisfaction. Paper presented to ASHE Annual Meeting, Minneapolis, October–November.

Oromaner, M. (1983) Professional standing and the reception of contributions to economics, *Research in Higher Education*, 19(3): 351–62.

Ozga, J. (2000) *Policy Research in Educational Settings: Contested Terrain.* Buckingham: Open University Press.

Padilla, A.M. (1994) Ethnic minority scholars, research and mentoring: current and future issues, *Educational Researcher*, 23(4): 24–7.

Pantin, C.F.A. (1968) *The Relations Between the Sciences.* Cambridge: Cambridge University Press.

Parker, M. (2000) *Organizational Culture and Identity.* London: Sage.

Parlett, M. (1977) The department as a learning milieu, *Studies in Higher Education*, 2(2): 173–81.

Parry, S. (1997) Doctoral study in its disciplinary context. Unpublished PhD thesis, LaTrobe University.

Patel, N. (1973) Collaboration in the professional growth of American sociology, *Social Science Information*, 12: 77–92.

Patrick, W.J. and Stanley, E.C. (1996) Assessment of research quality, *Research in Higher Education*, 37: 1.

Perry, R.P., Menec, V.H., Struthers, C.W. *et al.* (1996) *Faculty in Transition: The Adjustment of New Hires to Postsecondary Institutions*. Winnipeg, MB: Centre for Higher Education Research and Development.

Pickering, A. (1984) *Constructing Quarks*. Edinburgh: Edinburgh University Press.

Platt, J. (1976) *Realities in Social Research*. Brighton: Sussex University Press.

Platt, J. (1981) On interviewing one's peers, *British Journal of Sociology*, 32(1): 75–91.

Podgorecki, A. (1997) *Higher Faculties: Cross-national Study of University Culture*. Westport, CN: Praeger.

Polanyi, M. (1962) The republic of science, *Minerva*, 1(1): 54–73.

Pollitt, C. (1993) *Managerialism and the Public Services: Cuts or Cultural Change in the 1990s?* Oxford: Blackwell.

Popper, K. (1979) *Objective Knowledge*. Oxford: Oxford University Press.

Porter, M. (1984) Saint George or the dragon, *Network*, 29 May: 1–2.

Potts, A. (1997) *College Academics*. Charlestown, NSW: William Michael Press.

Price, D. (1963) *Big Science, Little Science*. New York: Columbia University Press.

Price, D. de S. (1965) Networks of scientific papers, *Science*, 149(3683): 510–15.

Price, D.J. (1970) Citation measures of hard science, soft science, technology and non-science, in C.E. Nelson and D.K. Pollock (eds) *Communication Among Scientists and Engineers*. Lexington, MA: Heath.

Price, D. and Beaver, D. (1966) Collaboration in an invisible college, *American Psychologist*, 21: 1011–18.

Prichard, C. (1999) Identity work – moving the 'theory of the subject' from 'division' to 'depth' in critical organizational analysis. Paper presented for the Critical Management Studies Conference, Manchester School of Management, UMIST, July.

Prichard, C. (2000) *Making Managers in Universities and Colleges*. Buckingham: SRHE/ Open University Press.

QAA (1998) *Quality Assurance in UK Higher Education: A Brief Guide*. Gloucester: QAA.

QAA (1999) Final Report on the Trials of Aspects of the New Framework for Review, November: www.qaa.ac.uk/trialsreport/page2.htm#stru (accessed October 24 2000).

Quinn, J.B. (1993) The tax payer vs higher education, *Newsweek*, 15 November, 51.

Raffe, D., Croxford, L. and Howieson, C. (1994) The third face of modules: gendered patterns of participation and progression in Scottish vocational education, *British Journal of Education and Work*, 7(3): 87–104.

Ramsden, P. (1994) Describing and explaining research productivity, *Higher Education*, 27: 207–26.

Ramsden, P. (1998a) *Learning to Lead in Higher Education*. London: Routledge.

Ramsden, P. (1998b) Managing the effective university, *Higher Education Research and Development*, 17(3): 347–70.

RAND (1997) *Breaking the Social Contract: The Fiscal Crisis in Higher Education*. Santa Monica, CA: RAND Corporation.

230 *Academic Tribes and Territories*

Ravetz, J.R. (1971) *Scientific Knowledge and its Social Problems*. Oxford: Clarendon Press.
Reif, F. (1961) The competitive world of the pure scientist, *Science*, 134(3494): 1957–62.
Reif, F. and Strauss, A. (1965) The impact of rapid discovery on the scientist's career, *Social Problems*, 12: 297–311.
Rendel, M. (1984) Women academics in the seventies, in S. Acker and D. Warren Piper (eds) *Is Higher Education Fair to Women?* Guildford: SRHE.
Reskin, B.F. (1977) Scientific productivity and the reward structure of science, *American Sociological Review*, 42: 491–504.
Reynolds, M. (1997) Learning styles: a critique, *Management Learning*, 29(2): 115–33.
Rhoades, G. (1997) *Managed Professionals: Restructuring Academic Labor in Unionized Institutions*. Albany, NY: State University of New York Press.
Riesman, D. (1958) *Constraint and Variety in American Education*. New York: Doubleday Anchor.
Rip, A. (1981) A cognitive approach to science policy, *Research Policy*, 10: 294–311.
Ritzer, G. (1975) Sociology: a multiple paradigm science, *American Sociologist*, 10: 156–67.
Ritzer, G. (1979) Toward an integrated sociological paradigm, in W.E. Snizek, E.R. Fuhrman and M.K. Miller (eds) *Contemporary Issues in Theory and Research*. London: Aldwych.
Ritzer, G. (1980) *Sociology: A Multiple Paradigm Science*, Revised edn. Boston: Allyn and Bacon.
Roberts, A.H. (1970) The system of communication in the language sciences, in C.E. Nelson and D.K. Pollock (eds) *Communication Among Scientists and Engineers*. Lexington, MA: Heath.
Roe, A. (1953) *The Making of a Scientist*. New York: Dodd, Mead.
Rorty, R. (1979) *Philosophy and the Mirror of Nature*. Princeton, NJ: Princeton University Press.
Rose, M. and Rose, S. (1974) Do not adjust your mind, there is a fault in reality, in R. Whitley (ed.) *Social Processes of Scientific Development*. London: Routledge.
Rothblatt, S. (1968) *The Revolution of the Dons*. London: Faber.
Rothblatt, S. (1985) The notion of an open scientific community in historical perspective, in M. Gibbons and B. Wittrock (eds) *Science as a Commodity*. Harlow: Longman.
Rothman, R.A. (1972) A dissenting view on the scientific ethos, *British Journal of Sociology*, 23: 102–8.
Ruscio, K.P. (1985) Specializations in academic disciplines. Mimeo, University of California, Los Angeles, Comparative Higher Education Research Group.
Ruscio, K.P. (1986) Bridging specialisations, *Review of Higher Education*, 10(1): 29–45.
Ruscio, K.P. (1987) Many sectors, many professions, in B.R. Clark (ed.) *The Academic Profession*. Berkeley, CA: University of California Press.
Russell, A.B. (1992) *Faculty Workloads: State and System Perspectives*. Denver, CO: Education Commission of the States.
Ryan, Y. (2000) *The Business of Borderless Education: US Case Studies and the HE Response*. Queensland: Queensland University of Technology.
Saldivar, J.S. (1997) Tracking English and American literary and cultural criticism, *Daedalus*, 126(1): 155–74.
Salmond, A. (1982) Theoretical landscapes: on cross-cultural conceptions of knowledge, in D. Parkin (ed.) *Semantic Anthropology*. London and San Diego: Academic Press.

Sanford, N. (1971) Academic culture and the teacher's development, *Soundings*, Winter: 357–71.

Sax, L., Astin, A., Korn, W. and Gilmartin, S. (1999) *The American College Teacher: National Norms for the 1998–1999 HERI Survey*. Los Angeles, CA: HERI at UCLA.

Schatzman, L. and Strauss, A. (1966) A sociology of psychiatry, *Social Problems*, 14: 3–16.

Scott, P. (1998) Massification, internationalization and globalization, in P. Scott (ed.) *The Globalization of Higher Education*, pp. 108–29. Buckingham: SRHE/Open University Press.

Scott, P. (1999) The research-policy gap, *Journal of Education Policy*, 14(3): 317–37.

Sheehan, B.A. and Welch, A.R. (1996) *The Academic Profession in Australia*. Canberra: Department of Employment, Training and Youth Affairs, AGPS.

Shinn, T. (1982) Scientific disciplines and organizational specificity, in N. Elias, H. Martins and R.D. Whitley (eds) *Scientific Establishments and Hierarchies*. Dordrecht: Reidel.

Shulman, L.S. (1987) Knowledge and teaching: foundations of the new reform, *Harvard Educational Review*, 57: 1–22.

Shulman, L.S. (1986) Those who understand: knowledge growth in teaching, *Educational Researcher*, 15(2): 4–14.

Singh, G. (1998) Race equality staffing policies in higher education, in T. Modood and T. Acland (eds) *Race and Higher Education*. London: Policy Studies Institute.

Slaughter, S. and Leslie, L.L. (1997) *Academic Capitalism: Politics, Policies and the Entrepreneurial University*. Baltimore, MD: Johns Hopkins University Press.

Slaughter, S. and Rhoades, G. (1993) Changes in intellectual property statutes and policies of a public university: revising the terms of academic labor, *Higher Education*, 26(3): 287–312.

Slaymaker, O. (1968) The new geography, *Geographical Journal*, 134(3): 405–7.

Small, H. (1978) Cited documents as concept symbols, *Social Studies of Science*, 8: 327–40.

Smart, J.C. and Ettington, C.A. (1995) Disciplinary institutional differences in undergraduate education goals, in N. Hativa and M. Marincovich (eds) *Disciplinary Differences in Teaching and Learning: Implications for Practice*, pp. 49–58. San Francisco, CA: Jossey-Bass.

Smeby, J-C. (1998) Knowledge production and knowledge transmission, *Teaching in Higher Education*, 3(1): 5–20.

Smith, D. (1982) Social history and sociology – more than just good friends. *Sociological Review*, 30(2): 286–308.

Smyth, J. (ed.) (1995) *Academic Work*. Buckingham: SRHE/Open University Press.

Snow, C.P. (1959) *The Two Cultures and the Scientific Revolution*. Cambridge: Cambridge University Press.

Snyder, B.R. (1971) *The Hidden Curriculum*. New York: Knopf.

Sokal, A. and Bricmont, J. (1998) *Intellectual Imposteurs*. London: Profile Books.

Spiegel-Rösing, I. (1974) Disziplinare stratagien die statussichering, *Homo*, 25(1): 11–37.

Sporn, B. (1999) *Adaptive University Structures: An Analysis of Adaptation to Socioeconomic Environments of US and European Universities*. London: Jessica Kingsley.

Spurling, A. (1990) *Report of the Women in Higher Education Project*. Cambridge: King's College.

Squires, G. (1990) *First Degree: The Undergraduate Curriculum*. London: SRHE/Open University Press.

Startup, R. (1980) The sociology of mathematics, *Sociology and Social Research*, 64(2): 151–67.

Steig, M. (1986) *The Origin and Development of Scholarly Historical Periodicals.* Alabama: University of Alabama Press.

Stern, N. (1978) Age and achievement in mathematics, *Social Studies of Science*, 8: 127–40.

Stevens, R.E. (1953) Characteristics of scientific literatures, *American Council of Learned Societies, Monograph*, 6.

Stoddart, D.R. (1967) Growth and structure of geography, *Transactions and Papers of the Institute of British Geographers*, 41.

Storer, N. and Parsons, T. (1968) The disciplines as a differentiating force, in E.B. Montgomery (ed.) *The Foundations of Access to Knowledge.* Syracuse: Syracuse University Press.

Strauss, A. and Rainwater, L. (1962) *The Professional Scientist.* Chicago, IL: Aldine.

Swain, H. (1999) Natfhe rails at 'endemic discrimination' in pay, *Times Higher Education Supplement*, 12 November: 64.

Swales, J. (1988) Discourse communities, genres and English as an international language, *World Englishes*, 7(2): 211–20.

Taylor, P.J. (1976) An interpretation of the quantification debate in British geography, *Transactions of the Institute of British Geographers N.S.*, 1, 2.

Teichler, U. (1988) *Changing Patterns in the HE System.* London: Jessica Kingsley.

Terman, L.M. (1954) Scientists and nonscientists in a group of 800 gifted men, *Psychological Monographs*, 68: 7.

Thagaard, T. (1987) Does the organization of research in universities further creativity? Mimeo, Dalarö 1987 International Conference, Swedish National Board of Universities and Colleges, Research on Higher Education Program.

Thomas, K. (1990) *Gender and Subject in Higher Education.* Buckingham: SRHE/Open University Press.

Thomas, P. (1985) *The Aims and Outcomes of Social Policy Research.* London: Croom Helm.

Thompson, T.H. (2000) Three futures of the electronic university. www.educause.edu/pub/er/review/reviewArticles/33234.html (accessed 15 October 2000).

Tierney, W. (1997) *Academic Outlaws: Queer Theory and Cultural Studies in the Academy.* Thousand Oaks, CA: Sage.

Tierney, W.G. (1999) *Building the Responsive Campus: Creating High Performance Colleges and Universities.* Thousand Oaks, CA: Sage.

Tierney, W. and Bensimon, E.M. (1996) *Promotion and Tenure: Community and Socialization in Academe.* New York: State University of New York Press.

Toma, J.D. (1996) Scholars and their inquiry paradigms: exploring a conceptual framework for classifying inquiry and inquirers based upon paradigmatic assumptions. Paper presented to the annual meeting of the American Educational Research Association, New York, April.

Tooley, J. and Darby, D. (1998) *Educational Research: A Critique.* London: OFSTED.

Toulmin, S. (1972) *Human Understanding*, vol. 1. Oxford: Clarendon Press.

Traweek, S. (1982) Uptime, downtime, spacetime and power. Unpublished PhD thesis, University of California Santa Cruz.

Troare, N., Godin, B. and Landry, R. (1996) An econometric analysis of the effect of collaboration on academic research productivity, *Higher Education*, 32(3): 283–301.

Trow, M. (1970) Reflections on the transition from mass to universal higher education, *Daedalus*, 90: 1–42.

Trow, M. (1972) *The Expansion and Transformation of Higher Education*. Berkeley, CA: General Learning Corporation.

Trow, M. (1976a) The public and private lives of higher education, *Daedalus*, 104: 113–27.

Trow, M. (1976b) The American university department as a context for learning, *Studies in Higher Education*, 1(1): 11–22.

Trow, M. (1987) Academic standards and mass higher education, *Higher Education Quarterly*, 41(3): 268–92.

Trow, M. (1989) The Robbins Trap: British attitudes and the limits of expansion, *Higher Education Quarterly*, 43(1): 55–75.

Trow, M. (1992) Thoughts on the White Paper of 1991, *Higher Education Quarterly*, 46(3): 213–26.

Trow, M. (1994) *Managerialism and the Academic Profession: Quality and Control*. London: QSC.

Trowler, P. (1998a) *Academics Responding to Change: New Higher Education Frameworks and Academic Cultures*. Buckingham: SRHE/Open University Press.

Trowler, P. (1998b) What managerialists forget: higher education credit frameworks and managerialist ideology, *International Studies in Sociology of Education*, 8(1): 91–109.

Trowler, P. (1999) Captured by the discourse? The socially constitutive power of new higher education discourse in the UK. Paper presented to Re-organizing Knowledge/Transforming Institutions Conference, Amherst, MA, 17–19 September 1999.

Trowler, P. (2001) Captured by the discourse? The socially constitutive power of new higher education discourse in the UK, *Organization*, 8(2): 183–201.

Trowler, P. and Knight, P. (1999) Organizational socialization and induction in universities: reconceptualizing theory and practice, *Higher Education*, 37: 177–95.

Trowler, P. and Knight, P. (2000) Coming to know in higher education: theorising faculty entry to new work contexts, *Higher Education Research and Development*, 19(1): 27–42.

Trowler, P. and Turner, G. (2001) Exploring the hermeneutic foundations of university life: deaf academics in a hybrid 'community of practice', *Higher Education*. Mimeo, Lancaster University.

Turner, R.J. (1960) Sponsored and contest mobility and the school system, *American Sociological Review*, 25: 855–67.

Turpin, T. and Garrett-Jones, S. (1997) Innovation networks in Australia and China, in H. Etzkowitz and L. Leydesdorff (eds) *Universities and the Global Knowledge Economy: A Triple Helix of University–Industry–Government Relations*, pp. 21–32. London: Pinter.

University Grants Committee (1987) *University Statistics 1986–87, Vol. 1: Students and Staff*. Cheltenham: Universities Statistical Record.

Urry, J. (1998) Contemporary transformations of time and space, in P. Scott (ed.) *The Globalization of Higher Education*. Buckingham: SRHE/Open University Press.

Välimaa, J. (1998) Culture and identity in higher education research, *Higher Education*, 36: 119–38.

van den Braembussche, A. (1979) The annales paradigm, in W. Callebaut, M. Demey, R. Pinxten and F. Vandamme (eds) *Theory of Knowledge and Science Policy*. Ghent: Communication and Cognition.

van den Daele, W., Krohn, W. and Weingart, P. (1977) The political direction of scientific development, in E. Mendelsohn, P. Weingart and R. Whitley (eds) *The Social Production of Scientific Knowledge.* Dordrecht: Reidel.

Waldo, D. (1975) Political science: tradition, discipline, profession, science, enterprise, in F. Greenstein and N. Polsby (eds) *Political Science: Scope and Theory.* Reading, MA: Addison Wesley.

Warren Piper, D., Nulty, D.D. and O'Grady, G. (1996) *Examination Practices and Procedures in Australian Universities.* Canberra: Department of Employment, Training and Youth Affairs.

Waterman, A.T. (1966) Social influences and scientists, *Science,* 151: 61–4.

Watson, D. (1996) Unit Public Funding. Paper presented to 'Dilemmas of Mass Higher Education' Conference, Staffordshire University, 10–12 April.

Watson, J.D. (1970) *The Double Helix.* Harmondsworth: Penguin.

Waugh, E. (1956) An open letter, in N. Mitford (ed.) *Noblesse Oblige.* London: Hamish Hamilton.

Wax, M.L. (1969) Myth and interrelationship in social science, in M. Sherif and C. Sherif (eds) *Interdisciplinary Relationships in the Social Sciences.* Chicago, IL: Aldine.

Weber, E. (1977) *Peasants into Frenchmen.* London: Chatto and Windus.

Webster, A. and Packer, K. (1997) When worlds collide: patents in public sector research, in H. Etzkowitz and L. Leydesdorff (eds) *Universities and the Global Knowledge Economy,* pp. 47–59. London: Pinter.

Weingart, P. (1974) On a sociological theory of scientific change, in R. Whitley (ed.) *Social Processes of Scientific Development.* London: Routledge.

Weinstock, M. (1971) Citation indexes, *Encyclopaedia of Library Information Science.* New York: Marcel Dekker.

Weiss, C.H. (ed.) (1977) *Using Social Research in Public Policy Making.* Lexington, MA: Lexington Books.

Wesseling, H.L. (1985) The identification of scientific advancement in history, in T. Hägerstrand (ed.) *The Identification of Progress in Learning.* Cambridge: Cambridge University Press.

Whitley, R. (1969) Communication nets in science, *Sociological Review,* 17: 219–33.

Whitley, R. (1976) Umbrella and polytheistic scientific disciplines and their elites, *Social Studies of Science,* 6: 471–97.

Whitley, R. (1977) The sociology of scientific work and the history of scientific developments, in S. Blume (ed.) *Perspectives in the Sociology of Science.* New York: John Wiley.

Whitley, R. (1982) The establishment and structure of the sciences as reputational organizations, in N. Elias, W. Martins and R. Whitley (eds) *Scientific Establishments and Hierarchies.* Dordrecht: Reidel.

Whitley, R. (1984) *The Intellectual and Social Organization of the Sciences.* Oxford: Clarendon Press.

Wiener, M. (1981) *English Culture and the Decline of the Industrial Spirit.* Cambridge: Cambridge University Press.

Wilder, R.L. (1981) *Mathematics as a Cultural System.* Oxford: Pergamon.

Williams, G. (1995) The marketization of HE: reforms and potential reforms in HE finance, in D. Dill and B. Sporn (eds) *Emerging Patterns of Social Demand and University Reform,* pp. 160–70. Oxford: IAU Press/Elsevier.

Williams, G. (1996) *Paying for Education Beyond Eighteen: An Examination of Issues and Options.* London: Council for Industry and Higher Education.

Williams, G., Blackstone, T. and Metcalf, D. (1974) *The Academic Labour Market.* Amsterdam: Elsevier.

Willmott, H. (1993) Strength is ignorance; slavery is freedom: managing culture in modern organizations, *Journal of Management Studies*, 30(4): 515–52.

Winter, R. (1995) The university of life plc: the 'industrialisation' of higher education?, in J. Smyth (ed.) *Academic Work*. Buckingham: SRHE/Open University Press.

Winter, R., Taylor, T. and Sarros, J. (2000) Trouble at mill: quality of academic worklife issues within a comprehensive Australian university, *Studies in Higher Education*, 25(3): 279–94.

Wolfe, D.M. and Kolb, D.A. (1979) Career development, personal growth and experiential learning, in D. Kolb, I. Rubin and J. McIntyre (eds) *Organizational Psychology*, 3rd edn. Engelwood Cliffs, NJ: Prentice-Hall.

Woods, P., Bagley, C. and Glatter, R. (1996) Dynamics of competition, in C. Pole and R. Chawla-Duggan (eds) *Reshaping Education in the 1990s: Perspectives on Secondary Schooling*. London: Falmer Press.

Wormald, E. (1985) Teacher training and gender blindness, *British Journal of Sociology of Education*, 6(1): 112–16.

Yates, P.D. (1985) Science and sensibility. Mimeo, University of Sussex.

Ylijoki, O.H. (2000) Disciplinary cultures and the moral order of studying, *Higher Education*, 39: 339–62.

Ziman, J. (1973) Foreword, in G. Gaston (ed.) *Originality and Competition in Science*. Chicago, IL: Chicago University Press.

Ziman, J. (1981) What are the options? Social determinants of personal research plans, *Minerva*, 19(1): 1–42.

Ziman, J. (1987) *Knowing Everything about Nothing*. Cambridge: Cambridge University Press.

Zinberg, D. (1985) The legacy of success, in M. Gibbons and B. Wittrock (eds) *Science as a Commodity*. Harlow: Longman.

Zuckerman, H. (1968) Patterns of name ordering among authors of scientific papers, *American Journal of Sociology*, 74: 276–91.

Zuckerman, H.A. (1970) Stratification in American science, *Sociological Inquiry*, 40: 235–57.

Zuckerman, H.A. (1977) *Scientific Elite: Nobel Laureates in the United States*. New York: Free Press.

Zuckerman, H. and Cole, J.R. (1975) Women in American science, *Minerva*, 13(1): 82–102.

Zuckerman, H. and Merton, R.K. (1971) Patterns of evaluation in science, *Minerva*, 9: 66–100.

Zuckerman, H. and Merton, R.K. (1973) Age, ageing and age structure in science, in R.K. Merton (ed.) *The Sociology of Science*. Chicago, IL: University of Chicago Press.

Index

The Society for Research into Higher Education

The Society for Research into Higher Education (SRHE) exists to stimulate and coordinate research into all aspects of higher education. It aims to improve the quality of higher education through the encouragement of debate and publication on issues of policy, on the organization and management of higher education institutions, and on the curriculum, teaching and learning methods.

The Society is entirely independent and receives no subsidies, although individual events often receive sponsorship from business or industry. The Society is financed through corporate and individual subscriptions and has members from many parts of the world.

Under the imprint *SRHE & Open University Press*, the Society is a specialist publisher of research, having over 80 titles in print. In addition to *SRHE News*, the Society's newsletter, the Society publishes three journals: *Studies in Higher Education* (three issues a year), *Higher Education Quarterly* and *Research into Higher Education Abstracts* (three issues a year).

The Society runs frequent conferences, consultations, seminars and other events. The annual conference in December is organized at and with a higher education institution. There are a growing number of networks which focus on particular areas of interest, including:

Access	Learning Environment
Assessment	Legal Education
Consultants	Managing Innovation
Curriculum Development	New Technology for Learning
Eastern European	Postgraduate Issues
Educational Development Research	Quantitative Studies
FE/HE	Student Development
Funding	Vocation at Qualification
Graduate Employment	

Benefits to members

Individual

• The opportunity to participate in the Society's networks

- Reduced rates for the annual conferences
- Free copies of *Research into Higher Education Abstracts*
- Reduced rates for *Studies in Higher Education*
- Reduced rates for *Higher Education Quarterly*
- Free copy of *Register of Members' Research Interests* – includes valuable reference material on research being pursued by the Society's members
- Free copy of occasional in-house publications, e.g. *The Thirtieth Anniversary Seminars Presented by the Vice-Presidents*
- Free copies of *SRHE News* which informs members of the Society's activities and provides a calendar of events, with additional material provided in regular mailings
- A 35 per cent discount on all SRHE/Open University Press books
- Access to HESA statistics for student members
- The opportunity for you to apply for the annual research grants
- Inclusion of your research in the *Register of Members' Research Interests*

Corporate

- Reduced rates for the annual conferences
- The opportunity for members of the Institution to attend SRHE's network events at reduced rates
- Free copies of *Research into Higher Education Abstracts*
- Free copies of *Studies in Higher Education*
- Free copies of *Register of Members' Research Interests* – includes valuable reference material on research being pursued by the Society's members
- Free copy of occasional in-house publications
- Free copies of *SRHE News*
- A 35 per cent discount on all SRHE/Open University Press books
- Access to HESA statistics for research for students of the Institution
- The opportunity for members of the Institution to submit applications for the Society's research grants
- The opportunity to work with the Society and co-host conferences
- The opportunity to include in the *Register of Members' Research Interests* your Institution's research into aspects of higher education

Membership details: SRHE, 3 Devonshire Street, London
W1N 2BA, UK Tel: 020 7637 2766. Fax: 020 7637 2781.
email: srhe@mailbox.ulcc.ac.uk
world wide web: http://www.srhe.ac.uk./srhe/
Catalogue: SRHE & Open University Press, Celtic Court,
22 Ballmoor, Buckingham MK18 1XW. Tel: 01280 823388.
Fax: 01280 823233. email: enquiries@openup.co.uk